## Future of Business anc

The Future of Business and Finance book series features professional works aimed at defining, describing and charting the future trends in these fields. The focus is mainly on strategic directions, technological advances, challenges and solutions which may affect the way we do business tomorrow, including the future of sustainability and governance practices. Mainly written by practitioners, consultants and academic thinkers, the books are intended to spark and inform further discussions and developments.

More information about this series at https://link.springer.com/bookseries/16360

Michael Kempf • Frank Kühn
Editors

# Navigating a Travelling Organization

## Insights, Ideas and Impulses from the 3-P-Model

Springer

*Editors*
Michael Kempf
Bad Honnef, Germany

Frank Kühn
Dortmund, Germany

ISSN 2662-2467 ISSN 2662-2475 (electronic)
Future of Business and Finance
ISBN 978-3-030-95328-7 ISBN 978-3-030-95326-3 (eBook)
https://doi.org/10.1007/978-3-030-95326-3



This Springer imprint is published by the registered company Springer Nature Switzerland AG
The registered company address is: Gewerbestrasse 11, 6330 Cham, Switzerland

# Contents

# Part I

# Introduction and Framing

# Further Development of the Application of the Three-Pillar Model

Michael Kempf and Frank Kühn

**Abstract**

This chapter describes how the Three-Pillar Model has evolved within a community of professionals and how, according to recent practical experience, it can be complemented by different application methods. The original model describes the Three Pillars themselves, i.e., Sustainable Purpose, Travelling Organization, and Connected Resources. The application methods describe in which form these Three Pillars can be brought up for discussion, for example, in leadership, in the management team, or in workshops, and become effective for the navigation of the Travelling Organization.

## 1 Introduction

It has now been at least four years since we started our journey with our first reflections on the core principles of future-oriented organizations in a multinational community of authors. We have since presented the 3-P model and its application in two books that have been much appreciated by our professional readership (Wollmann et al., 2020, 2021). The model has been developed by a multinational community of practitioners, academics, and consultants. We have developed the model based on many years of experience and in view of the challenges of our time, reflected on it in numerous chapters and discussed its applications.

M. Kempf
Bad Honnef, Germany
e-mail: michael@kempf-cp.com

F. Kühn (✉)
Dortmund, Germany
e-mail: frank@kuehn-cp.com



M. Kempf, F. Kühn (eds.), *Navigating a Travelling Organization*, Future of Business and Finance, https://doi.org/10.1007/978-3-030-95326-3_1

These two first books have been followed by the question in which direction a further deepening could go. The discussion has resulted in two diverse focuses, so we decided to publish two further books, both offering many insights from our professional community.

Thanks are due to Peter Wollmann and Reto Püringer for the joint development. They will edit one of the two books focusing on next step transformations based on the Travelling Organization concept. This focus is coming from conversations with C-level managers from global players and other potential readers who showed a significant need in supporting and guiding organizations' next step transformations with strategic and fundamental dimensions and building the capability for this challenge.

The other book, now on the table in front of us, focuses on the challenge of how to navigate a Traveling Organization toward future success under uncertain conditions such as crisis, disruption, and continuous change. The basis is clearly visible in the first book and further developed and outlined. We developed this book as a reader for the 3-P application, offering effective approaches and perspectives, inspirations, and fresh thinking for navigating organizations towards future success.

The chapters in this book contribute valuable ideas and experiences. The authors come from companies, public institutions, the church, the cultural sector, and consulting and they describe what is important in navigating, what the opportunities and hindering factors are, and what solutions or even unfamiliar approaches might look like. The book is dedicated to readers who want to face urgent and future challenges, enrich their own professionalism, and therefore think outside the box. And for both of us, as editors and authors of this chapter, it is another big step in 23 years of working together in consulting and supporting organizations on their exciting journeys.

## 2 The Three-Pillar Model as an Open Approach

We defined the Three-Pillar Model as an experience-based, open approach, that can be further differentiated and concretized to make it suitable for the specific challenges of any organization or transformation. For example, the objective of applying the 3-P model can vary:

- We can use the Three Pillars as design principles from the very beginning of a program or project: How to create solutions that meet the Three Pillars?
- Or we can use the Three Pillars to reflect and validate the current organization and leadership situation.
- Or we can apply them to align tools, management processes, and ways of working within the organization, e.g., we can ask whether our performance management meets the principles of the model.

The contributions in the previous two books followed all these tracks and presented interesting use cases. This book continues this by focusing on good

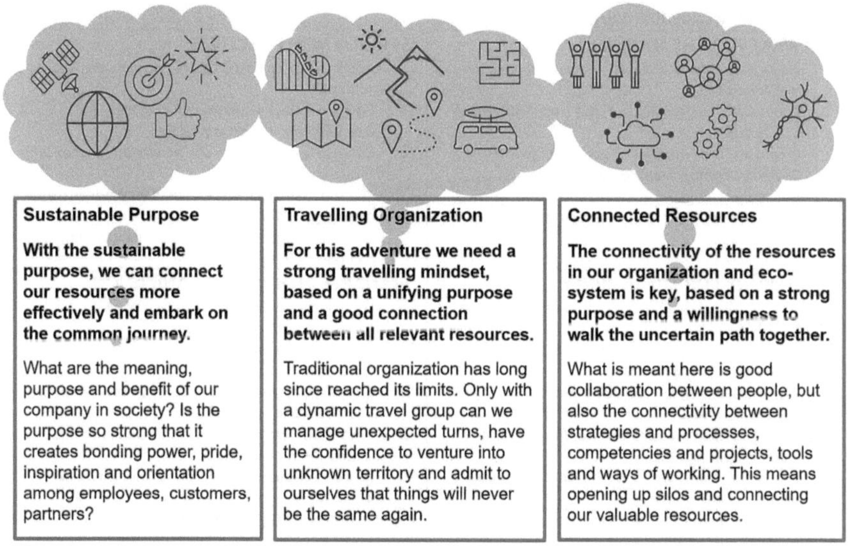


**Fig. 1** Definition of the Three-Pillar Model (Wollmann et al., 2020, 2021) (Illustrated by the authors, used with permission. All rights reserved)

practices for navigating traveling organizations in a forward-looking way. In this chapter, we provide four examples of how the Three-Pillar Model can be applied and brought into a fruitful discussion.

In the first example, we use the original definition of the Three Pillars (Fig. 1). The discussion then can be: What exactly do these Pillars mean to us? Where do we see a need for action in the navigation of our organization, journey, or transformation? This is a very open approach to creating a common understanding of the Three Pillars and how they can be applied to a specific challenge.

Based on this definitional approach, we have interlinked the Three-Pillar Model with three concrete applications.

## 3 Application Via Inspiring and Stimulating Questions

The first application consists of a questionnaire that is used to review the organizational journey and its need for navigation. This questionnaire is kept generic; the first step toward practical application is to invite your management team to discuss and, if necessary, supplement the questionnaire from a company-specific perspective. Which questions are relevant for navigating our organization? Based on the authors' experience, this is an important step to establishing a common understanding about the Three-Pillar Model (Fig. 2).

| App 1: Generic Questionnaire | |
|---|---|
| **(1) AWAKE FOR THE JOURNEY**<br>☐ Explore and create a shared understanding of the VUCA world<br>☐ Commit to a sustainable purpose that inspires staff and customers<br>☐ Create a shared mindset of agility and journey<br>☐ Develop a commitment to the next steps of transition<br>☐ Ensure sponsors accept the uncertainty and risks of the journey | **(5) BUILD NEW PRACTICES**<br>☐ Apply the three pillars to develop activities and solutions<br>☐ Develop collective platforms, practices, and interventions that attract talents<br>☐ Connect the enterprise and ecosystem to cope with future challenges<br>☐ Question technical systems that are inadequate for managing VUCA issues<br>☐ Apply problem-solving practices appropriate to the complexity of the challenges |
| **(2) INTERLINK FOR THE JOURNEY**<br>☐ Connect all personal and organizational resources for the journey<br>☐ Create a collective mindset to overcome silos between units and levels<br>☐ Organize learning and development loops along the common endeavor<br>☐ Use diversity of opinions and working styles as learning opportunities<br>☐ Provide full transparency of the facts and figures needed for the journey | **(6) ENABLE PEOPLE & ORGANIZATION**<br>☐ Use crises and disruptions to overcome hurdles towards collaborative culture<br>☐ Facilitate teams and employees to interconnect and co-create results quickly<br>☐ Create a transparency and climate that encourages people to take responsibility<br>☐ Learn from retrospectives in terms of purpose, journey, and connectivity<br>☐ Recruit and support people with curiosity, openness & agility |
| **(3) PRACTICE THE FUTURE MODE**<br>☐ Develop outside-in: from market dynamics to future-fit organization<br>☐ Ensure that all parts of the organization contribute to the purpose<br>☐ Apply collective tools, e.g., micro-projects, to create quick results<br>☐ Practice discursive loops to cope with crucial, even insoluble challenges<br>☐ Use alternative ways (e.g., impro theatre) to better understand the journey | **(7) NAVIGATE THE JOURNEY**<br>☐ Transfer purpose, journey, & connectivity into products, processes, structures<br>☐ Co-create an entrepreneurial compass that helps navigate the complexity<br>☐ Include the dynamics of crisis, disruption and change in the navigation system<br>☐ Coordinate the navigation of entities, subsidiaries, and the ecosystem as a whole<br>☐ Update and develop your compass and navigation practices on a regular basis |
| **(4) LEAD ON THE JOURNEY**<br>☐ Understand and practice leadership as a serving or shareable task<br>☐ Share, connect and commit the leadership concept in the entire system<br>☐ Apply the 3 pillars to explore the expectations and perspectives in your team<br>☐ Develop psychological safety from collective behavior<br>☐ Promote leadership culture via qualification, coaching, feedback practices etc. | **(8) DEVELOP HYBRID SETTING**<br>☐ Work with the hybridity of a traveling organization (start-up & institutionalized)<br>☐ Coordinate the journeys & developments carefully, even counter-cyclical ones<br>☐ Include crisis mode as a managed part of the hybrid organization<br>☐ Learn from different organizational set-ups, work modes and good practices.<br>☐ Secure your start-ups or spin-offs within the surrounding organization |

**Fig. 2** Learning from questions developed from use cases—how good are we at the presented aspects? (Wollmann et al., 2020, 2021) (Illustrated by the authors, used with permission. All rights reserved)

## 4 Supporting the Application via Impulses and Examples

The second application draws attention to a variety of tools and practices that can support the realization of the Three Pillars. Related to this is the need to examine the compatibility of existing tools and practices with respect to the Three-Pillar Model. Do the tools and practices support the Three Pillars? This approach, as displayed in Fig. 3, provides an initial overview of the multitude of options, so it certainly needs

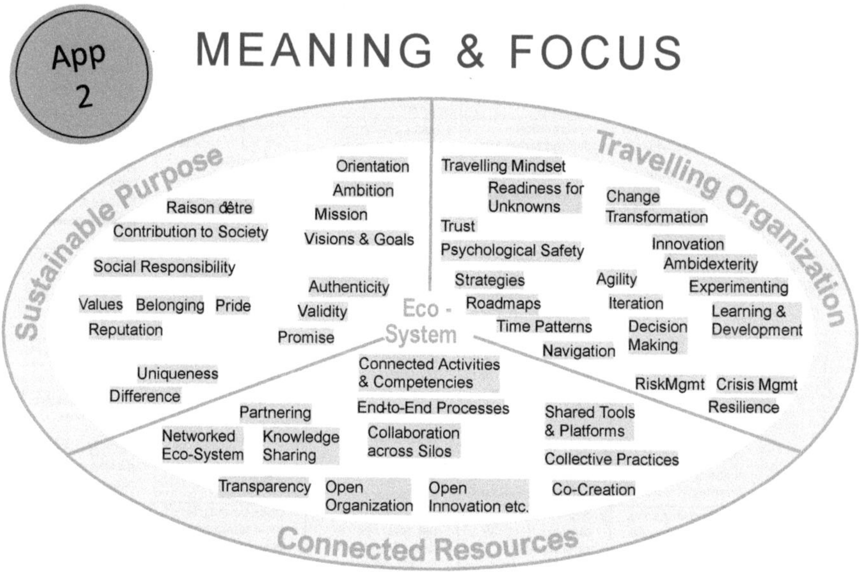


**Fig. 3** What are the main issues in our ecosystem? How compatible are our tools? (Illustrated by the authors, used with permission. All rights reserved)

to be supplemented further: What is helpful in navigating the organization, where do we prioritize the use of tools and practices?

The practical application has meanwhile proven to be very practical and effective, as exemplified in the following case.

***Aligning Organization Development***

*The discussion for the organizational design of a start-up has been continuously related to the Three-Pillar Model and the organizational characteristics assigned. Our Vision—does it support the Purpose? Our personal values—are they compatible with the Purpose? Our intended product roadmap and personnel development plan—are both flexible enough for our journey? Our partnerships and communication structures—are they effective enough to quickly connect our internal and external competencies? With these questions, the development was reflected and aligned and could be quickly readjusted at all critical points.*

## 5 Using the Three-Pillar Model to Discuss the Situation and the Vision

The third application (Fig. 4) translates the Three-Pillar Model into a development model (cf. Glasl & Lievegoed, 2004; Laloux, 2014), which helps to identify the current situation of the organization and the vision of the organizational journey: Where are we today, where do we want to navigate our travelling organization, what are the milestones we want to achieve in this year? Experience shows that the

| App 3: Development Route | | | | | |
|---|---|---|---|---|---|
| Route / Pillars | **Starting**<br>Pioneering*<br>Tribal, Impulsive** | **Structuring**<br>Differentiating*<br>Traditional, Conformist** | **Expanding**<br>Integrating*<br>Modern, Performance-Oriented** | **Partnering**<br>Associating*<br>Post-Modern, Pluralistic** | **Self-Evolving**<br>Evolutionary, Integral, Systemic** |
| **Sustainable Purpose** | ■ Enthusiasm for own idea and creativity<br>■ Charisma of the founder<br>■ Everything for the customer | ■ Systematically defined target group and market position<br>■ Performance and efficiency as an ambition | ■ Focus on competitive advantage, profit & expansion, shareholder expectations & customer requirements | ■ Vision and position defined in business and society<br>■ Focusing benefits of stakeholders in the eco-system | ■ Formulated contribution to society as a strong core and primary binding force for employees and partners |
| **Travelling Organization** | ■ Steering by central person<br>■ Improvisation<br>■ Learning & development loops, also reinvention of the basic idea possible<br>■ First trials of consistent documentation and learning structures | ■ Technocratic formalisms for planning & control of routines, projects and changes.<br>■ Standardization and automation, systems setting conditions for further development<br>■ Episodic change according to rules of external consultants | ■ Control via cascaded target agreements for performance and development<br>■ Self-organized implementation by managers and teams – with support by central functions<br>■ Roadmaps and processes for learning organization | ■ Change mindset, to develop together with the ecosystem and with partners<br>■ Organization outside-in, to support interactions with customers and market<br>■ Self-organized teams and shared leadership | ■ With high VUCA awareness, everyone can lead and steer<br>■ Radical transparency for teams' self-navigation<br>■ Rapid & iterative approaches<br>■ Agile decision-making and conflict resolution practices |
| **Connected Resources** | ■ Sworn community, structured around central person<br>■ Direct exchange and interlinking via personal contact<br>■ Strategies, projects and processes connected ad-hoc | ■ Separation: strategic/tactical/ operational etc.<br>■ Different languages at different functions and levels<br>■ Communication & connectivity hierarchically determined<br>■ Executives as top experts and connectors | ■ Communication becomes central issue: teamwork, communities, networking across areas<br>■ Connections through matrix<br>■ IT offering collaboration tools<br>■ Knowledge transfer from external consultants | ■ Open boundaries of the organization, open innovation<br>■ Joint learning & development<br>■ Defined exchange of resources in the eco-system<br>■ Consultants as development partners | ■ Collaboration as a principle<br>■ Transparency via platforms, working out loud etc.<br>■ Flexible connections around activities and initiatives<br>■ Flexible exchange with ecosystem and labor market (e.g., digital nomads) |

**Fig. 4** What is our current situation and our vision? The development route is based on models proposed by (*) Glasl and Lievegoed (2004) and (**) Laloux (2014) (Illustrated by the authors, used with permission. )

discussion about the current situation and the vision in the management circles is very lively and triggers an important pull-effect for joint development. So this application provides a tool that starts navigation at the very first step.

But with reference to the aforementioned development models, we must realize that this journey is not uniform and never ends in a linear process (Fig. 5). On the one hand, there are always new business requirements or management and navigation models that lead to some kind of "re-starting" the company or parts of it. Thus, parts of the organization need to develop faster, while others persist longer. Some start working in an agile way, others rely on stable routines. Some even stop at the structuring phase, while others have a broader ambition.

***Progressive Practices Lost in the Merger***

*The company had been very successful in developing a modern project management concept that greatly advanced the entire collaboration culture, which could be attributed to the self-evolving phase. Then the company was bought by a larger corporation. This corporation was not even ready for the partnering phase, and the whole group reverted to*

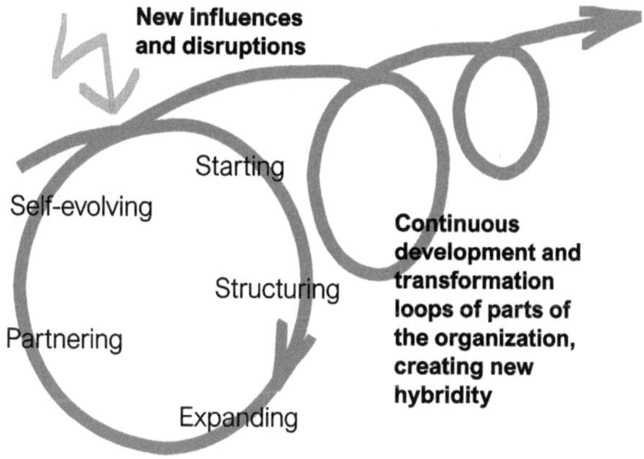


**Fig. 5** The development loops repeat, usually also for individual parts in the organization (Illustrated by the authors, used with permission. All rights reserved)

*the structuring phase. Today, after 10–15 years, parts of the company have returned to the self-evolving phase.*

From this, a natural diversity, or even hybridity, develops with different subcultures and navigation approaches, again and again. A meta-level navigation must ensure that the interaction between the different parts works.

***Failure Due to Diversity***

*A spin-off was formed from the chemical company to quickly realize a highly attractive product idea and bring it to market. The work started with a highly dedicated team. However, the spin-off was soon hampered by the controlling ambitions of the parent company. Finally, the spin-off was reincorporated and became a business unit in the overall organization. The most dedicated employees left the company, and the new product was not realized.*

## 6 The Results Count

We have brought into the dialogue three applications of the Three-Pillar Model, all of which serve the same purpose: to examine, significantly evolve, or redefine the performance and resilience of organizations, and thus make them key navigation factors in the cockpit of the travelling organization.

The approaches to discussing Sustainable Purpose, Travelling Organization, and Connected Resources may vary, as shown. Others are possible. What is important is that the chosen approach works in the process and situation in the team, with colleagues, or with the entire workforce. It must have an impact there: In exploratory discussions, in the management team's future workshops, in feedback workshops with the staff, in design workshops for corporate processes and functions. Together with the right application, the Three-Pillar Model will lead to a sustainable movement in the company.

These considerations result in three key takeaways:

- The objective of the application method for the Three-Pillar Model must be concretely clarified: What should the result be? A diagnosis of the organization and its tools? An orientation for joint organizational work? A status and future picture for the company? Concrete needs for action and an action plan?
- The success of the model is based on accompanying aspects: clarity of the application goal, a group of participants with open thinking, appropriate application method, and lively agenda with committed and dedicated people.
- The results of the application of the Three-Pillar Model are never final. Incidentally, this is true for all interventions in travelling organizations. From the beginning, reviews of the achieved application results and retrospectives of the application process must be agreed upon, which is part of the navigation. This allows the application to be iteratively reviewed, adjusted and to achieve maximum effectiveness.

## References

Glasl, F., & Lievegoed, B. (2004). *Dynamische Unternehmensentwicklung*. 3. Aufl. Haupt.

Laloux, F. (2014). *Reinventing organizations.* Nelson Parker.

Wollmann, P., Kühn, F., & Kempf, M. (Eds.). (2020). *Three pillars of organization and leadership in disruptive times—Navigating your company successfully through the 21st century business world.* SpringerNature.

Wollmann, P., Kühn, F., Kempf, M., & Püringer, R. (Eds.). (2021). *Organization and leadership in disruptive times—Design and implementation of the 3-P-model.* SpringerNature.

**Michael Kempf** has been an experienced Management Consultant for over 20 years. The driving force of his professional activities is his strong ambition to design processes and organizations in a sustainable manner. He relishes identifying key challenges, diagnosing complex relationships and assisting in shaping the future. Gaining experience and learning something new are indispensable parts of his life, which is why he likes to seize new opportunities. He began his career as a carpenter before studying social work, education, and business administration. His career has spanned various jobs in social work, 10 years as a manager (HR and logistics) in industrial and retail companies and, since 1998, in advising people, leadership teams as well as working teams and organizations that are all very different. Michael has co-authored numerous publications in the field of leadership and organizational development.

**Frank Kühn** has been supporting companies and institutions in the areas of transformation, organization, and leadership for many years. His clients involve him as a development partner for both their urgent change projects and sustainable future concepts. Frank has a degree in engineering and a doctorate in work science. In leading positions in research and industry, he was responsible for labor management, production strategies, and project management. In the early 1990s, he joined HLP Hirzel Leder & Partners in Frankfurt and later co-founded the ICG Integrated Consulting Group Germany in Berlin and was a partner in the European group in Graz. Today, he is an independent consultant, business partner of ICG and is associated with other project partners and think tanks. He brings his experience to the development of methodologies such as the Three-Pillar Model and has published numerous articles in management journals and books.

# Navigating a Travelling Organization Toward Future Success: How to Inspire and Co-create the Joint Endeavor

Michael Kempf and Frank Kühn

**Abstract**

This chapter combines the experiences from many years of consulting practice with the reflections and results of the authors in this book. The fact that the topics complement and connect each other is of course not coincidental in a community but intentional and part of the power that arises from a dialogue. In the discussion and synthesis, a new perspective on creative starting points for the navigation of a travelling organization emerges. This understanding of navigation is not about keeping the organization in familiar waters, but about opening new opportunities. Otherwise, transformation, a new beginning, or a journey are not possible. In this sense, this chapter also cross-references the other chapters of this book.

## 1 From Controlling to Navigating

These days, traditional management, organization, and control have long since reached their limits and new approaches are required. Centralized command and control or checks and balances can no longer meet complex requirements with the necessary speed and quality. It is not for nothing that old, repackaged, or genuinely new concepts attract great interest—or are met with skepticism when managers cannot imagine implementing them in their established organizational concepts, structures, and cultures: Digitalization? Agilization? Self-organization? Distributed leadership? Evolutionary concepts?

M. Kempf
Bad Honnef, Germany
e-mail: michael@kempf-cp.com

F. Kühn (✉)
Dortmund, Germany
e-mail: frank@kuehn-cp.com



M. Kempf, F. Kühn (eds.), *Navigating a Travelling Organization*, Future of Business and Finance, https://doi.org/10.1007/978-3-030-95326-3_2

We appreciate new approaches. However, we have to be careful that these approaches do not crystallize into dogmatism again, are understood as a panacea, and are "missionized" in consulting offers. That, too, is part of navigation. It is not just about the route, but also about the appropriate practices.

So, what does it come down to? It sounds simple: what matters is the expedient, the impact that will lead us to a good future in our society and our organizations. But that means understanding what navigation is really about, rather than hastily adapting new fashions in strategy and organization. It also means breaking free from the familiar, understanding new time patterns, learning to think and decide in new ways.

How can organizations navigate their journey through the terrain of uncertain market demands and creative solution possibilities? How can this navigation be understood as a system performance that pays into the organization's purpose (not individual interests), that supports the organizational journey into the future (not the fulfillment of outdated goals), that meaningfully interlinks the capabilities, motivations, processes, and practices in the organization (not developed separately)? The Three-Pillar Model focuses precisely on these dimensions: Sustainable Purpose, Travelling Organization, Connected Resources (Wollmann et al., 2020, 2021). They also describe the cornerstones of navigating the joint journey.

So, how do we get to what is purposeful, intended, and effective? What is it all about? And how do we develop the navigation that will lead us into the future?

## 2 Navigation Is a Systemic Challenge

When it comes to systems—like an organization—their navigation must also be considered systemically. Otherwise, the navigation process will be under-complex. Just as we know that we cannot meet the complex challenges of the VUCA world with complicated answers; we cannot meet uncertainty and ambiguity with even more sophisticated controlling templates. It is absurd to want to secure what cannot be secured.

Navigation is based on decisions, and decisions are made by everyone in the company, at every level, in every function, in every area, every day. These decisions need to be aligned with the business purpose, embedded in the business journey, linked together; this is exactly what the Three Pillars are all about. In doing so, individual navigation tasks—like all other tasks in the company—can be assigned to defined roles or described as capabilities of key people (Scherer, 2022), or we can connect appropriate practices for the decisions on a case-by-case basis, as envisaged in approaches such as consent or delegated decision-making (Oestereich & Schröder, 2019; Trapp, 2022).

This is not just about effective decision-making per se, but about vitalizing and dynamizing the system as a whole, about the Travelling Mindset as a lasting competitive advantage. It is about people who understand their role in leading and navigating the company, who keep moving to do so, and who know that, in the VUCA world, their lives are changing (Sloterdijk, 2009; Wallner & Völkl, 2022;

Raman, 2022). Only in this way can resilience develop, and be prepared for the joint endeavor.

Therefore, it will always be a matter of ensuring that all players in the organizational system are effectively involved. Otherwise, the efficiency of navigation will be low, and the purpose of the company and the strategic goals will only be implemented sub-optimally in day-to-day business, in the projects, or in the transformation process (Kühn, 2022).

## 3 It Is About Success

So let us start with success, because this term is comparatively resistant to crisis and change. Its content, however, is not. What does success mean? Personally, in the team, in the company, in the institution? In the past, today, in a crisis, in the future? It has to do with what contribution we want to make in our world, what we want to achieve, how we want to measure that, and how we want to create the shared journey with our resources.

That is exactly what is reflected in our Three-Pillar Model. We must share the ideas about this in the organization (Fig. 1); otherwise, there is a great danger that we will drift apart in our thinking and actions, that we will waste our skills, energies, and motivations. That would truly not be a success, neither in the sustainability of the company in the society and the markets nor in its financial results and value.

On the journey, we have to interact with external conditions and developments: Market dynamics, technological trends, climate crisis and migrations, global customer worlds, new business models, proclaimed management fads and terms. What is relevant to the future success and journey of our organization is what we need to examine. The criteria are called meaningfulness and purposefulness. What, in terms of transformation, digitalization, globalization, agilization, and others, is meaningful and serves our purpose?

| What does success mean to us? | | | |
|---|---|---|---|
| Yesterday | Today | Tomorrow | Day after tomorrow |
| ☐ Fulfillment of financial targets (market share, revenue, profit, value)<br>☐ Competitiveness, e.g., global presence<br>☐ Secure jobs | ☐ Financial survival in the crisis<br>☐ Performance with virtual forms of work<br>☐ Learning from the crisis for organization design | ☐ Sustainable performance and supply chains<br>☐ Resilient structures<br>☐ Attractive on the labor market: a good place to be, to work and to learn | ☐ Success together with ecosystem partners<br>☐ Pro-adaptive (evolutionary) structures<br>☐ A good journey to join and co-develop |

**Fig. 1** Develop and share understandings of "success," here with some examples from current discussions. The representation on the timeline makes meanings and differences clear. (Illustrated by the authors, used with permission, all rights reserved)

This cannot be solved with recipes and certificates. They are copies of past concepts. That is why the challenge sometimes seems unfamiliar: In order to assess meaningfulness and expediency, we have to familiarize ourselves with the possibilities, make more substantial decisions, and repeatedly check them for their relevance to success. And then we have to iteratively plan and follow through with implementation in the dynamics of the ecosystem—as long as the decisions pay off in terms of success. Otherwise, we need to make new decisions and review the success criteria. Navigation must do this; it is not just about information and intervention, but also about creating the conditions: the faster-paced communication, decision-making, and implementation processes as well as the attitudes and mindset of the Travelling Organization on its unpredictable and unplannable journey.

## 4 Releasing Old Structures and Tracks

For us, navigating does not mean following familiar tracks. Rather, the question is: what are the new tracks? How reliable are they? We may have to do without tracks altogether, because tracks are the past, and they quickly become blurred. Finding them nevertheless is the art of pathfinding. But the future has not yet left any paths. That is why the picture does not fit. That is why we have to try out new and previously unknown things in a rapid sequence of steps and decisions (Dörner, 1997).

Complex and disruptive developments cannot, therefore, be countered with complicated organizational structures that may have fit in the past. They tend to be counterproductive. When the market is changing rapidly, it does not help to make the controlling process even more sophisticated, to expand Management by Objectives (MBO) even further instead of looking at more agile approaches such as Objectives and Key Results (Wirl & Luge, 2022). It also does not help to stick to decisions about projects and priorities once they have been decided, instead of applying a rapid prototyping approach to the project portfolio as well and managing the portfolio iteratively end-to-end (Püringer & Kühn, 2022).

However, calling ourselves agile but not being so makes things even more confusing. Then we have to cultivate an additional illusory world—in which no one believes. It is the same with a Code of Conduct if we do not live it consistently.

However, releasing is difficult (Raman, 2022); this also applies to familiar structures in which we have found our place. In many cases, we continue projects against our better knowledge, even if we would be better off terminating them. We stick to outdated understandings of roles that expect management to take initiative, over and over again, not release or quit (Gustafsson et al., 2022). Therefore, people and organizations are overloaded, tired, and exhausted. Therefore, it is courageous as a manager not only to push a new business idea forward but also to put one's own understanding of management's role and role behavior to the test, to change oneself (Wallner & Völkl, 2022).

Navigation of a travelling organization must initiate and support this kind of change and transformation. It refers to the uncertain course of the organization, the reinvention of roles, the definition of the new collaborative practices, tools and attitudes, the structural and cultural conditions.

## 5 Navigation Means Critical Engagement

Being courageous—that also means exposing the spread between current hierarchical culture and postmodern or even evolutionary development (Laloux, 2014). This can then be discussed. Where do we want to go? Not because everyone is promoting it that way, but because it is expedient for us. We can present this in the form of a grid (Fig. 2) or a roadmap, discuss it in the organization, and further develop it continuously. Employees no longer work only *in* the organization, but also *on* the organization; systemic navigation emerges.

However, this motivation must come from within. Just like imagining new things that we want to try out. Leadership must encourage this, even if it does not always understand it itself straight away. Openness to new things and trying them out make all the difference in the culture.

However, we can only achieve this development if we receive, accept, interpret, and process the findings, signals, and ideas from our ecosystem: the suggestions of our employees, the impressions and findings from customer discussions, the information about markets. All of this must guide our development (outside-in) and we must develop our contribution to markets and society from it (inside-out) (Oestereich & Schröder, 2019). Then we might no longer even talk about customer–supplier relationships, but about partnerships.

After all, we want all of us to do well. That has something to do with peace. At least with social peace. It has something to do with Sustainable Purpose, with the

| | |
|---|---|
| **Maintain**<br>☐ Composition of the teams<br>☐ Measurement against business performance indicators<br>☐ Change forums<br>☐ Resonance meetings on important developments | **Try out**<br>☐ Self-management of teams, stand-ups<br>☐ OKR<br>☐ Distributed leadership<br>☐ Work hacks |
| **Omit**<br>☐ Individual bonuses<br>☐ Management by Objectives<br>☐ Company suggestion scheme<br>☐ Budget constraints and dilemmas | **Introduce**<br>☐ Team Monitors<br>☐ Bonus based on company success<br>☐ Retrospectives of organization development<br>☐ Transformation roadmaps with flexible budgets |

**Fig. 2** Coming into exchange—cf. Blue Ocean Grid (Kim & Mauborgne, 2015). (Illustrated by the Authors, used with permission, all rights reserved)

commonality of the journey, with the connectivity of our resources, skills, and motivations (Kempf & Schlaud-Wolf, 2022).

Outdated concepts and convenient recipes are seldom of any help. The solutions and reflections in this book therefore also include unfamiliar considerations, new impulses, and approaches to thinking that require a certain amount of engagement on the part of the reader. But how can this be achieved when "cognitive ease" (Kahneman, 2012) is demanded everywhere, so that management can reach speedy decisions on the basis of familiar presentation formats, well-formulated statements, and habitual categories of thought?

## 6 Navigation: On a Confrontation Course Between the Old and the New

Questioning familiar communication formats is difficult. But we also have to confront the organizational models that we have developed, consulted on, and established over a long period of time. We can do this by remembering our common sense again and turning to very obvious solutions for fast action. Many large organizations do not dare to do this, cannot imagine it, are not allowed to formulate it, or have in fact blocked their own way with their legacy systems or administrative overkill. Was there no sustainable discussion about fast pacing, small-scale solutions, time-based decisions? And what about today?

Developments are often delayed in relation to one another, resulting at best in creative tension or at worst in energy-consuming drifts between technology, organization, and people (Przybilla & Kühn, 2022). Innovative technology is pushed where it can in digitalization and artificial intelligence, or it is tied up for years in investment in a large chemical plant. People are quick to use the apps and media that make their lives easier or support their power play. Or they work by the book using outdated tools. They often experience the organization as limiting and obstructive if it does not support entrepreneurial development and collaboration among people—which would be its very purpose. And this is exactly where navigation along the lines of the three pillars is called for: How can it all be aligned more effectively, support the dynamics, connect the movements?

Of course, hierarchical pyramids can also be appropriate when it comes to the vertical and horizontal division of labor, to applying the principle of command and control. However, this reaches its limits when it comes to flexibility and using people's experiences, talents, and motivations in their entirety. For this, much more natural principles are obvious than any organizational over-determination (Kempf & Schlaud-Wolf, 2022).

Navigation needs unified competence to move the organization somewhere between diverse and conflicting information, beliefs, and experiences toward the future.

## 7 Doing What Is Obvious

In the course of organizing and navigating, there are concepts that seem expedient, obvious, and logical in their basic ideas (Fig. 3). We need to look a little deeper into their principles; simple labels of centralized or decentralized, flat or slim, pyramid or circle, etc. are not sufficient for fruitful discussion.

For example, the seemingly logical role distributions proposed in the agile Scrum concept (Sutherland, 2015) are obvious: The product owner is responsible for his wish list and ranking of his wishes (the backlog) and the expert teams for their statement of what they can realistically accomplish in 2 weeks. Honesty instead of overpressure. Responsibility for what only we can take responsibility for. Pull instead of push: control of input—how much time do we have and what fits in? That is so obvious! How else could it be done? Everything else is just the illusion of power and feasibility: accepted perceptual biases because we shy away from the energy expenditure of conflict (Kahneman, 2012). For effective navigation, however, it is critical that realistic tasks are addressed to be implemented within clear time frames. This is also the basis of so-called micro-projects: strategic topics are worked on and implemented in four workshops (Kühn & Kempf, 2014, 2021).

Similarly, the concept of the Viable Stepping Stones applies the idea of the Minimum Viable Product (MVP) to the testing and implementation of business execution in the travelling or transforming organization (Turnwald & Zirn, 2022). Such effective business execution also means focusing on the customer touchpoints, aligning teams and activities to them, and developing appropriate solutions under

| Obvious | Practiced |
|---|---|
| We take on roles and decisions that we can implement responsibly, with commitment and competence. | We are assigned formal roles that are outlined in the organizational chart, in function descriptions and decision matrices. |
| We discuss meaningful goals, solutions and achievements, appropriate timelines, and how to move forward. | We try to achieve annually agreed goals. There is a review every six months. |
| We distribute leadership to those who are good at a task and to whom the colleagues will follow. | Leadership is attributed to those who are superior to us in the hierarchical pyramid. |
| We accept the diversity of perceptions and definitions and agree on what makes sense in common. | We follow current management fashions and dominant interpretations by some individuals. Discussions are limited |

**Fig. 3** Obvious versus practiced approaches. (Illustrated by the Authors, used with permission, all rights reserved)

volatile conditions. This requires effective processes and settings so that the result is right at the time it is delivered (Turnwald et al., 2022).

Or in the concept of Objectives and Key Results (OKR), for example, the quickly timed comparison of what has been accomplished on the target track, what the results mean, whether it makes sense to continue in this way (Doerr, 2018; Wirl & Luge, 2022) is obvious. How should it work differently? Achieving annual goals and sanctioning failure just because goals are agreed upon and needed to measure performance against? Formal enforcement instead of meaningful work? Everyone wants to do meaningful work; the proof to the contrary is still missing. This is also supported by the regular studies on job satisfaction, alienation, or so-called "internal resignation," which repeatedly put the focus on good or weak leadership. From the point of view of navigation, the Sustainable Purpose must translate directly into the meaning of work, the Travelling Mindset into the joint further development of work, the Connected Resources into the interaction in the organization.

Distributed leadership, for example, is obvious. In progressive thinking, leadership is no longer understood as a position to be defended, but as a task, and this can be distributed according to expediency. Perhaps coaching the team and shaping the communication process remains the task of the department head; but we should not need him or her to moderate a meeting to make it proceed efficiently. Others may take on project leadership, running the meeting, coordinating the communication process, facilitating the team calendar, taking the lead in change tasks. How leadership tasks are distributed can be mutually agreed upon. This also creates personal responsibility and development. How else should it work?

The advantage is obvious if we jointly design the appropriate organizational and navigation concept, beyond general fashionable terms and personal "sovereignty" over the interpretation. It just has to be clear and sustainable: What is important to us, what needs to be done, for which terms do we need to agree on meanings in order to make navigation effective? We can talk about development, change, or transformation, we can go by proposed definitions (Höfler et al., 2018), but in the end, the company has to choose the meaningful and appropriate one. Do we want to talk about efficiency, performance, or ambition? We need to agree together on what it should mean; otherwise, the navigation will not work.

## 8 Organization Is Interaction

How do we solve all this? First, we have to understand that companies consist of communication (Luhmann, 1995) and even more concrete: Interactions (Kühn & Wollmann, 2012; Kühn, 2022), i.e., messages, conversations, meetings, workshops. This is where knowledge is exchanged, energy is generated, people get involved, and organization developments end and begin (Raman, 2022). Whether we like it or not. That is where orientation, influence, opinion-forming, appointments, in short: navigation happens, constantly and systemically, at all levels. Whether we want it or not. Everything else is initially just a blueprint, an effective one, admittedly: Organizational charts, process charts, decision matrices, etc. But these only become real in

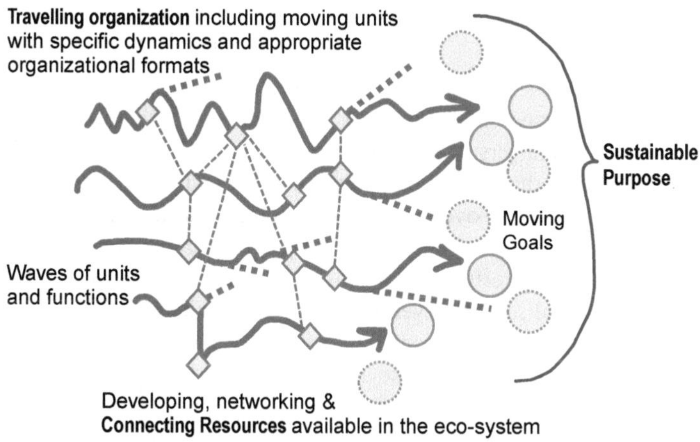


**Fig. 4** Connected Journeys. (Illustrated by Frank Kühn, used with permission, all rights reserved)

interactions with each other, with all the familiar informal, socio- and psychological influences.

This can be a challenge. For example, where personal self-realization is sought and any influence is avoided, individuals withdraw from interaction. They go on their own journey, and they do not want to link it to the journey of any system, for good reason. They form their own bubbles and echo chambers, perhaps with some like-minded people. They enter the interaction only temporarily where it promises them material benefits, for example. Then they play the game for a moment (Haselbach & Kühn, 2022). Beware of the iceberg model. We must keep this in mind.

But let us follow the path of interactions. Once we have shared the Sustainable Purpose and agreed on the next steps in the Travelling Organization, we can set off. Each team follows its journey as best it can with its skills and capacities. To keep the different journeys together, we again need a common situation: Connecting Resources. The situations are also called Gathering Points (Winnen & Kühn, 2022) (Fig. 4). It is like eye contact between two people: If we lose it even briefly, we end up on different journeys. These gathering points are crucial for navigation: This is where joint exchange, strategic coupling, feasibility statements, and directional decisions take place. This is all the more relevant when the subsystems involved follow their own logics, as we know from the university sector with science, administration, and politics (Reimers, 2022), the clerical sphere (Kempf & Schlaud-Wolf, 2022) with its very own, multilayered logics or from the cultural sector with funding agencies, cultural institutions, and the artists themselves (Haselbach & Kühn, 2022).

## 9 Navigation Needs Difference and Disruption

Developments that are focused on the future need a language that does not limit us to models that are rehearsed in the familiar language of business or are currently "trending." Management jargon should not be underestimated. Today, if you do not speak the language that is adequate to the hierarchical level, you have to watch out. We have to consciously overcome these language barriers. It is not enough to discuss the core terms at the beginning of a project (which happens rarely enough), but it can be enormously effective to consciously use other terms and language worlds (Gustafsson et al., 2022). Even if this is inconvenient. For example, it is not about neatly formulated "requirements" to a solution, but about real needs, hopes, fears of other people and groups. These are alien to us, however, and yet we need to understand them before we think of our favorite solutions. To do this, we need to change our perspective; design thinking and personas, for example, try to do just that.

That is the subject of effective navigation. Navigation requires market-relevant knowledge, and this is more likely to arise in practical customer contact than in the boardroom. Navigation is therefore a challenge for the entire system. How do we bring together information, competencies, and attributions of authority so that viable decisions can be made? Outside-in, from the periphery of the company (Oestereich & Schröder, 2019). Decisions are more likely to have to be made locally in large organizations. This has nothing to do with decentralized or centralized organization, just as the OKR mindset is substantially different from MBO. It has something to do with agile and collaborative practices and processes (Wirl & Luge, 2022).

## 10 Leadership Is a Promise

Where do people find support in the organization? The purpose can change in the medium term, the journey in the short term, and connectivity by the minute. And no one knows what the future will hold and what will be necessary in the future. What else can we promise the people in companies? The least we can do is provide information about the shared journey and how to navigate it (Przybilla & Kühn, 2022); and then we must keep this promise.

People in the organization are aware of the uncertainties. It is not for nothing that discussion about good leadership has come more to the fore in recent years, when the traditional structures were increasingly no longer able to provide security. And when we talk about leadership, it is essentially about attitude. This also applies to distributed leadership: When leadership is no longer seen as a contested position, but as a role and service to the team. And leadership tasks can also be distributed among several shoulders.

Attitude is carefully perceived and observed by people. Reliable attitude and behavior are a high expectation; we can measure this by the disappointment that comes when this attitude is not "delivered" fulfilled. Then leadership and navigation in troubled waters also function only to a limited extent. That is why we need to broaden our view of navigation to include such aspects.

At the same time, we need to take a closer look at leadership itself. What are the expectations in terms of attitude, behavior, and action? I must not only reflect on this with reference to my own company, because people also compare how leadership is perceived and exemplified in the ecosystem and in society, in politics, and also interculturally. Against this background, I have to review my thinking and my attitude if I want to get into leadership action and develop new insights for myself as well (Wallner & Völkl, 2022).

## 11 The Opposite of Arbitrariness

Wherever the journey takes us, we all know that no one can know beforehand, including all the people in the organizations, where we will ultimately end up. However, this does not give us any right to arbitrary action, but instead even demands a higher level of commitment on the shared journey. There will be all the more need for a purpose and goal statement, but that can change quickly. There will be process and role agreements, but they can change even faster. There will be decisions, but they will only last until we know better. A lot of information only emerges along the way. Waiting will not help, only trial and error. However, this will not work haphazardly, but according to reliable agreements. And then we stick to what we say; and if it does not work, we say so and agree on adjustments.

There will be strategy or organization consultants and "evangelists" who will explain agile and post-agile and many other terms to us and offer solutions and concepts, but these must ultimately be realized from inside the organization. Because the most important thing is the reliability of organizing and navigating, and that needs inner commitment, "This is ours." This requires real discipline and consistency. Agile teams, for example, experience that this works when they meet on time for their stand-up. We experience it when colleagues reliably fulfill their roles. When we keep promises, walk the talk, talk the walk. And when we think that is a good thing.

It is different from traditional hierarchies. There, we may have retreated into our functional bubble. Now it is all about agreement, behavior, and feedback. That gives us security on the Journey, nothing else. And it is much faster.

## 12 Conclusion

The navigation of a travelling organization is a completely different undertaking than maneuvering a ship safely along a nautical chart. We have no nautical chart. Therefore, our findings are different:

- Where nautical charts and structures provide less data, navigation places greater demands on leadership. Leadership requires a personal, systemic, and social attitude in a world that people perceive as uncertain and disruptive. Navigation is therefore also essentially realized in leadership. What are the demands on leadership? How, for example, can the concept of distributed leadership be applied effectively? How can new leadership practices be tried out and evaluated in relation to the Travelling Organization?

- Navigation must stimulate and support the development of collaboration and communication concepts that empower the organization for the journey. What do appropriate communication processes look like? What interactions are needed?
- This issue also affects the subsystems of the travelling ecosystem: the company's own business, business partners, legislators, and other stakeholders. They all need quickly timed interactions to align and, if necessary, integrate their navigation.
- It is not just about navigating an uncertain route, it is also about appropriate practices. That is, navigation also involves the meaningful conceptualization of navigation itself, of the navigation process, of the situations in which navigation happens. Navigation itself becomes the subject of a regular decision-making process. What kind of navigation does our company need to succeed in the ecosystem? What do we have in our backlog of decisions that we want to try out?
- What is useful and expedient for navigation needs to be reviewed regularly regarding effectiveness and impact because, in the VUCA world, the scales are also constantly shifting. The Three-Pillar Model offers benchmarks for orientation: How does navigation support Purpose, how does navigation support the travel group on its uncertain path, how does navigation support the connectivity of needed resources?
- Navigation needs quickly available information from direct market and customer contact. This information needs to be quickly evaluated within the company and combined into viable decisions. The need for navigation determines the design of corresponding fast processes and agile practices. Navigation influences the organization, and organization influences navigation.
- This means that navigation also involves regularly asking ourselves what we need to start anew and what we need to let go of. This applies to the product portfolio, structures, processes, skills, and cultural aspects. This can mean giving up what we have practiced and using something else that is more obvious, more natural, less over-determined. This process of "letting go" often still has to be explicitly practiced.
- Navigation must also address the areas of tension and connectivity: For example, how do we develop the tension between organization, technology, and people? How do we navigate the organization between creative tension and necessary compatibility of the resources involved?

Sustainable Purpose, Travelling Organization, and Connected Resources: This also results in three key issues for navigation, asking questions about relevant topics instead of providing ready-made answers. This, too, we have come to know as a challenge, because the more complex our VUCA world, the greater the desire for simple patent remedies and populist explanations. And we are finding that navigation needs new questions and new answers, and finding new questions and answers is itself becoming part of navigation. All of this requires a new culture of commitment: Where structures give us less support, we must be able to rely on our competencies and behaviors. They, too, become the subject of navigation.

## References


Doerr, J. (2018). *Measure what matters – OKRs*. Penguin.

Dörner, D. (1997). *The logic of failure: Recognizing and avoiding error in complex situations* (4th ed.). Perseus.

Gustafsson, T., Kühn, F., & Sølvberg, J. (2022). Navigating travelling organizations means beginning – What prevents us from the new? In M. Kempf & F. Kühn (Eds.), *Navigating a traveling organization – Insights, ideas and impulses from the 3-P-model*. SpringerNature.

Haselbach, D., & Kühn, F. (2022). Why cultural policy has such a hard time with travelling. In M. Kempf & F. Kühn (Eds.), *Navigating a traveling organization – Insights, ideas and impulses from the 3-P-model*. SpringerNature.

Höfler, M., Bodingbauer, D., Dolleschall, H., Schwarenthorer, F., et al. (2018). *Adventure Change Management*. Franfurter Allgemeine Buch.

Kahneman, D. (2012). *Thinking, fast and slow*. Penguin.

Kempf, M., & Schlaud-Wolf, J. (2022). Dilemma to navigate a rock. In M. Kempf & F. Kühn (Eds.), *Navigating a traveling organization – Insights, ideas and impulses from the 3-P-model*. SpringerNature.

Kim, W. C., & Mauborgne, R. A. (2015). *Blue Ocean strategy: How to create uncontested market space and make the competition irrelevant*. Harvard Business Review Press.

Kühn, F. (2022). *Unternehmen agil entwickeln*. Hanser.

Kühn, F., & Kempf, M. (2014). *Time flies – Integrate timelines with commitment and results*. In: Integrated Consulting Group: Change. Graz 3/2014.

Kühn, F., & Kempf, M. (2021). Transformation in the field of production: A five-day micro project. In P. Wollmann, F. Kühn, M. Kempf, & R. Püringer (Eds.), *Organization and leadership in disruptive times – Design and implementation of the 3-P-model*. SpringerNature.

Kühn, F., & Wollmann, P. (Eds.). (2012). *Interaktion als Organisationsstrategie*. ICG Integrated Consulting Group.

Laloux, F. (2014). *Reinventing organizations*. Nelson Parker.

Luhmann, N. (1995). *Social systems*. Stanford University Press.

Oestereich, B., & Schröder, C. (2019). *Agile Organisationsentwicklung*. Vahlen.

Przybilla, W., & Kühn, F. (2022). Industrial excellence meets travelling organization. In M. Kempf & F. Kühn (Eds.), *Navigating a traveling organization – Insights, ideas and impulses from the 3-P-model*. SpringerNature.

Püringer, R., & Kühn, F. (2022). Navigating investments for transformation in a travelling organization. In M. Kempf & F. Kühn (Eds.), *Navigating a traveling organization – Insights, ideas and impulses from the 3-P-model*. SpringerNature.

Raman, M. (2022). Beating the Normal curve – Finding the path for a travelling Organization in Disruptive Times. In M. Kempf & F. Kühn (Eds.), *Navigating a traveling organization – Insights, ideas and impulses from the 3-P-model*. SpringerNature.

Reimers, M. (2022). Navigating the ivory tower. In M. Kempf & F. Kühn (Eds.), *Navigating a traveling organization – Insights, ideas and impulses from the 3-P-model*. SpringerNature.

Scherer, J. (2022). The role of "Navigators" in travelling organizations. In M. Kempf & F. Kühn (Eds.), *Navigating a traveling organization – Insights, ideas and impulses from the 3-P-model*. SpringerNature.

Sloterdijk, P. (2009). *Du mußt dein Leben ändern. Über Anthropotechnik*. Suhrkamp.

Sutherland, J. (2015). *Scrum – The art of doing twice the work in half the time*. Crown Business.

Trapp, D. (2022). Decision making in travelling organizations – How to-principles and practices. In M. Kempf & F. Kühn (Eds.), *Navigating a traveling organization – Insights, ideas and impulses from the 3-P-model*. SpringerNature.

Turnwald, S., Jennings, T.-A., & Zirn, J. (2022). Agile and design-based methodologies in sales and service delivery. In M. Kempf & F. Kühn (Eds.), *Navigating a traveling organization – Insights, ideas and impulses from the 3-P-model*. SpringerNature.

Turnwald, S., & Zirn, J. (2022). Viable stepping stones along transformation journeys. In M. Kempf & F. Kühn (Eds.), *Navigating a traveling organization – Insights, ideas and impulses from the 3-P-model*. SpringerNature.

Wallner, H. P., & Völkl, K. (2022). The Leader's personal approach to navigating a travelling organization. In M. Kempf & F. Kühn (Eds.), *Navigating a traveling organization – Insights, ideas and impulses from the 3-P-model*. SpringerNature.

Winnen, M., & Kühn, F. (2022). Gathering points creating momentum. In M. Kempf & F. Kühn (Eds.), *Navigating a traveling organization – Insights, ideas and impulses from the 3-P-model*. SpringerNature.

Wirl, D., & Luge, S. (2022). Objectives and key results – How navigating travelling organizations might succeed. In M. Kempf & F. Kühn (Eds.), *Navigating a traveling organization – Insights, ideas and impulses from the 3-P-model*. SpringerNature.

Wollmann, P., Kühn, F., & Kempf, M. (Eds.). (2020). *Three pillars of organization and leadership in disruptive times – Navigating your company successfully through the 21st century business world*. SpringerNature.

Wollmann, P., Kühn, F., Kempf, M., & Püringer, R. (Eds.). (2021). *Organization and leadership in disruptive times – Design and implementation of the 3-P-model*. SpringerNature.

**Michael Kempf** has been an experienced Management Consultant for over 20 years. The driving force of his professional activities is his strong ambition to design processes and organizations in a sustainable manner. He relishes identifying key challenges, diagnosing complex relationships and assisting in shaping the future. Gaining experience and learning something new are indispensable parts of his life, which is why he likes to seize new opportunities. He began his career as a carpenter before studying social work, education, and business administration. His career has spanned various jobs in social work, 10 years as a manager (HR and logistics) in industrial and retail companies and, since 1998, in advising people, leadership teams as well as working teams and organizations that are all very different. Michael has co-authored numerous publications in the field of leadership and organizational development.

**Frank Kühn** has been supporting companies and institutions in the areas of transformation, organization, and leadership for many years. His clients involve him as a development partner for both their urgent change projects and sustainable future concepts. Frank has a degree in engineering and a doctorate in work science. In leading positions in research and industry, he was responsible for labor management, production strategies, and project management. In the early 1990s, he joined HLP Hirzel Leder & Partners in Frankfurt and later co-founded the ICG Integrated Consulting Group Germany in Berlin and was a partner in the European group in Graz. Today, he is an independent consultant, business partner of ICG and is associated with other project partners and think tanks. He brings his experience to the development of methodologies such as the Three-Pillar Model and has published numerous articles in management journals and books.

# Part II

# Concepts and Instruments

# Navigation Means Beginning: What Prevents Us from the New?

Tommi Gustafsson, Frank Kühn, and Jan Sølvberg

**Abstract**

This chapter discusses approaches and examples of how effective navigation can be realized by focusing on unknown future challenges rather than keeping to the well-known practices of the past, and by freeing ourselves for exploratory thinking rather than being restricted to classical business language. The organizational system, business language, and thinking patterns are closely interconnected; they can condition, support, and hinder each other. Thus, by intervening in terminology and language use, we can influence the course of the traveling organization.

The authors analyzed their experiences with organizational development and transformation projects as well as with the latest research and prioritized five words that make a difference: Ending, Suddenly, Waving, Treasure, and Laughter. Working with these words and their concepts in business environments will create significant aha moments or eureka effects. It will help navigate the company toward the future with an engaged and informed workforce and a management team that is prepared for surprising perceptions, paradoxical thinking, unusual ideas, and astonishing results.

T. Gustafsson
Tuusula, Finland
e-mail: tommi.gustafsson@innotiimi-icg.com

F. Kühn (✉)
Dortmund, Germany
e-mail: frank@kuehn-cp.com

J. Sølvberg
Stabekk, Norway
e-mail: jan@solvberg.com

 
M. Kempf, F. Kühn (eds.), *Navigating a Travelling Organization*, Future of Business and Finance, https://doi.org/10.1007/978-3-030-95326-3_3

## 1 How the Journey of the Authors and Their Contribution Evolved

We navigated ourselves through a writing journey that started many years ago on a bench under a tree in Austria near the Hungarian border during a conference, where we preferred to share our experiences in a smaller team. This continued with conversations that made us explore project experiences with many companies across all industries, all of them looking for good examples of how to navigate their exciting journey in their uncertain business worlds.

We found that our most successful projects have been run with people who trusted in their teams, appreciated unusual inspiration, used disruption to create different approaches, juggled established and quirky concepts, approached new ideas with nonjudgmental openness, delighted in sudden insights—i.e., wanted to develop navigation practices to not only fulfill the known plan, but to shape the uncertain future.

*Without deviation from the norm, progress is not possible. (Frank Zappa)*

They have also realized that navigation happens always and everywhere in the organization, whether we like it or not, that decisions are made by everyone based on more or less transparency, and that not to make a decision is also a decision.

As the pandemic has shown, people are ready to move quickly beyond the standard navigation, decision-making practices, and predefined boundaries that prevented them from experiencing remote or hybrid work and working at maximum efficiency.—What now? Continue this good experience with people who can organize themselves well? Or revert to the former "normalcy" instead of learning that everyone is waiting to help navigate the organization through new realities and future challenges? We know that an engaged workforce often makes faster decisions and surprises its leaders with reality. Conversely, we have learned, through many corporate failures, that hierarchical decision-making makes the situation worse.

## 2 Words for Navigating the Travelling Organization

Let us continue as we were, or shall we rock the boat? Since established navigation routines are shaped over many years, along with the structures that are perhaps no longer effective today, we think it takes a disruptive approach to open our minds to new possibilities.

**Practices for Thinking Differently**

There are several practices from the field of problem and conflict resolution that use different images, scenarios, or languages to create a different perspective and free us from ingrained thought patterns.

Some examples:

- Discussing a solution in a foreign language, which creates a helpful defamiliarization, provides a different vocabulary and mindset as well as the common ground for all the limitations of dealing with a foreign language.
- The hero analogy: how would Robin Hood deal with the problem? What daring tactics and strategies would he use with his Merry Men and his bow and arrow?
- The so-called Disney approach (people take on the role of dreamer, realist, or critic) or De Bono approach (different colors and hats for different roles in a discussion) that gets us thinking about the problem from different perspectives.
- Describing the problem in terms of an animal, such as a cow, leads to an analogous and sometimes astonishing short story.
- Crazy thinking that thrives on differences and liberation: How would we normally solve the problem? Or differently? Or in a crazy way? And what would not work at all? We see that much more is possible than we ever thought.
- A selection of postcards with daily motifs, or picking up things in the forest, or finding images online, then a topic is explained based on these findings.
- Thinking circles that promise sudden aha moments—like those of the authors.

We can use these practices to explore the words and topics that give us new inspiration to navigate and with which we can continue to work. To do this, the words must be meaningful.

**Different Terminologies**

Language creates and constrains organizational reality and vice versa. We are trapped by and in language. At present we are being confronted with new terminologies from the digital or agile world. We resist or adopt them, often without really understanding their meaning or the methodology behind them. So, we developed an "exercise of creating words that make a difference to our jargon" to overcome the business language that reflects current organizational systems and vice versa.

We set out to find words that make a difference in navigating the travelling organization and challenge the ingrained self-image of "professional management" and "business language" that we all use to be part of the club. The words we think about are meant to create resonance with people in the organization, to interlink with their experience and imagination, to foster openness, to support the psychological safety necessary for this to happen, which has been proven to be a key requirement for high-performance teams—which can be shopfloor teams as well as management teams (Duhigg, 2016; Clark, 2020).

Five of these words are discussed below. Feel free to define others that make a difference for you and your organization, tailored to your situation, and that inspire creative solutions.

*Ending*—Every navigation means a beginning, sets a course toward the future. This is what we expect from managers. The more challenging task is to end situations, projects, and dysfunctional patterns, thus freeing the situation, the people, and their minds for the new. The first step is to determine, prioritize, and schedule the endings.

*Suddenly*—New ideas and insights are food for creative navigation. Many of them developed over a period of time, need a safe and inspiring situation to show up, and suddenly they are there, expecting to be dealt with appreciatively and effectively to keep this valuable resource available.

*Treasures*—There are many treasures in the organization: knowledge, talents, ideas, questions, concerns. How do we deal with them? Leave them where they are so as not to disrupt navigation, or dig deeper to open up the navigation and the future to new opportunities?

*Waving*—Personal life, teams, organization, ecosystem, economy, and nature are all seeking their future. On this journey, we experience waves of energy that we ourselves or others create, hypes, fashions, and feasibility, ups and downs. Waves are not predictable, and they are never linear, even if some of them have a certain regularity. We chose the verb form "waving" instead of a noun (a wave) because it is more interesting.

*Laughter*—Creativity, engagement, and high performance need conditions that make them possible. Pressure and cynicism are hindrances. Shared, authentic laughter frees us from stress: The situation is fine, the safety is there, we can open up and share our suggestions. These are reasons why recent research analyzes this phenomenon.

In the following text, you will find some diversity in the way we have described these words. There is indeed both inherence and diversity in the way we developed it: We found the words, then we distributed the task of writing the paragraphs on the words between us, and after these personal journeys, we assembled the text.

**Application of the Three-Pillar Model**

The Three Pillars (Wollmann et al., 2020, 2021) are defined as:

1. Sustainable Purpose—The raison d'être of an organization, bringing new orientation and certainty to the people for their joint endeavor and success.
2. Travelling Organization—The mindset of an organization in a permanent state of flux, interacting with the market and customer journey, with rapid adaptivity.
3. Connected Resources—Interconnecting all needed resources inside and outside the silos, creating consistency between goals and concepts, strategies and processes, competencies, and roles.

This chapter focuses on how to realize navigation that vitalizes the travelling organization, lets ideas flourish, lifts treasures, gives new energy for a purposeful journey. This needs to disrupt established thinking. This chapter offers this disruption by questioning professional jargon and trying alternative words that change perception and thinking and create a new connectivity in this joint endeavor.

## 3 Ending

To have the capacity and energy to begin, we need to end something else, free resources and make profitable beginnings possible. That is why travelling needs endings, and even endings are part of navigation. If not, we will create a monster of beginnings and loose ends. This means we will need to find a way to create good endings and make them happen more frequently—it is often easier to hold on than to let go. Family reunions are so much easier than goodbyes. Useless projects are continued instead of cancelled. Hierarchical structures are maintained and remain overcomplicated instead of transformed into new organizational formats. Is it an evolutionary inheritance that humans tend to add more aspects rather than take something away when looking for solutions to problems (Klotz, 2021)?

Examples of endings could be tidying a room; feeling the satisfaction of completion knowing it will need to happen again before long; the use of To-Do lists; crossing off completed tasks that will not reappear; a funeral; saying goodbye to a loved one. In a work setting, ending a doomed project is difficult but better than letting it continue. Still, we push through so as not to lose our prestige, position, and pride relying on "politics" and emotions to pave the way.

***Using the urgent situation for management learning***

*Bill wanted to cancel the project he had enthusiastically initiated eight months ago (and which now increasingly seemed obsolete to him) and use the resources for a much more urgent and sustainable task. But he was afraid to suggest the decision because he felt the expectation on him as a manager to initiate and follow through on things. He remembered his sales colleague saying: Are you a sheep or a wolf—think about it. He found that it was not just a technical decision that needed to be made, but also a change in leadership mindset that he wanted to share and develop: (1) As a manager, I need to be courageous enough to make business decisions beyond manager stereotypes. (2) We need to make smaller and earlier decisions—try fast, fail fast, which also means constructing future projects differently, more agilely. Because ending has nothing to do with arbitrariness but is a professional option. So ending creates a double opportunity: to start something new that is more valuable, and to experience a valuable new management practice.*

How can endings be supported?

Often, as in the case described above, entrepreneurial decision-making processes are supported by professional coaching of the key person to overcome individual barriers, explore new possibilities, and encourage new behavior. This is why ending is a fundamental question in professional coaching.

***Coaching situation***

*Ann had worked in the same company for almost all her life. With just basic education she had worked her way up to a respectable position and had almost unlimited powers in the execution of her daily work, as management trusted her with the biggest projects in the organization's history. This meant she could provide financially for her family in a different way to what she had experienced herself as a child. Everything was taken care of but there was still something missing for Ann. Her job satisfaction had been declining lately and inner questions about the origins of this had emerged. A journey of analysis of the situation began which also meant exploring options inside and outside her current organization which could re-ignite her lost "fuel."*

Being aware of the situation and realizing that "enough is enough" is the first step in such a process. Finding and evaluating the options is the next—both of which might not be that difficult. But then the hard part starts: For Ann, it would mean putting an end to something that had been inherent for the best part of her life.

What are the challenges? We have listed some obstacles and ideas for overcoming them.

**What can prevent us from ending something?**

- *We feel safer in our well-practiced behaviors, processes, etc.*
- *Things we own are more valuable to us than others.*
- *Everything is someone's preferred solution/tool/etc.*
- *Things have worked so far—why change anything?*
- *We believe in sayings such as "Never change a winning team."*
- *We do not believe in the new, or our ability to make it work.*
- *We do not take the right decision because the consequences are hard.*

**What could help us?**

- *Try the following exercise: Check 100% of your work this year. What 10 percent of your work do you not want to continue and what new 10 percent do you want to start instead?*
- *Where will you be in 6 months if you haven't changed, i.e., begun something new and ended something instead?*
- *What can we do from next Monday on so that <u>nothing</u> will change? Then do the opposite.*
- *As a manager, remember that you are paid for decision-making, which means both starting and ending things. What prevents you from ending things?*
- *Create a Not-to-do list or a list of things to be ended.*
- *Discuss hints such as these with your team and co-create new ideas and welcome the paradoxical ones.*
- *Try a regular exercise: How good are we at deciding together to end things (on a scale of 1–10)? What can we end right now?*

Thinking of personal, team, and company activities from beginning to end would be helpful to have resources available for next tasks. Often, for example, the transition from projects to operations is not clear, which makes people feel insecure and wastes resources. Why not celebrate the delivered outcome and then thank the people for the work they have done—instead of never-ending stories overloading the people and organization? Agile practices such as sprints ease this practice. Therefore, the end needs a clear will and, above all, management discipline.

**What do we need to make good decisions?**
Try the ARC concept.

We identified three aspects to make effective decisions. If navigation is defined as a process of making decisions, including putting an end to something, we must ensure the preconditions of these decisions.

- *Authority*: This is the formal, role-related, or situationally delegated authority and/or personal authority which is acknowledged by other people.
- *Responsibility*: This means taking responsibility for the people concerned by the decision, for the communication, implementation, and results of the *decision*.
- *Competence*: This means really knowing what the decision is and having the personal, social, technical, organizational, ecosystemic skills to understand it.

## 4 Suddenly

### Navigation Needs Suddenlies, and Suddenlies Need Navigation

A travelling organization needs beginnings and endings as a part of its navigation, and both need "suddenlies"—moments where a new insight or idea emerges or the sudden realization when you realize the project needs to end. We benefit from suddenlies because they bring something new to the moment which will help the organization to navigate forward, or even set a new course which is then subject to navigation.

***The Oceanos story: How suddenlies can trigger disconnected behavior***

*In 1991, off the coast of South Africa, the cruise ship Oceanos, carrying 571 people onboard, was having problems. The problem, stemming from a combination of leaving port in the middle of a storm and an engine problem resulting in seawater leaking into the ship due to faulty repair, meant the ship was starting to list.*

*As this got worse, some of the staff, but not the ones you would think, started to realize that no one was taking charge. The guitarist and bass players of the ship's band, joined by the magician, understood that if anything was to happen it would have to be them who would have to organize everything from alerting the coast guard and rescue service to launching the lifeboats. Needless to say, the coastguard and ships answering their mayday call were slightly surprised when they asked the person's rank and the answer was: "I have no rank—I'm the guitarist—the captain is nowhere to be found."*

*Thanks to the swift and resolute response of these three and a few others, all passengers were able to leave the ship, by helicopter or life raft, and survived before the ship sank. Most of the crew fled in "empty" lifeboats—there was space for about 50 more people in that boat but they left almost alone.*

*This story leads to some reflections about crises and other suddenlies: When do appointed leaders act in a selfish way, and how do stakeholders promote this kind of behavior? How does one create a culture that impacts and hurts others and is sometimes dangerous?*

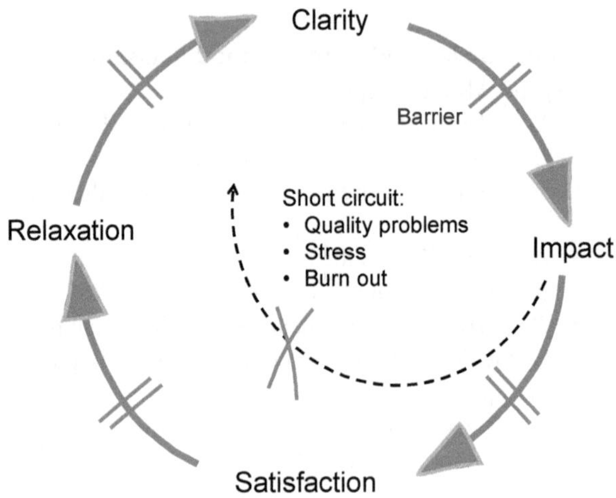


**Fig. 1** This cycle of sensitivity (Kurtz, 1990) shows stages that follow each other. Humans can have barriers between the stages, e.g., they come into action, but do not manage to draw satisfaction and relaxation from it, which is necessary for new clarity. (Illustrated by the authors, used with permission. All rights reserved)

How do suddenlies best come about? There are a few ways that suddenlies could happen or appear. Here are some examples:

- Suddenlies could come from an accident (like the Oceanos) or a global crisis (like COVID-19).
- Another source is a disruption or uncontrollable event/conditions from a third party. A changing priority or a new need for customers, markets, technological trends, and opportunities such as digitalization.
- Or they come from opposing views, like in a debate. In this case, it would still be productive to respect each other's opinions but also disrespect might trigger some new ideas. Does the debate support or hinder suddenlies? This makes the fundamental difference: Is the debate for joint learning or for the right and the wrong? (Senge, 1990).
- Relaxation supports suddenlies, freeing our minds during non-work-related activities (Kurtz, 1990, Fig. 1): Good job-related ideas often come when you are not thinking about work, such as when doing outdoor activities (running, gardening, etc.), taking a shower, going to the cinema, etc.
- At night, a work-related problem may "buzz" in your head making it difficult to fall asleep. But in the morning the problem is solved "magically" by itself. To push on is often not the answer when major breakthroughs are to occur, at least when a bit of novel brain work is required.
- The path to a more productive organization lies perhaps in taking small groups and going to a new mental place to create better ways of working together, where people will suddenly have ideas, the navigated turn into navigators.
- Suddenlies appear when a group of like-minded people come together and create new insights and ideas. With like-mindedness we mean they have similar values, there is a dialogue-based interaction, and everyone is at "the same level"; no one is perceived as being more expert or senior than the others: There is a feeling of

equilibrium in the group. In this scenario "golden moments" will suddenly occur depicting an idea or insight that no one in this group had thought of before.

## Coming from Personal Experiences

Some might say that these "suddenlies," moments when brilliant ideas occur, are a condition for living a full life. It is about self-development, fulfilment, and contribution, supporting a lively organization with teams that are looking forward to their exciting corporate journey. In this case, navigating a travelling organization also includes developing this quality of precondition.

Such preconditions can also serve to provide individuals and teams with the opportunity to learn how best to develop their engagement and creativity, for example, by focusing on tasks. We all know the situations where we try to focus but are prevented from doing so by something else in our minds. In the end, neither gets resolved properly. So, it is not only a question of safety but also providing the space, time, and priorities for effective focusing.

***When conditions are in disfavor—John's story***

*John was going to do the week's shopping so he sat down to write a list of everything the family might need. The only problem was his mind was at work thinking about a suggested process change that had been proposed which would have a serious impact on their working hours for him and his colleagues. This prevented him from fully focusing on the shopping list—no golden moments to be found—and only getting half of what he needed to when visiting the supermarket.*

***Mary's Story***

*Mary, a mechanical engineer who was now working as a consultant, was in the process of writing a book about previous job experiences but in recent months, she had struggled to produce new material. She wanted to write more but increased demand from her work as a result of more contracts being won meant she had more work on her mind, increasing the emails in her inbox and also having to engage with an increasing number of stakeholders. Moreover, she had taken on a volunteer role in the engineer association, which made her put in more hours, especially in the evenings. As a result, the book did not get prioritized.*

*The constant switch of tasks and projects meant a lot of "downtime" for her brain when switching from one task or project to the other. It became clear to her that, much like a tool change in a CNC machine, the machine is idle and not productive while the tool is being swapped for another that can do the next operation. When many such swaps occur in the human brain, we too get less productive as the brain overloads with information and leads us to a state of mental fatigue. So, the mental coordination of tasks prevents the brain from working on them productively and creatively. When trying to focus on more than one thing at a time (sometimes, perhaps falsely, referred to as multitasking) "nothing" substantial gets done!*

In the two examples above there is no room for opening up to suddenlies as there are too many other thoughts occupying the brain.

## Leadership for Suddenlies

The role of the leader is to support the beginnings, endings, and between, i.e., create the conditions to make them happen in the organization. This needs attention, mindfulness, and listening because there is sometimes only a small time slot to make things happen. As psychology tells us, the present tense lasts only a few seconds, then it becomes the past tense. So, we have to consider team meetings, customer interactions, shareholder conversations key moments of suddenlies that need consonance among peers, mutual understanding and respect, a nonjudgmental attitude. Otherwise, the opportunity and the sudden treasure get lost in the past.

What are the challenges here? We have again listed some obstacles and ideas for overcoming them.

**What can prevent us from suddenlies?**

- *We do not like surprises (unless they come from ourselves).*
- *We have no practice in dealing with suddenlies.*
- *No budget for suddenlies.*
- *I am not sure how to behave in such situations.*
- *Our customers want more of the same but cheaper.*
- *Contributing ideas and insights is not appreciated when culture puts a dampener on them.*
- *How do the suddenlies fit our KPIs?*
- *Setting up a Sudden Management System with Key Suddenly Indicators (KSI).*

**What could help us?**

- *Describe the role of a virtual Chief Suddenly Officer and learn from this exercise.*
- *Ask in the warm-up round of a meeting: What have your biggest suddenlies been in the week?*
- *Ask: What could surprise you or others in this meeting?*
- *How could you imagine surprising your peers or your managers?*
- *What would create suddenlies for our customers—negatively or positively?*

No budget or KPIs for suddenlies? Businesses strive to be financially productive, establishing controls increasing predictability. These controls occasionally lead to absurd decisions and priorities since the world is not predictable.

Indeed, many suddenlies will not deliver immediate measurable success according to the current strategy, otherwise, they would not be suddenlies, but they are the precondition for future success. Offering space for suddenlies makes the difference between leadership and management.

## 5 Treasure

*A mind is like a parachute. It does not work if it is not open. (Frank Zappa)*

Most people are ready to change if they understand the need and urgency for making their company fit for the future; but they are prevented from unleashing their talents, motivation, and ideas by overdetermined organizations that provide smart managers with centralized power, strategy consultants with expensive assignments and "stories" detached from reality based on partial information; and themselves with KPIs, outdated policies or agile recipes, and increasing mental workload.

But real life is different. Market and customer feedback reach employees on the ground first (or to use another metaphor, at the organizational periphery with its touchpoints to the broader ecosystem). The employees are interested in handling situations properly with both customer satisfaction and the health of the business in mind. We have never experienced this in any other way—as long as the collaboration within the teams, with their leaders, across the structure was fair, respectful, and trusting. Good contact and cooperation between people are human needs and dealing with them is a human competency. The concepts of servant or distributed leadership are based on such insights.

***Finding treasures in reversing the impact chain***

*In a mail order company, the employees in the returns department performed their tasks at silo-like workstations, timed by a central conveyor belt. KPIs were defined top-down, fulfillment was expected and sanctioned, communication among employees was not allowed. Now one of the managers, triggered by impulses in his professional community, was brave enough to initiate a workshop with the employees. This was a surprising management idea, and they tried the experiment. In the workshop, the participants formulated smart ideas about how to reorganize the department and support their motivation and engagement more effectively. Thus, each team took responsibility for its process end to end. The teams were supported in their self-organization, and they were asked what kind of support, information, and data they needed to coordinate their work in the best way possible. Ultimately, the navigation chain was turned 180 degrees, from push to pull: From "what do you have to do" to "what do you need." This was one of the key outcomes and opened a sudden treasure in their traveling organization.*

How can we leverage such treasures? The treasure is not the one that pirates seek on a desert island. The treasure we are talking about is very close to us, standing with us every day, evolving and changing rapidly, ready to be developed; it is the people in the organization. The challenge is not to dig deep, but to appreciate and respect people for what they can contribute. It is a matter of attitude and behavior. Everyone has a good sense of that because the evolution of humankind is based on empathy and cooperation even if nowadays the survival of the fittest is re-interpreted in business terms of competition, fighting, tactics, which may be a wanted bias of perception in favor of our growth-driven society (Gruen, 2007).

But in many companies, we have obscured these treasures by means of organizational constructs, KPIs, job descriptions, and power play. Management is delegated to navigation tools, and people respond accurately or try to beat the navigation system's perfection.

***Hidden energies to hack the perfection***

*Colleagues from the IT department announced that they had installed the perfect security system. But it only took two days for it to be hacked by other colleagues, which was celebrated throughout the company with some degree of Schadenfreude. Was this reaction a result of the silo-ing of resources and creativities competing with each other? Or was it a rare outburst of hidden energies rebelling against the system that prevented them from exciting co-creative and explorative co-navigating?*

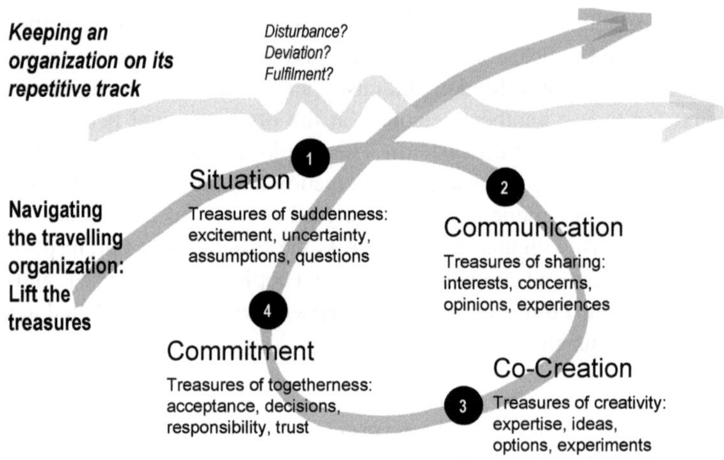


**Fig. 2** Welcome the sudden situations that bring in questions, ideas, impulses. Even uncertainty is a treasure if we take it seriously. Such situations make the organization a living system. The purpose of navigation is to make this possible. (Illustrated by the authors, used with permission. All rights reserved)

Facing challenges, contributing energy and creativity and creating solutions are both human needs and assets. How can they be made to flourish in shared navigation?

Following the idea of valuable treasures, this is an exciting addition to the Three-Pillar Model and its concept of connecting resources. Strategies, roadmaps, products, structures, budgets, agile practices, profiles of people, skills, etc. are necessary resources but they are not treasures. They are quickly spread by managers and consultants who move from organization to organization; after all, they have even been standardized, audited, and certified, and we have to pay for copied solutions. Is not that strange?

The treasures we speak of are not paid for, they pay for themselves when we explore them, see them, listen to them (Fig. 2). This means encouraging and involving people; opening up their surprising perceptions; learning from their uncertainty, concerns, and questions; discussing their paradoxical thoughts and unusual ideas. This level of navigation means giving up control, engaging with new thoughts and thinking patterns. It is not holding onto past patterns but facing future and unknown challenges.

Coming back to the idea of waves, we see in Fig. 2 two different qualities of waves: There are some smaller ones to keep things on track. And there are much bigger ones (here drawn as an exemplary loop) to challenge and reshape the organization again and again. Both have to be navigated in parallel, which needs ambidextrous management.

At the same time, striving for control means disconnecting oneself from the wealth of information, feelings, and creativity of the system as a whole and instead of following one's individual emotions, fears, hopes, traumas, illusions of power and influence. Which we do not consider a treasure at all—unless we share them.

***Hotspot of navigation as a treasure trove of people and organization***

*In the excellence project of a company in the food industry, an open change forum was set up next to the canteen. Here, joint project events were hosted, or the forum simply offered the opportunity to take colleagues by the hand and talk about the intended changes. The results of working groups were immediately exhibited on the forum, new tasks were taken, conflicts were discussed and solved. Developments were shared, feedback and ideas were taken on board. Thus, the forum became the factual hotspot of navigation. This radical openness and inspiration were the prerequisites for bringing in all the treasures of experience and creativity that people discovered within themselves.*

So, what can prevent us from the treasure hunt?

- I do not believe in treasures, only in what I see.
- We have enough other things to do.
- We do not like surprises—what is in the box?
- We do not have a budget to dig deep.
- Others will claim it, no need for conflict.
- I think I know people—there are no treasures to be found!
- If there is a treasure here, it is me.

From this, the challenges to leadership become clear. It is about welcoming people with all their possibilities as well as any kind of surprises, about providing conditions such as time, and about humility and confidence toward the treasures offered in the world, even if they are still hidden.

## 6 Waving

### Meaning of Waves in Navigating a Travelling Organization

*Navigare necesse est*—We must always navigate because the dynamic world around us moves and so do we. Navigating means determining the direction and the pace we take on the different planes we are moving on. The organization, the process, the product, the customer are all dynamic, moving entities: they are all parts of our shared ecosystem, at the same time all of them are on waves of their own.

This exactly is not the intention of hierarchical pyramids which intend to cement the past into the future—which is not predictable. Hierarchies have always existed between parent and child, old and young, strong and weak, master and apprentice. In a small group, these hierarchies are balanced by knowing, caring, trusting, and a sense of travelling together. In a large organization, the hierarchies need to be respected and to survive: a compelling common story with control mechanisms based on reward and threat, even on violence. The top of the hierarchy mostly determines the direction of travel. The more predictable the world and the more routine the output of an individual in an organization seems, the easier the organization is to navigate via hierarchical control—thus, this explains the historical success of large religions, armies, and industries with rituals and standardized operations guiding their members.

In contrast to this static understanding of organizations, the metaphor of waves and waving can help us to create a broader understanding of the corporate journey and how to navigate it. And this means much more than aligning the organization and its journey linearly or simply extrapolating any development. We have rerouted rivers in a straight line and given them a linear shape, which has always led to flooding; rivers prefer to take the natural form of irregular waves that allow them to flow most easily—there are so many learning opportunities.

Staying with the metaphor—what do we know about waves?

- They are a source of energy and information.
- They consist of up-and-down cycles.
- Their size is different—and changing quickly.
- They have their own timing, rhythm, speed, and unpredictability.
- They bring something new that we cannot anticipate.
- They may be critical even for the largest boats.

In companies, the metaphor has been used in a simple form so far, so a broader consideration will lift some treasures in the world. This needs an open mind and will then give us some additional ideas for good practice in organization, collaboration, and leadership.

**Waves of Change**

These kinds of waves are not only the ones described as the well-known change curves (Lewin, 1947), today overlapping at breathtaking speed, building waves of their own, barely achieving their goals. This seems similar to the waves we can observe on the beach. But there is a fundamental difference: The waves in the ocean contribute to a wonderful natural spectacle. The waves in the organization, however, are—put simply—defective if they cannot respond adequately to the disruptions of our time.

***Stories of waves***

*There is a saying about change projects in the workforce: The next wave is sure to come. Let us keep our heads down; then the wave will wash over us. Another saying is about surfers: They always stay on top, ride from wave to wave, and make their career that way.*

Even systemic loops are waves if you pull on them long enough—surprise! But they describe a very different quality of waves, each of them an iterative step of conceptualizing, trying, and committing to face the fast dynamics in the ecosystem. A loop is a cycle is a wave over time.

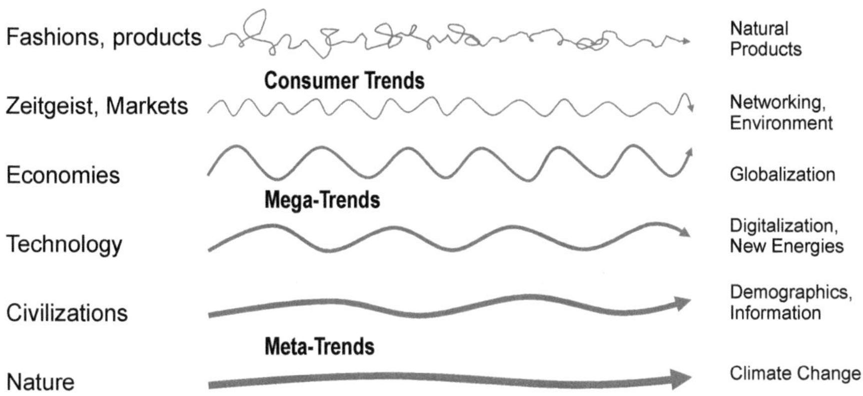


**Fig. 3** The long waves influencing the travelling organization and its navigation concept. (Illustrated by Frank Kühn, used with permission. All rights reserved)

## Waves between Humans

> *... and the least we can do is wave to each other. (John Minton)*

In the English language, the meaning of the word includes waving at people. This waving is full of communicative meaning. Is it attentive, shameful, disparaging, too fast or too slow, royal or humble? We see it every day on the street and on the high stage of political events—across many cultures. It is a very basic outward expression of the relationship between people. In any case, it seems to be a fundamental need since we already ask our toddlers to wave to other people, who enjoy this very much.

To stay with this picture, there are the proverbial wavelengths between humans, and they should fit in collaborative organizations. The same is true between individuals, groups and organizations. Even though we need good diversity to develop organizations, we need a shared basic understanding about this context and must be able and willing to discuss it (Kühn et al., 2021).

## Waves in the Business World

Waving is much more than timing, rhythm, frequency. It includes energy, height, content, messages, like music. But “New Wave” is not only music but also social media, next generation, next mode after the pandemic.

The business world is made of waves. There are more or less regular waves, which we then also call cycles, with technological upheavals, often associated with social upheavals. Well-known are the economic cycles that brought us the steam engine, railroads, automobiles, information, and digitalization (Fig. 3).

Pandemics are also predicted in waves, at least once per century. And each pandemic is itself made up of several waves, we have already learned that. We try to learn from each pandemic wave to increase the resilience of economies and businesses. But each wave will also bring something new.

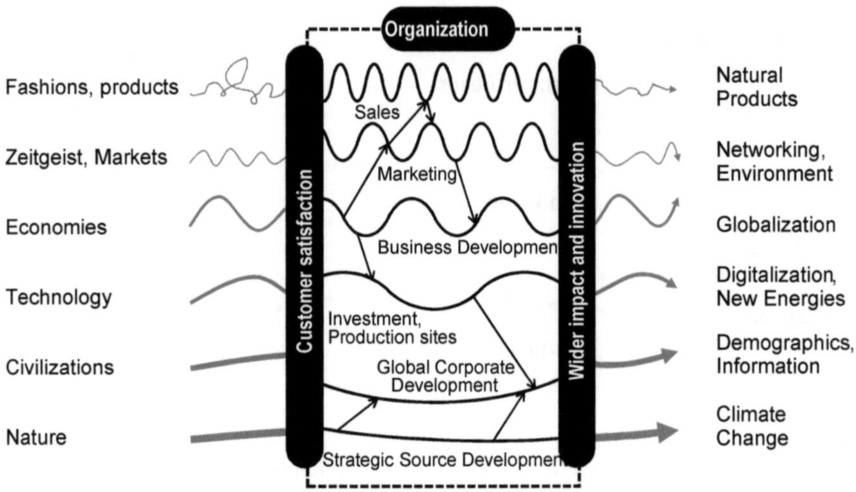


**Fig. 4** The organizational waves interacting with the environment and themselves (Kühn, 2022). (Illustrated by Frank Kühn, used with permission. All rights reserved)

There are several waves running in the organization that we need to know about in order to navigate the company (Fig. 4). They determine the course and speeds, which are seldom aligned, leading to typical conflicts and needs for interaction. A good management exercise is to let the participants draw and explain the waves they see.

Of course, the waves are by no means as regular as shown in the drawings (Fig. 5). The travelling organization is a system of waves that are determined by searching, experimenting, paying attention to an engaged and informed workforce that often makes quicker decisions and surprises its leaders with valuable reality.

We "feel in control" even on an uncertain journey when we have a sense of navigating together with a group we know and trust. We see progress and growth, and we know everyone will do their best if obstacles get in the way. We feel most in control when things are getting better, we trust the people we work with, and we know they also take responsibility for navigating. An organization that learns, meaning leaders that listen and learn, induces hope for a better future and allows for a story that energizes us.

Consider the paradox: Controlling others leads to a sense of distrusting them and to a loss of control. Trusting others leads to them taking responsibility for navigating and you feeling in control but with a totally different understanding of control.

## 7 Laughter

*Other primates maintain social contacts by mutual grooming, which also induces endorphin release. This is, however, very time-consuming. (Robin Dunbar)*

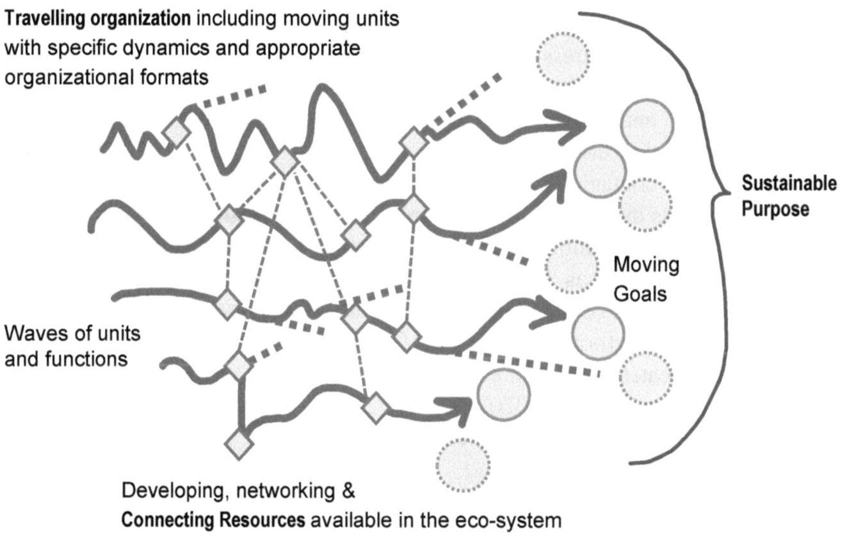


**Fig. 5** Waves of entities—how are they interconnected? (Kühn, 2022). (Illustrated by Frank Kühn, used with permission. All rights reserved)

### Laughter as a Natural Human and Social Need

This observation continues as follows: "Because social laughter leads to a similar chemical response in the brain, this allows significant expansion of human social networks: laughter is highly contagious, and the endorphin response may thus easily spread through large groups that laugh together." (Manninen et al., 2017)

Why did the King, with powers believed to come from God, need a court jester, a joker? Because the jester could say things that others were not allowed to express, the jester brought relief to absurdities and made things more bearable for everyone by making it possible to laugh at them. The late-night comedian serves a similar purpose for society today.

When a new idea, a new mental path suddenly opens for us, we often laugh even though it was not originally meant to be a joke. Sometimes a joke becomes a new idea that can be implemented. This is because a new idea is structurally like a joke for the brain. It is a new connection between things, a sudden change in our perceived world. The change proposed by the idea at first seems ridiculous, thus the laughter comes.

### Laughter as a Sudden Indicator in High-performance Organizations

Laughter, induced by our ability to see something new, funny, or even good about a new situation, maybe one of the indicators of our ability to deal with the new situation. Organizations that cannot laugh at themselves are probably governed by fear. Fear makes things stale, you avoid mistakes and do not rock the boat, you keep quiet. A leader who laughs with a relaxed joy is sending the message that the situation is not so bad after all, there is nothing to fear here.

There are studies by major universities (e.g., Manninen et al., 2017) that show that as laughter relieves stress and boredom, it also boosts resilience, engagement, and well-being. Mentally it spurs not only creativity and collaboration but also analytic precision and productivity! It almost seems that all good things in the world are connected to laughter.

And laughter is contagious. How does this work? "Shared laughter accelerates a feeling of closeness and trust. For example, when pairs of strangers were prompted to laugh together for five minutes before completing a self-disclosure exercise, their interactions were viewed as 30% more intimate than pairs who conversed without laughing first." (Aaker & Bagdonas, 2021) And besides collaboration there is a direct influence on performance factors. "Our brain releases dopamine—a neurotransmitter that creates a sense of euphoria. Dopamine can enhance learning, motivation, and attention" (Black, 2020).

So try this quick check to briefly review the challenges.

**What can prevent us from good laughter?**

- *Fear, lack of hope.*
- *Our culture wants us to be "business-serious."*
- *My boss could be confused or irritated: "Why are they laughing, they should be working?", or: "Managing this business is no joke."*
- *We do not have time or budget for idle laughter.*
- *Cultural, personality differences (they do not understand my humor, I do not understand theirs...)*

If one of these items fits you should be concerned about your company's performance, creativity, and future viability.

**What to do?**

- *"Fear & no hope"? Take your feelings seriously. Clarify what "no hope" means to you. Perhaps discuss it with your peers to countercheck the situation.*
- *Try to understand cultures by discussing what they are laughing about (speaking about laughter will make us laugh).*
- *Analyze what hinders you from laughing (as a person, in the team).*
- *Discuss your culture—incl. "laughter"—yesterday / today / tomorrow.*
- *Change the job or organization.*
- *Ask applicants to tell a story of a personal mistake in a previous job and see whether they are able to laugh about it. Recruit the ones who can.*
- *Try some amusing and useful methodology in your workshops.*
- *Use the first 5 min to try something to make people laugh, e.g., pair work: How could you make me laugh?*
- *Try explicitly "unprofessional" approaches for gaining new ideas, ask your children, or your grandmother.*

**What do you think about the following recommendations?**

- *Organize and schedule laughter times and locations.*
- *Serious business laughter is explicitly allowed.*
- *Install a laughter KPI—is there enough laughter (at least 30 min/day)?*

So let us get serious about laughter: it makes us both creative and intelligent. Which organization, team and individual dos not need this?

As mentioned, laughter can be the quickest form of team building, resonating in laughter together is a strong experience with endorphins and oxytocin being released and stress hormones being released and consumed, leading to relaxation. Other primates groom and tickle each other for social connection and play, people use social laughter.

**Laughter Means Taking the Opportunity**

But laughter is also a way for our minds to introduce a new idea in a non-threatening way; later, the more analytical parts of our mind can work on the actual consequences of the new thought. Thus, when we suddenly laugh, our lives may change and a new reality is created. But because at that moment the new idea seems ridiculous it may take a conscious effort by courageous people to advance it, leading to the common observation that it is the unreasonable people who change the world.

Visiting or perhaps inhabiting Mars will be one of the next big adventures for our unreasonable explorers. What has been found in studies of long-term isolated teams working on challenging things is that a joker needs to be included on the team to make the absurdities of the situation bearable and to enable new solutions to new situations to be found together.

Even more important for the explorers may be that all team members find joy in the project. The joy of work does not have to include explicit laughter, but it means that the purpose of the work is inherently meaningful for the participants.

If you try to force the idea of laughter, it will not bring joy to people and will not be a reason to laugh. Laughter is precious feedback that comes from the deepest well-being of people who have the freedom to welcome it sincerely.

## 8 Conclusion

Navigation means beginning—What prevents us from the new?—Let us start the conclusion with a comparison to our human mind and body. This may be appropriate as organizations understand themselves more and more as organisms.

What do we humans do when we start something new, when we need courage, when we finish something difficult, when we need fresh thoughts when we see the open sea in front of us? We take a deep breath, exhale stale air and inhale new air. This creates relief and gives us new energy. As humans, we have different ways of breathing, depending on the situation. And all kinds of breathing affect the mind and body substantially.

How can organizational organisms develop mindfulness to perceive, understand and draw insights from their breathing? How do established management language and power behaviors prevent organizations from taking a deep fresh breath?

This is also part of navigation: creating the conditions for the new, creating different views, creating fresh insights that support the organization in its transformation and on its journey on uncertain territory.

## 9 Lessons Learned

The following takeaways cover both the need for reinventing our thinking patterns for highly effective navigation and results from prototyping this approach using the words: Ending, Suddenly, Waving, Treasure, and Laughter.

- Navigating the travelling organization toward a good future needs fresh thinking: How can you find your own "thinking-bench" under a tree to overcome boundaries and open yourself to sudden insights for navigation? (Fig. 6)
- Sometimes it is even inspiring enough to question our choice of words and the professional jargon we use in the organization, based on the desire for, and illusion of, total manageability. Let us check the terminology you are using, its meaning and its limits. What are the different words that can be used to free us from entrenched planning and controlling patterns, and open our minds for the navigation that we really need on our journey in the VUCA world?
- There are also well-proven team exercises that challenge our thought patterns and lead us to new insights on how to better navigate the travelling organization. Make sure that every idea, no matter how silly it seems, is appreciated. Respecting and appreciating the commitment of the individual makes all the difference in a high-performing navigation system.
- To have the capacity and energy to begin something new, we need to end something else, free up resources. Therefore, travel needs endings, and endings are also part of navigation. So, our action plans should always include enough things to end and help us implement an effective ending culture. This also means a new understanding of the role of management, which traditionally includes taking the initiative and moving things forward.
- Navigation needs such effective decisions, either to start something or to end it, and effective decisions need at least three prerequisites: Authority (delegated or acknowledged by others), responsibility (for people, communication, implementation, and results), and competence (in personal, social, technical, organizational, ecosystemic terms). Only if these are connected will decisions be effective and sustainable.
- A travelling organization needs beginnings and endings, and both need "suddenlies"—moments when a new insight or idea emerges, or the sudden realization that a project needs to end. How well prepared is our navigation system to quickly incorporate suddenlies into the flow of the travelling organization?

**Fig. 6** Find your thinking bench. (Illustrated by the authors, used with permission. All rights reserved)

- To improve our systemic navigation skills, we can analyze the barriers between exploration, clarity, and action: What prevents us from recognizing the need for action and then taking action? This analysis will always deliver hints for structural and cultural improvement.
- Using the term "treasure," we find much more than pain points, high potentials, and agile practices. They are relevant but are not treasures. The treasures we speak of are not identified in advance, they are not paid for, they pay for themselves when we explore them, see them, listen to them: individuals full of energy and ideas, crazy approaches for better processes, deep desires to make things different. Things that we normally do not have the awareness, time, and budget for. Navigation must include this.
- Navigating a travelling organization is not about steering the boat through familiar waters, or even following a sophisticated change curve. Rather, we cannot predict the waves and how they will evolve: Pandemics, climate crises, political change, market dynamics, technological and social upheavals, or even the diverse ambitions and turns of the organizational functions such as research

and development, purchasing, production, and sales. Thus, it is necessary to be constantly aware of what is happening in the ecosystem and to interact quickly rather than merely reacting.

Navigating a travelling organization means doing it together with a group we know and trust. Controlling others leads to a sense of distrust and a loss of control. Trusting others leads to taking responsibility for having the authority and competence to navigate together toward the future.

What does it mean in terms of the Three-Pillar Model? The journey needs a collaborative navigation set-up, following a Sustainable Purpose, sharing a Travelling Mindset, Connecting Resources that are much more than workforce capacities and person-days. Take, for example, laughter: It is a sudden indicator in high-performance organizations facing unforeseeable endeavors. Organizations that cannot laugh at themselves are likely to be dominated by fear, preventing organizational journeys, shared navigation, joint inspiration to follow the sustainable purpose. Organization development and transformation have to provide situations that free individuals from fear and create new experiences.

Enjoyment of work means that the purpose of the work is truly meaningful. Joy of work, high performance, and curiosity for the new are siblings. Navigation, then, includes social awareness and concern for good leadership for supporting the corporate community on this journey. We can explore this by asking: What in our culture prevents us from navigating our journey with enjoyment?

## References


Aaker, J., & Bagdonas, N. (2021, February 5). How to be funny at work. *Harvard Business Review*. https://hbr.org/2021/02/how-to-be-funny-at-work

Black, J. S. (2020, May 27). Laughter will keep your team connected—Even while you're apart. *Harvard Business Review*. https://hbr.org/2020/05/laughter-will-keep-your-team-connected-even-while-youre-apart

Clark, T. R. (2020). *The 4 stages of psychological safety*. Berrett-Koehler Publishers.

Duhigg, C. (2016, March 25). What Google learned from its quest to build the perfect team. *New York Times*.

Gruen, A. (2007). *The insanity of normality: Toward understanding human destructiveness*. Human Development Books.

Klotz, L. (2021). *Subtract—The untapped science of less*. Flatiron.

Kühn, F. (2022). *Unternehmen agil entwickeln*. Hanser.

Kühn, F., Sølvberg, J., & Ndrevataj, M. (2021). Nature eats culture for lunch: About consonances and dissonances shifting or limiting harmony. In P. Wollmann, F. Kühn, M. Kempf, & R. Püringer (Eds.), *Organization and leadership in disruptive times—Design and implementation of the 3-P-model*. Springer Nature.

Kurtz, R. (1990). *Body-centered psychotherapy: The Hakomi method*. LifeRhythm.

Lewin, K. (1947). Frontiers in group dynamics. *Human Relations*, 1/1.

Manninen, S., Tuominen, L., Dunbar, R. I., Karjalainen, T., Hirvonen, J., Arponen, E., Hari, R., Jääskeläinen, I. P., Sams, M., & Nummenmaa, L. (2017, June 21). Social laughter triggers endogenous opioid release in humans. *Journal of Neuroscience, 37*(25), 6125–6131. https://doi.org/10.1523/JNEUROSCI.0688-16.2017

Senge, P. (1990). *The fifth discipline: The art and practice of the learning organization.* Doubleday.

Wollmann, P., Kühn, F., & Kempf, M. (Eds.). (2020). *Three Pillars of organization and leadership in disruptive times—Navigating your company successfully through the 21st century business world.* Springer Nature.

Wollmann, P., Kühn, F., Kempf, M., & Püringer, R. (Eds.). (2021). *Organization and leadership in disruptive times—Design and implementation of the 3-P-model.* Springer Nature.

**Tommi Gustafsson** "Engaged organizations will perform better, and better performance wins." This optimistic view of the future of work is what Tommi believes in and promotes. Whether it is about shared, engaging leadership, social and personal learning or creative, unexpected development: He claims the outcome will be a better and more productive place to work. With an engineering background and 30 years of international consulting experience, he has a wide array of concepts and methodologies for the benefit of the client. The client process is often unique and experiential, aimed at high impact. He is a consultant in the ICG-Innotiimi Group.

**Frank Kühn** has been supporting companies and institutions in the areas of transformation, organization, and leadership for many years. His clients involve him as a development partner for both their urgent change projects and sustainable future concepts. Frank has a degree in engineering and a doctorate in work science. In leading positions in research and industry, he was responsible for labor management, production strategies, and project management. In the early 1990s, he joined HLP Hirzel Leder & Partners in Frankfurt and later co-founded the ICG Integrated Consulting Group Germany in Berlin and was a partner in the European group in Graz. Today, he is an independent consultant, business partner of ICG and is associated with other project partners and think tanks. He brings his experience to the development of methodologies such as the Three-Pillar Model and has published numerous articles in management journals and books.

**Jan Sølvberg** spent the first 15 years of his working life in the IT industry as a sales engineer, trainer, leader and project manager and the next 15 years as an organizational development consultant specializing on coaching, leadership development and change processes as a partner in ICG—Integrated Consulting Group. Today he is an independent consultant cooperating in various constellations, mainly in the EMEA region, and is the preferred Executive coach of a number of international organizations. He is also the President of the Norwegian chapter of ICF—International Coaching Federation. To the clients, he brings a mix of a coaching approach, experiences from the emerging agile trends of software development, his business insights and a nose for the practical.

# The Role of "Navigators" in Travelling Organizations

Jürgen Scherer

**Abstract**

The VUCA business world requires a more fluid and agile organizational setup to master the enterprise journey. This setup must help connect activities, build bridges, and synchronize projects. Navigation is defined as proactive workplace behavior by leading from within the organization, and by initiating, planning, and controlling the course of action. Navigators are the people within organizations that mobilize resources, make bold decisions, have a passion for executing on and achieving results, and transform agility in a business enterprise.

## 1 Introduction

> Navigating means finding your location, setting your destination and steering your way there. The higher form of navigation is the ability to find one's way in uncertainty—when the location is unknown, the targets are moving, and the paths are varied (Malik, 2015). (Fredmund Malik, Austrian economist, *1944)

Volatile, uncertain, complex, and ambiguous (VUCA) business conditions require a new and different mindset from organizations. While a certain level of structure is still needed for resilience and stability, there is a strong quest for a more "fluid" organizational setup, for accelerated agility and adaptability to address "a state of constant flux" (Bryant, 2020). Hence, it is vital for a travelling organization to be self-reflective, curious, and experimental, to constantly explore the best path between poles, alternatives, and options (Wollmann et al., 2020).

This translates into a new set of skills and traits for the workforce beyond traditional capabilities. As organizations open (Whitehurst, 2015) to incorporate

J. Scherer (✉)
Düsseldorf, Germany

 
M. Kempf, F. Kühn (eds.), *Navigating a Travelling Organization*, Future of Business and Finance, https://doi.org/10.1007/978-3-030-95326-3_4

outside resources and partially break up silo structures to mobilize internal know-how, boundary-spanning skills are needed to facilitate efficient interface permeation. Rather than traditional top-down leadership, open organizations demand a flexible mix of vertical, horizontal, and lateral structures. They enable "circular management" (Hesselbein, 2002) and "circular leadership" (Roebuck, 2019) in "web"--shaped organigraphs (Mintzberg & van der Heyden, 1999). Recent research results confirm the "power of hidden teams," driven by literally "*anyone* who has successfully recruited a group of people to work on something" (Buckingham & Goodall, 2019). So-Called "orbit organizations" consist of employees who connect, bring together, build bridges, synchronize projects, and "agilize" an entire organization from within (Schüller & Steffen, 2019). "This coordination, leadership and orientation activity can be summarized with the term *navigation*" (Huchler, 2013).

> Navigation is the process of directing others and ourselves toward some destination. To navigate is to chart a course for getting from where you are to where you want to go. Getting there is the process of planning, recording, and controlling the course and our progress to our destination. Guiding yourself and others through a series of inter-related behaviors not only determines how and when you get there but what you are when you get there. Navigation goes beyond craft and cleverness. It is the measure of yourself in relationship with others and their relationship with you. (Wohl & Wolter, 2011)

New York Times bestselling author John C. Maxwell describes "The Law of Navigation" as one of "The 21 Irrefutable Laws of Leadership" (Maxwell, 2007). Preparing, listening, and communicating are essential to convey confidence, to monitor progress and to ease some of the fear of the unknown. "Navigators see the path ahead and make mid-course corrections to avoid dangerous water, relying on past experiences as a source of information and wisdom. They solicit the advice of others, examine conditions before making commitments, and have faith in others while dynamically balancing optimism and realism, intuition and planning" (Gilley & Maycunich, 2000). They constitute the kind of leadership required in travelling, developmental organizations striving for competitive readiness through employee growth and development (Gilley & Maycunich, 2000).

Navigators are particularly focused on the "relationship between vision and action," "unafraid to make decisions," "both practical and caring," "masterful at implementation," and "passionate about results and arriving successfully at their destination" (Spencer, 2004). They identify "white spots" (Maletz & Nohria, 2001; Griffin et al., 2012), mobilize untapped resources, recognize opportunities others do not, as if they possessed a kind of "sixth sense." Navigators can deal with ambiguity and paradox in a business context, addressing conflicts and disagreements and guiding toward solutions, change, and adaptation. By doing so, they enable and enhance the agility and adaptability within and between organizations.

The aim of this chapter is to define the role of navigators in organizations by:

1. Illustrating the analogy to monitoring and controlling the mobility of objects and vehicles in different, often difficult physical conditions.

2. Describing the generic skill set beyond functional and/or hierarchical organizational structures ("wirearchy").
3. Conceptualizing the conditions in which navigators are highly motivated for best performance.
4. Showcasing the importance of navigation as a proactive workplace behavior.

**Application of the Three-Pillar Model**
The Three Pillars (Wollmann et al., 2020, 2021) are defined as:

1. Sustainable Purpose—The raison d'être of an organization, bringing new orientation and certainty to the people for their joint endeavor and success.
2. Travelling Organization—The mindset of an organization in a permanent state of flux, interacting with the market, and customers journey, with rapid adaptivity.
3. Connected Resources—Interconnecting all necessary resources inside and outside the silos, creating consistency between goals and concepts, strategies and processes, competencies, and roles.

This chapter describes who, how, when, and where navigation happens in travelling organizations. It is not "the organization" as such, but individuals—"navigators"—within organizations that chart the course (who). They proactively map, team, and maneuver important projects in order to realize opportunities and/or overcome obstacles (how). The organizational setup is key to providing favorable framing conditions and effective motivation for successful navigators (when). In open organizations, so-called "boundary spanners" are predestined navigators, as their roles are like sensing antennas at the internal and external interfaces (where). The interview showcases such an important navigator role.

## 2 Art and Science of Navigation

> The rules of navigation never navigate a ship. The rules of architecture never built a house. (Thomas Reid, Scottish philosopher, 1710–1796)

The Global Positioning System (GPS) based on satellite navigation has replaced various pre-twenty-first century forms, reaching back as far as 6000 years of early nautical navigation systems. At that time, Polynesian tribes already travelled the open Pacific Ocean using wayfinding techniques based on the know-how and experience of highly ranked navigators. American actress and producer Elizabeth Kapu'uwailani Lindsey, a native Hawaiian raised by indigenous elders, has described how her mentor, Pius "Mau" Piailug taught her the famed celestial ("Ethno"-) navigation without the use of maps and instruments (Lindsey, 2020).

Thousands of years later, the invention of the magnetometer compass by the Chinese, devices like Jacob's staff, the sea astrolabe, and the sextant enabled more precise measurements of the distance between visible objects in astronomical navigation.

Terrestrial and aerial navigation comprises visual navigation (piloting) and so-called "dead reckoning (DR)," calculating the distance by means of recorded heading, speed, and time. Charles Lindbergh on the first nonstop transatlantic flight in 1927, and Harold Charles Gatty, an Australian aeronautical navigator on his flight captained by Wiley Post breaking the world record for circumnavigating the earth in 1931, revolutionized the ability to navigate in cloudy, obscure conditions, using DR. Gatty, known as the "Prince of Navigators" believed that "a man with a good sense of direction is quite simply an able pathfinder—a natural navigator—somebody who can find his way by the use of the five senses, developed by the blessing of experience and the use of intelligence."

Albert Segars, Professor of Strategy and Entrepreneurship at the University of North Carolina, Kenan-Flagler Business School, has described navigation as one of seven "tribal instincts" to be found in the DNA of innovative organizations. It is the ability to capture, formulate, and interpret numbers (data/metrics) coupled with conventional wisdom (expert opinion) in order to sense surrounding dynamics and adapt accordingly (Segars, 2020).

Therefore, despite the indubitable achievements of modern technology, i.e., radar and satellite radio navigation, there is still no autopilot system that can fully replace human experience and expertise, particularly in challenging and changing conditions. Two well-known events in recent civil aviation and marine transportation history illustrate the importance of the human impact.

In January 2009, pilot Chesley B. Sullenberger ("Sully") navigated US Airways flight 1549 onto the Hudson River—the most successful ditching in aviation history, saving all 155 people on board. After both aircraft engines had been disabled by a bird strike shortly after take-off at New York LaGuardia airport, Sullenberger decided, based on his vast experience as an Air Force fighter pilot and civil airline captain, not to attempt a landing at one of the nearby airports as suggested by air traffic control, but instead manually flying for a landing on water (Langewiesche, 2009; Hoffman, 2021).

Three years later almost to the day, in January 2012, cruise liner captain Francesco Schettino made a navigation error in a so-called sail-by salute maneuver. The Italian cruise ship, with 4250 passengers and crew members aboard, ran aground and later sank in shallow waters after striking an underwater rock off Isola del Giglio in Tuscany, Italy. The tragic incident resulted in 32 fatalities. The captain was sentenced to sixteen years in prison, guilty of manslaughter, causing the disaster, and abandoning his ship. Maritime lawyer David Y. Loh concluded that "steering a large vessel like the Costa Concordia cruise liner should never rely solely on electronic navigation systems (...) overriding common sense" (Eulich, 2012). Instead, interacting and communicating among the team is essential for navigation (Marquet, 2012; Bailey et al., 2016).

## 3 Skills and Traits of Navigators

> It is very difficult to teach navigation theory to someone who clings to the shore. (Carol Bly, American teacher, 1930–2007)

Applying the insights of navigation systems and theory to today's business environment, navigators need to combine the benefits of extrinsic knowledge generated from data analysis and derived information insights with an intrinsic instinct, a sense of practicality and applicability. It requires a triad of skills and traits, which can be generally described as a balanced portfolio of "head, heart and hand," also known as the holistic learning approach, coined by Swiss pedagogue Johann Heinrich Pestalozzi.

The cognitive dimension (head) provides the factual clarity needed for identifying the current position, the status quo of a business (position A). It is the ability to read and interpret the signals, to call for action toward a new position, to define the targeted state of business (position B) and to outline various options for direction. In order to facilitate the convergence from A to B, the necessary skills include guiding, planning, *mapping*, and particularly open-minded and creative thinking in terms of "and/or" instead of "either/or" alternatives (Wollmann et al., 2020).

The emotional dimension (heart) positions the navigator to mobilize the (human) resources for the journey from A to B. Based on strong internal (across business units, functions, regions) and external (across companies) networking capabilities, the buy-in and commitment are achieved through active communication, strong relationship skills, and empathy. Amy C. Edmondson, Professor of Leadership and Management at the Harvard Business School underlines the importance of horizontal relationships within and across organizations (*teaming*), by "building bridges and being an adhesive" through empathy and cultural brokerage (Edmondson, 2019), also "Velcro organization" (Prahalad, 2009).

However, it is the explicit volition, the will for change, the "maker instinct" (Johansen & Euchner, 2013) that ultimately puts the organization into gear and sets it in motion. This behavioral dimension (hand) of navigators is responsible for generating the agility to get from A to B, for getting things done (Agnihotri et al., 2019) as well as the adaptability to overcome obstacles and hurdles along the way. They "must be able to manage surprises, to cope with complexity and volatility" (Kühn et al., 2020). Therefore, decisiveness and initiative need to be well balanced with flexibility and resilience. Especially the interfaces within and across complex organizational structures demand capabilities in dealing with adversities, *maneuvering* and thriving in often "permanent white water" (Kinsinger & Walch, 2012) conditions.

The navigators' vision (cool head), inspiration (warm heart), and execution (working hands) are equally important for organizational development and transformation. Too often, projects are "heavy-headed" (*cerebral*), and hence potentially stall and stumble, not paying enough attention to heart and hands (Hemerling et al., 2018).

The described navigator skills and traits can be learned and developed. However, traditional development and training methods (on-the-job training, job rotation, coaching, mentoring) are increasingly falling short. Instead, simulation, scenario thinking, and game-based learning are much better suited to trigger and train the desired adaptability and resilience competencies in navigation (Lawrence, 2013; Johansen & Euchner, 2013; Porschen-Hueck, 2017). Thus, besides assessing these competencies when recruiting, organizations are better off hiring for attitude and training for skills.

# 4 Conditions and Context for Navigators

> It is not the ship so much as the skillful sailing that assures the prosperous voyage. (George William Curtis, American writer, 1824–1892)

The motivation for successful and active navigation in organizations is highly dependent on motivational factors, integrating implicit and explicit motives with perceived abilities (Kehr, 2004). Regarding intrinsic motivation, American author Daniel M. Pink has identified autonomy, mastery, and purpose as the decisive factors for drive (Pink, 2011). Based on studies at the Massachusetts Institute of Technology (MIT) and other universities, employee satisfaction and performance positively correlate with the desire to be self-directed (autonomy), the urge to get better skills (mastery), and the wish to do something meaningful (purpose). This is predominantly relevant for, but not restricted to, Generation Y employees.

An open organization committed to developing navigation as a core competence needs to provide a structure and culture to nurture, and incentivize navigator activities and projects, providing sufficient extrinsic motivation. According to the Institute for Social Science Research (ISF) in Munich this includes three core organizational competencies. The "care competence" stands for the awareness and recognition, for the expressive support for self-initiated activities at intra- and interorganizational interfaces including incentives for proactive involvement and engagement. The so-called "create/play competence" ensures sufficient space for creativity, for bottom-up innovation, a culture of continuous organizational learning, and lateral thinking for unconventional solutions. Thirdly, within the "framework competence" the organization provides the necessary order and structure and a feedback mechanism for perspective and orientation (Porschen-Hueck & Huchler, 2016).

The perceived abilities of an organization by its major stakeholders, including its employees are largely driven by transparency, empowerment, and collaboration (TEC model, Puckett, 2020). Transparency relates to data and information, to plans and intentions, results, and impact of one's own work and is thus a strong trust-building and motivational component. The empowerment consists of the freedom to create and innovate, the self-determined direction and speed and the self-perceived ownership of action and change. Collaboration depends on the ability of an organization "to co-explore the territory and co-create the future" (Kühn et al.,

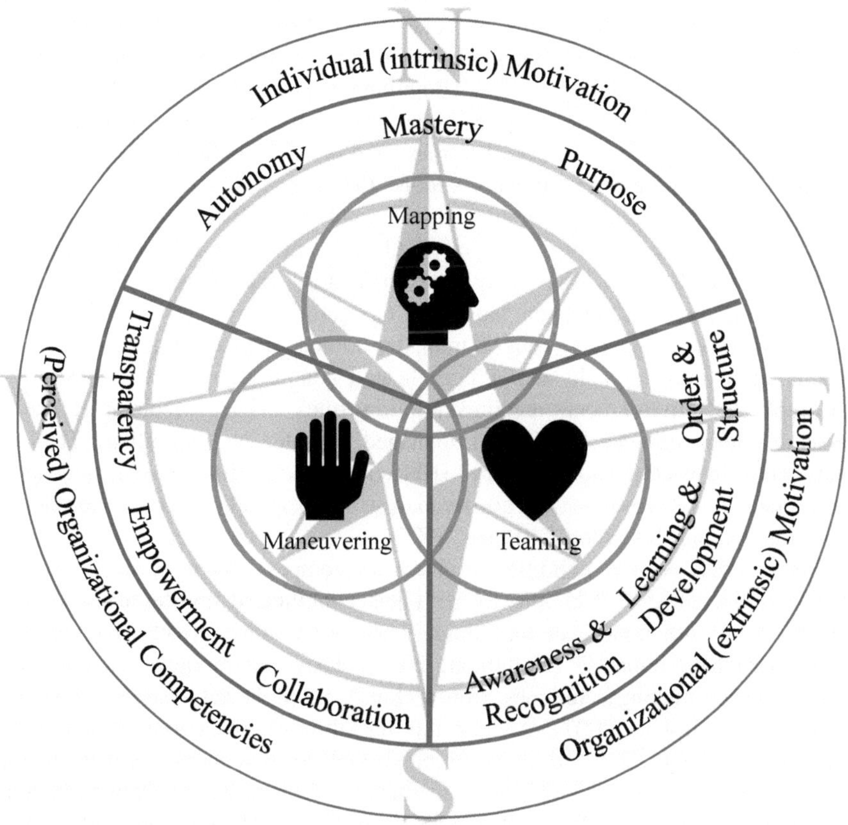


**Fig. 1** Navigator model. (Illustrated by the author, all rights reserved)

2020), to jointly learn and grow, to exchange know-how, and ultimately contribute to a larger purpose.

Figure 1 summarizes the individual and organizational components of business navigation.

## 5 Navigators in Boundary-Spanning Roles

And the winds and the waves are always on the side of the ablest navigators. (Edward Gibbon, English historian, 1737–1794)

Stephen Mirante, long time CHRO and recent CAO of the American television and radio network CBS addresses the role of a "chief navigator": "balance science and art—blending the ability to define root causes, analyse data and build trust up, down and across the organization. They typically have both left- and right-brain capabilities, combining a strong analytical mind and decisiveness with the ability to build relationships with a range of stakeholders. Navigators can articulate their position on key issues while integrating (and appreciating) others' points of view. Being a good listener during conflict, combining an enterprise view with a keen eye for detail, connecting dots and resources across business lines and functions, demonstrating a profound sense of fairness and creative problem-solving (...) are the foundation of the chief navigator's tools" (Mirante, 2020).

In principle, according to Mirante, this role can be taken by anyone in the C-Suite. IMD Professor Emeritus of Technology and Innovation Jean-Philippe Deschamps refers to the CTO as the "corporate navigator" (Deschamps, 2008), other publications see the CFO as an "advanced navigator" (Weber et al., 2009; Crook, 2013). However, this represents a more traditional understanding of leadership operating in rather simple and/or complicated conditions of "ordered context." "Complicated environments are linear, follow rules and are predictable; like an assembly line, they can be planned, managed, repeated and controlled. They are maximised by routine and efficiency" (Heffernan, 2020). Here, most organizations still practice a "sense → categorize/analyse → respond" type of "top-down" decision-making (Snowden & Boone, 2007).

By contrast, VUCA conditions, which are complex, often even chaotic, are "unordered contexts." "Complexity isn't just complicated on steroids. Complex environments are non-linear and fluid, where very small effects may produce disproportionate impacts" (Heffernan, 2020). They require new emergent and novel decision-making techniques "from within," i.e., "probe/act → sense → respond" (Snowden & Boone, 2007). Against this backdrop, a much more experimental (head), sensitive (heart), and adaptive (hand) skill set is required, as it is inherent with navigators at various levels of an organization. Lois Kelly and Carmen Medina, co-authors of "Rebels at Work: A handbook for leading change from within" have coined the term "tugboat pilot" for some of these most valuable members navigating the organizational landscape. "Tugboat pilots are masters of context and of reading people. They seem to have recognized early in their careers that their innate skills are suited to guiding others and embrace that mission with enthusiasm... Unfortunately, they don't wear name tags identifying themselves" (Kelly & Medina, 2014).

Boundary-spanning roles within and between organizations are predestined conditions for navigators. The Business Relationship Management Institute (BRMI) defines three subsequent steps in the management of successful business relationships: (1) connecting, (2) orchestrating, and (3) navigating in order to mobilize projects and programs, drive value and facilitate convergence (Jesuthasan, 2017).

Dennis W. Organ, Professor of Personnel and Organizational Behavior at Indiana University described this very context fifty years ago. In "turbulent fields," boundary agents are the "linking pins" between their organizations and the environment, functioning as "sensory organs." As "**it is not really organizations that interact—*it is people*,**" "**one must presume that leaders of organizations would have considerable interest in the type of person who is best suited for these roles...with rather distinctive profiles of abilities, traits, and values**" (Organ,

1971). However, "comparatively little attention is accorded to the pivotal role of individual actors in the management of [...intra- and] inter-organizational relationships" (Williams, 2002).

As there is hardly any literature showcasing the specific proactive workplace behavior in boundary-spanning roles, the author of this chapter initiated a research project, capturing navigation within and between organizational boundaries through a series of semi-structured qualitative interviews. The following is the transcript of a 90-minute interview with Melissa[1], a US-based R & D manager, as a prime example of navigation in an intra-organizational project context.

## Navigator Interview

Melissa has worked for almost 20 years for a large global Fortune 500 company with double-digit billion-dollar revenues. Based on a strong technical background in Chemical Engineering, and a fast-track international career in various R & D roles, her passion is bridge-building between the technical and commercial sides of business. Consequently, she extended her education with an MBA while working full-time to further master her skill set and business understanding.

At the end of 2018, Melissa was involved in a very complex company project, seeking to develop and market a new technology in her industry. Two years in, the project had already absorbed a substantial amount of money, time, and resources. Yet, increasing complexity and frustration between numerous dispersed technical experts and commercial partners, made it look more and more like a dead-end street. As Melissa recalls: *"The status quo of this important company initiative was murky, the project members almost created their own obstacles and were stuck in their closed silos."* Although there was no defined role for her, no script for her engagement, she recognized the need for clarity and simplicity, for "connecting the dots." She was inspired by the opportunity to provide the "bigger picture" and shape the decision-making process. She understood that the ineffective journey of continuous small step changes had to be stopped. Instead, her target was to trigger the uncomfortable but inevitable last experiment, that would ultimately prove or fail the business case. In order to get there, she had to start sharing risks, open communication, and speak the same language. As Melissa describes it: *"Going on the journey to simplify complexity is often as rewarding as the outcome."*

She immediately built rapport with all project stakeholders involved, most of them outside her own area of responsibility. In many one-on-one sessions, and "not afraid to ask the silly questions," she empathetically listened and developed a relationship with each project contributor. *"I introduced myself to all the characters of the movie, but I still had to learn how they can act. I was curious to render their emotions, to understand their state of mind, to put myself into their shoes."* Melissa felt that particularly working collaboratively with those experts who "where not getting on the bus" was mission critical. Often indirectly influencing them by leveraging peers in other departments or inserting a junior person into the project with an unbiased view, helped to "massage" the key stakeholders. *"Instead of breaking their functional territory, my intentions were rather getting different stakeholders step-by-step on the same page, trusting and believing in each other."* The fascinating part of teaming up with all the involved project members is "to crack the best out of everyone," to develop the best possible mix of expertise, like in a "mosaic of talents."

[1]The interview took place on October 8, 2021, via video. The name of the interviewee has been changed to protect their identity. All rights reserved with the author.

The project was one of the largest company initiatives with very deep vertical (= functional) knowledge, but one of the least horizontally (= cross-functionally) connected. The technical community was afraid to point out the challenges and risks, fearing adversity from the business units with repercussions of ending funding and support. The commercial side could not fully comprehend the benefits and was impatient at the speed of step-change progress, increasingly losing confidence. Thus, the project required a mix of adaptability, flexibility, and patience. A key moment was a long-anticipated presentation by the technical leads to the decision makers about the project business opportunity. When Melissa realized that there was "no hook" for the business side, "no story to tell," she took the lead, translated technical language into business-relevant terms, addressing the project realities openly and honestly. *"That was like cracking the code."* She was able to release the deadlocked approval and funding for a pilot line, and consequently, the results lead to the project being halted and resources being redeployed.

In review, Melissa summarizes her navigator role as "non-linear," driven by the desire to seek experimental opportunities with autonomy, and to discover new organizational playgrounds for value creation—almost like being *"energized by an adrenaline rush from the unknown."*

## 6 Conclusion

Travelling organizations need a holistic agility in their mindset and DNA, a readiness to embrace change, and an eagerness to deliver. Increasingly, this requires their organizational members to be curious, open, self-reflective, and experimental in order to cope with uncertainty, special challenges, and unforeseen obstacles (Wollmann et al., 2020). "Organizations with effective teams of navigators can spot opportunities, potential dangers, and emerging changes. With more sets of eyes on the prize, they're able to see around corners in a way that fragmented organizations cannot" (Price, 2017).

Using a metaphor, a shrewd navigator combines the ability to measure ("thermometer"), to adjust ("thermostat", Whitehurst, 2015), and to keep the temperature at an equilibrium ("thermoregulation") despite changing conditions. Their success is "deeply human, derived from curiosity, imagination and not a little bravery, prepared to navigate the unknown in pursuit of the ill-defined because they realise that the only way to know the future is to make it" (Heffernan, 2020).

## References

Agnihotri, R., Yang, Z., & Briggs, E. (2019). Salesperson time perspectives and customer willingness to pay more: Roles of intraorganizational employee navigation, customer satisfaction, and firm innovation climate. *Journal of Personal Selling & Sales Management, 39*(2), 138–158.

Bailey, N., Housley, W., & Belcher, P. (2016). Navigation, interaction and bridge team work. *The Sociological Review, 54*(2), 342–362.

Bryant, F. D. (2020, September 1). 3 ways to improve your adaptability and manage your life. www.evernote.com

Buckingham, M., & Goodall, A. (2019, May 14). The power of hidden teams. www.hbr.org

Crook, S. (2013, October 28). Finance as the navigator and not the "support function". www.pwc.blogs.com

Deschamps, J.-P. (2008). The Chief Technology Officer—Corporate navigator, agent of change and entrepreneur. In P. Bottger (Ed.), *Leading in the top team—The CXO challenge*. University Press.
Edmondson, A. (2019, September 10). Fostering collaboration across silos. Webinar summary. www.hbr.org
Eulich, W. (2012, January 16). Why navigation can 'fail' and other cruise ship questions. www.businessinsider.com
Gilley, J. W., & Maycunich, A. (2000). *Beyond the learning organization: Creating a culture of continuous growth and development through state-of-the-art human resource practices*. Perseus.
Griffin, A., Price, R. L., & Vojak, B. A. (2012). *Serial innovators: How individuals create and deliver breakthrough innovations in mature firms*. Perseus.
Heffernan, M. (2020). *Uncharted: How uncertainty can power change*. Avid Reader Press.
Hemerling, J., Kilmann, J., & Matthews, D. (2018, November 5). The head, heart, and hands of transformation. www.bcg.com
Hesselbein, F. (2002). *Hesselbein on leadership*. Jossey-Bass.
Hoffman, B. (2021, July 17). Top decision-making expert says leaders need to get comfortable with uncertainty. www.forbes.com
Huchler, N. (2013). *Wir Piloten. Navigation durch die fluide Arbeitswelt*. Edition sigma, Berlin.
Jesuthasan, M. (2017, December 5). Business relationship management: BRM as a role. www.westmonroepartners.com
Johansen, R., & Euchner, J. (2013). Navigating the VUCA world: An interview with Bob Johansen. *Research Technology Management, 56*(1), 10–15.
Kehr, H. M. (2004). Integrating implicit motives, explicit motives, and perceived abilities: The compensatory model of work motivation and volition. *Academy of Management Review, 29*(3), 479–499.
Kelly, L., & Medina, C. (2014). *Rebels at work: A handbook for leading change from within*. O'Reilly.
Kinsinger, P., & Walch, K. (2012, July 9). Living and leading in a VUCA world. http://www.thunderbird.edu/article/living-and-leading-vuca-world
Kühn, F., Kempf, M., & Chamberlain, J. (2020). The concept of purpose, travelling and connectivity: Three Pillars of organization and leadership. In P. Wollmann, F. Kühn, & M. Kempf (Eds.), *Three Pillars of organization and leadership in disruptive times—Navigating your company successfully through the 21st century business world* (pp. 27–39). Springer Nature.
Langewiesche, W. (2009, May 5). *Anatomy of a miracle*. www.vanityfair.com
Lawrence, K. (2013). Developing leaders in a VUCA environment. www.execdev.unc.edu
Lindsey, E. (2020, October 16). *We, the Navigators*. www.elizabethlindsey.com
Maletz, M. C., & Nohria, N. (2001). Managing in the whitespace. *Harvard Business Review, 79*(2), 102–111.
Malik, F. (2015). *Navigieren in Zeiten des Umbruchs: Die Welt neu denken und gestalten*. Campus.
Marquet, L. D. (2012). *Turn the ship around: How to create leadership at every level*. Penguin Publishing Group.
Maxwell, J. C. (2007). *The 21 irrefutable laws of leadership: Follow them and people will follow you* (10th anniversary ed.). HarperCollins.
Mintzberg, H., & van der Heyden, L. (1999). Organigraphs: Drawing how companies really work. *Harvard Business Review, 77*(5), 87–94.
Mirante, S. (2020, October 2). Does your organization have a "Chief Navigator". www.ceoworld.biz
Organ, D. W. (1971). Linking pins between organizations and environment: Individuals do the interacting. *Business Horizons, 14*(6), 73–80.
Pink, D. H. (2011). *Drive: The surprising truth about what motivates us*. Riverhead Books.

Porschen-Hueck, S. (2017). Kompetenzen in der Offenen Organisation in qualitativer Sicht. In S. Porschen-Hueck, N. Huchler, S. Sauer, M. Burgenmeister, & S. Pfeiffer (Eds.), *Kompass für Open Organisation*. Institut für Sozialwissenschaftliche Forschung.
Porschen-Hueck, S., & Huchler, N. (2016). Offene Organisation: Anforderungen, Strategien, Kompetenzen. *PERSONALquarterly, 68*(2), 9–15.
Prahalad, C. K. (2009, September 10). In volatile times, agility rules. *Business Week*.
Price, H. (2017, May 17). How to navigate business growth as a team. www.blog.jostle.me
Puckett, S. (2020). *The agile culture code: A guide to organizational agility*. BusinessVillage.
Roebuck, L. (2019). *Circular leadership: Together we rise*. Capucia.
Schüller, A. M., & Steffen, A. T. (2019). *Die Orbit Organisation: In 9 Schritten zum Unternehmensmodell für die digitale Zukunft*. Gabal.
Segars, A. H. (2020). *Ideas and innovative organizations: A tribal perspective*. Peter Lang.
Snowden, D. J., & Boone, M. E. (2007). A leader's framework for decision making. *Harvard Business Review, 85*(11), 68–76.
Spencer, S. A. (2004). *The heart of leadership: Unlock your inner wisdom and inspire others*. Rider.
Weber, J., et al. (2009). *Der CFO als advanced navigator*. Wiley.
Whitehurst, J. (2015). *Open organization: Igniting passion and performance*. Harvard Business Press.
Williams, P. (2002). The competent boundary spanner. *Public Administration, 80*(1), 103–124.
Wohl, R. A., & Wolter, L. J. (2011). *Navigating organizations through the 21st century: A metaphor for leadership*. Xlibris.
Wollmann, P., Kühn, F., & Kempf, M. (2020). Three Pillars of organization and leadership. In P. Wollmann, F. Kühn, & M. Kempf (Eds.), *Three Pillars of organization and leadership in disruptive times—Navigating your company successfully through the 21st century business world*. Springer Nature.
Wollmann, P., Kühn, F., Kempf, M., & Püringer, R. (Eds.). (2021). *Organization and leadership in disruptive times—Design and implementation of the 3-P-model*. Springer Nature.

**Jürgen Scherer** holds a MBA and PhD from Cologne University in Germany. He has 30 years spanning broad industry experience in Executive positions for global corporations in Germany and the USA, namely FMCG company Henkel, Specialty Chemicals company Cognis (acquired 2010 by BASF) and Industrial Packaging company Mauser. He has published various papers in business journals and readers and has presented Business-to-Business Management topics at international conferences. Since 2019 he is a Business Consultant & Coach with www.bxb-exchange.com and is lecturing at various Business Schools in Europe and in the USA.

# Viable Stepping Stones along Transformation Journeys: Ensuring Business Execution while Transforming Diverse Organizations

Stefan Turnwald and Julia Zirn

**Abstract**

In transforming organizations, the concept of Viable Stepping Stones helps keep the focus on business execution. While different parts of the organization transform at different speeds, the Viable Stepping Stone sets the temporary focus point on the business execution. All sub-projects of the transformation are aligned and complemented. The viability of the stepping-stone is ensured by the thorough analysis and alignment of all relevant steps and tools along the business process. Temporary solutions close the gaps caused by elements of the business process that are either not yet able to deliver against the requirements at the Stepping Stone or for parts that have developed past these requirements already. Adding the Viable Stepping Stones to the transformation tools allows for balancing the progress of the transformation journey with excellence in business execution.

The concept of the Viable Stepping Stones translates the idea of the Minimum Viable Product (MVP) from product design into the temporary platform for the testing and improvement of critical steps in the business execution along the transformation journey. In return, the transformation initiative and its sub-projects are updated and adapted to changes in the marketplace and altering needs of the business. After the detailed outline of the Viable Stepping Stone process, the link and the synergies with the Three-Pillar Model are discussed. The chapter concludes with the suggestion to leverage Objectives and Key Results (OKR) cycles along the Viable Stepping Stone process to set and manage

S. Turnwald (✉)
Zug, Switzerland
e-mail: stefan.turnwald@compski.onmicrosoft.com

J. Zirn
Bonn, Germany
e-mail: zirn@cidpartners.de



M. Kempf, F. Kühn (eds.), *Navigating a Travelling Organization*, Future of Business and Finance, https://doi.org/10.1007/978-3-030-95326-3_5

objectives for the sub-projects of the transformation as well as for the business teams.

# 1 Introduction: Transformation Management in Diverse Organizations

## 1.1 The Challenge

Driving sustainable change in diverse organizations is a challenging and often cumbersome task. Transformation in organizations with a high degree of diversity is even more difficult to accomplish. The reasons for the highly diverse situation may be manifold:

- Affiliates in different geographies or cultures.
- Affiliates at different stages of organizational development.
- Operational silos with specific responsibilities and tasks along critical business processes.
- Large business operations with limited alignment across the various building blocks.

The more diverse the organization is, the more effort is required to achieve sufficient alignment across all relevant building blocks of the organization and the viability of the business execution. In addition, the organizational pluralism of short-, medium-, and long-term foci, i.e., the potential conflict of transformation goals and the short-term business execution requires attention (Hoenig de Locarnini & Kühn, 2021).

## 1.2 The Three-Pillar Model

Peter Wollmann, Frank Kühn, and Michael Kempf (Wollmann et al., 2020) introduced the three pillars of Sustainable Purpose, Connected Resources, and the Travelling Organization as a versatile model for managing transformation. These three pillars are suited to give the transformation the required direction—guiding leaders and associates along the change journey, to leverage and to align resources, and to take the progress of the change into account when managing the transformation.

▶ **Application of the Three-Pillar Model**
The Three Pillars (Wollmann et al., 2020, 2021) are defined as:

1. Sustainable Purpose—The raison d'être of an organization, bringing new orientation and certainty to the people for their joint endeavor and success.
2. Travelling Organization—The mindset of an organization in a permanent state of flux, interacting with the market and customer journey, with rapid adaptivity.
3. Connected Resources—Interconnecting all required resources inside and outside the silos, creating consistency between goals and concepts, strategies and processes, competencies, and roles.

This chapter focuses on how to ensure the viability of business execution while the diverse organization is travelling along its transformation journey. The concept of the Viable Stepping Stones is introduced for connecting resources and the temporary optimization and updating of the business processes to the progress of the transformation. Furthermore, the Viable Stepping Stone offers a controlled environment for testing outcomes from the sub-projects of the transformation and the updated business processes. This allows for the adjustment of the transformation, for the further improvement of the business execution, and for the renewal of the sustainable purpose. The authors suggest complementing the Viable Stepping Stone process with OKR (Objectives & Key Results) cycles for breaking the conceptual approach into tangible goals and tasks.

## 1.3 What this Chapter Offers

The authors Stefan Turnwald and Julia Zirn introduce the concept of Viable Stepping Stones and lay out the opportunities that this framework offers to the planning, monitoring, and management of transformation projects based on the Three-Pillar Model. Furthermore, the Viable Stepping Stones process will be complemented with OKR (Objectives & Key Results) cycles (Doerr, 2018). The combination of OKRs and the Viable Stepping Stones will provide you with the framework to identify, set, and manage relevant goals to ensure successful business execution while driving transformation.

- If you are managing transformation in diverse organizations, you will be provided with a robust conceptual approach for aligning the change journey with the ongoing business execution.
- If you are familiar with the Three-Pillar Model, you will be offered the tools to enable successful business execution during transformation by bringing the three pillars to life.
- If you are interested in or using the OKR approach already, you will learn about the synergies between OKRs and Viable Stepping Stones within the Three-Pillar Model.

## 2 From Checkpoints to Viable Stepping Stones

Transformation projects come with a multitude of change tasks. The breakdown of the transformation project into smaller easier-to-handle sub-projects is a common approach in management in transformation (Fig. 1). For the leader of the transformation project, it is important to understand the benefits, dynamics, and challenges to the management of transformation by sub-project.

### 2.1 The Challenges to Transformation in Large and Diverse Organizations

The culture and way of working of the transforming organization may impact the set-up and management of the transformation project.

- The formation and staffing of the sub-projects often reflect the responsibilities and competencies of individuals and teams. If the functions, teams, and individuals lack sufficient alignment in daily business, this challenge is likely to be transferred to the management and alignment of the sub-projects.
- Sub-projects are led by highly specialized subject matter experts. The members of the sub-project team are recruited based on their expertise and competencies. The high degree of specialization bears the risk of missing out on the perspectives and needs of the other sub-projects.
- Each of the sub-projects addresses specific change tasks. Accountable for the completion of the specific change tasks, the leader of the sub-project may prioritize its completion over alignment with the other sub-projects.

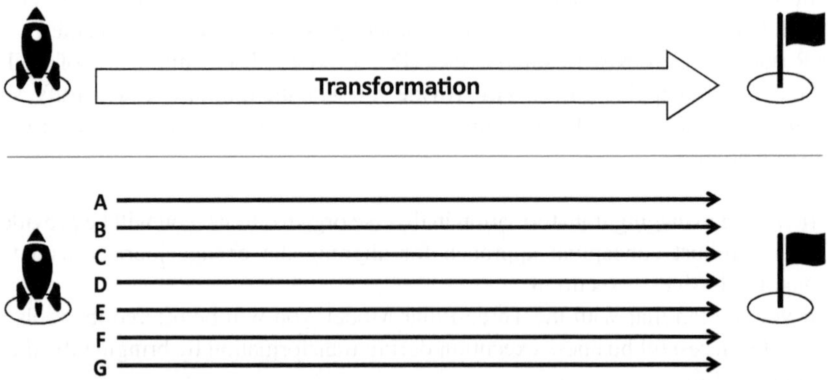


**Fig. 1 Transformation Projects**—Large transformation initiatives are broken down into task-specific and easier-to-manage projects and sub-projects (Illustrated by the authors, used with permission, all rights reserved)

The more fragmented the sub-projects are, the more effort will be required to align the management and to harmonize its outcomes to ensure the success of the overall transformation.

## 2.2 The Timing and Phasing of Sub-Projects

Of particular importance in the management of transformation initiatives is the timing and phasing of the sub-projects (Fig. 2).

### Continuation, Discontinuation, and Initiation of Sub-Projects

While some sub-projects cover topics that are of continuous importance from launch to the end of the transformation (Fig. 2 A, B, C), others lose relevance and will be discontinued along the transformation journey (Fig. 2 D). Discontinued sub-projects might be picked up again or be substituted with new ones (Fig. 2 E). In addition, new sub-projects are launched to address topics of increasing relevance along the transformation journey (Fig. 2 F, G).

### Progress of the Sub-Projects

Some sub-projects are at the desired state from the beginning of the transformation initiative (Fig. 3 A). The sub-projects that require change may be initiated and achieve their goals earlier (Fig. 2 B, F), or later (Fig. 2 C, E, G). Critical elements

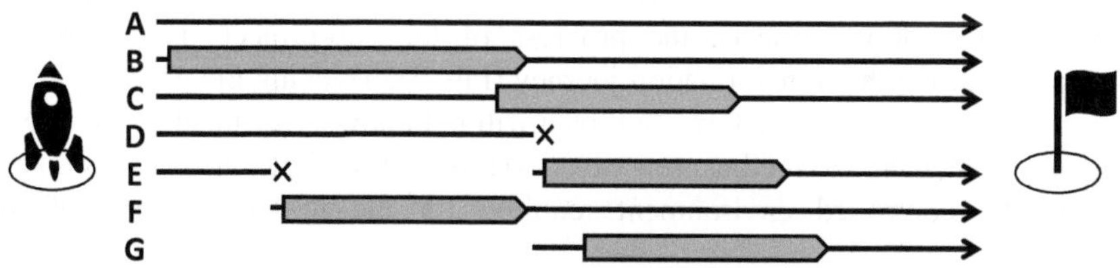


**Fig. 2** **Timing of the Sub-Projects**—In diverse organizations, the work on the sub-projects of the transformation initiative may start and end at different times. Also, sub-projects are likely to progress at different speeds (Illustrated by the authors, used with permission, all rights reserved)

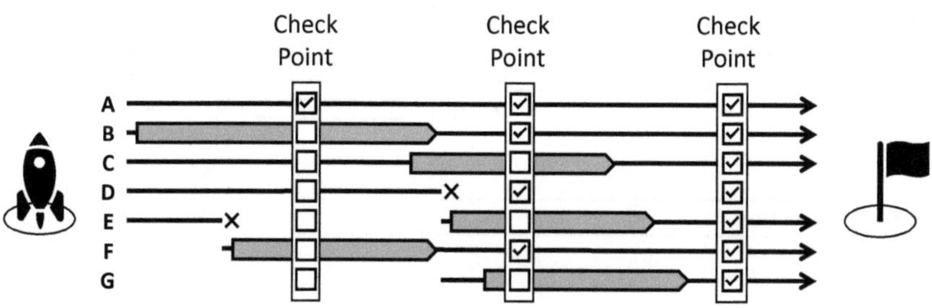


**Fig. 3** **Check Points along the Transformation Journey (I)**—Tracking the progress of the sub-projects against the plan (Illustrated by the authors, used with permission, all rights reserved)

of the business process may not be covered as sub-projects have been discontinued and others have yet not been initiated to close the gap. More subtle reasons for poor business execution may stem from the sub-projects progressing at different speeds. While some of them move ahead, others lag behind.

## 2.3 Change-Centered Transformation Initiatives

Higher competitiveness and performance, more efficient business processes and future readiness are common goals for transformation initiatives in business organizations. Despite the business-related drivers and objectives, the transformation project may disconnect from the day-to-day business execution. Then, transformation and its sub-projects solely center around the change tasks. Change-centered transformation often coincides with the focus on the assessment and tracking of the progress of the sub-projects against the plan (Fig. 3). In the change-focused transformation, the completion of change tasks is rated and valued more highly than its impact on the business execution.

## 2.4 Tracking Progress against the Transformation Plan

Change-centered transformation tracks success against the transformation plan. In many transformation projects, the progress of the sub-projects is assessed at checkpoints along the transformation journey (Fig. 4). Tracking the progress of the sub-projects against the transformation plan will not allow assessment of the effects of the applied change to the business execution. In addition, the checkpoints do not provide the controlled environment required for the in-depth testing of the

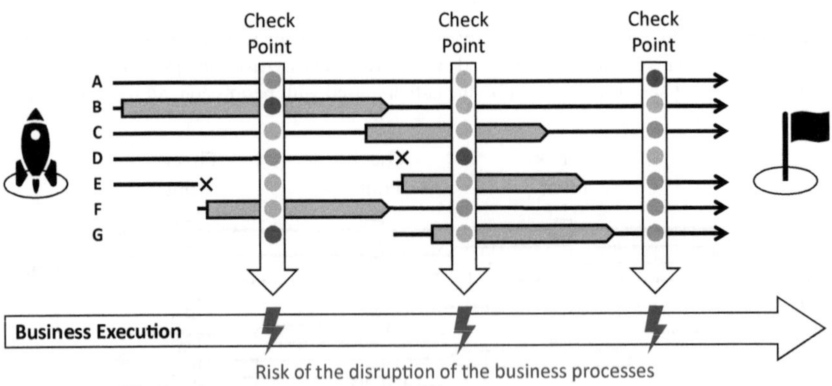


**Fig. 4 Checkpoint along the Transformation Journey (II)**—Snapshots of the fit of the sub-projects with the business process provide limited clarity on the contribution of the single transformation tasks (Illustrated by the authors, used with permission, all rights reserved)

deliverables from the single sub-projects in the context of whole transformation and its impact on business execution.

## 2.5 Viable Stepping Stones Refocus the Transformation on the Business Execution

The idea of the Viable Stepping Stones builds on the checkpoints along the transformation journey described above. Instead of merely tracking the status of the sub-projects, the Viable Stepping Stones process analyses, aligns, and complements the sub-projects in anticipation of the viable business execution. It ensures the viability of the business process and thereby the successful business execution on the timeline of the Viable Stepping Stone (Fig. 5).

The Viable Stepping Stone process culminates in a temporary high-performing environment, and establishes the platform for the business-centered transformation through:

- Adaptation of business processes to the transforming organization and to changes in the external environment.
- Controlled testing and improvement of the sub-projects.
- Evaluation of employee and customer experiences and feedback.
- Updating of the individual and team role and purpose along the transformation.
- Fine-tuning of the transformation goals and journey.

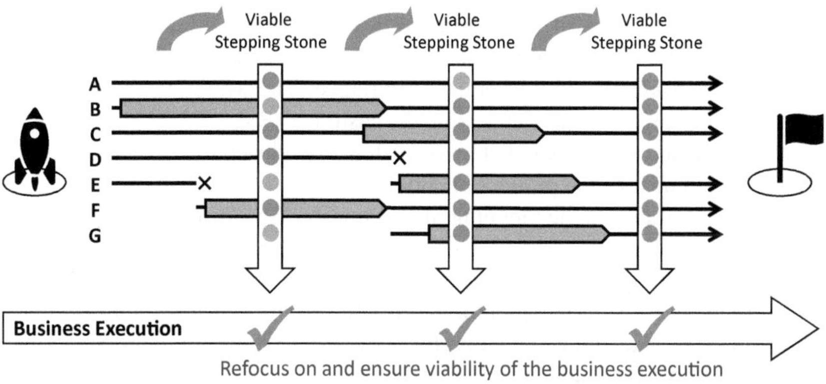


**Fig. 5 Viable Stepping Stones along the Transformation Journey**—The Viable Stepping Stone process prepares for, and ensures viability of, the business processes at the Viable Stepping Stone (Illustrated by the authors, used with permission, all rights reserved)

# 3 The Roots of the "Viable Stepping Stone" Idea

The concept of the Viable Stepping Stones applies and combines different ideas and methodologies onto the business-centered management of transformation. Of particular importance is the concept of the Minimum Viable Product (MVP) and design-based methodologies such as Design Thinking and similar approaches to the customer-focused and iterative development of solutions. The Three-Pillar Model offers the framework embedding the Viable Stepping Stones into the transformation process. In return, the concept of the Viable Stepping Stones refocuses individuals and teams on relevant change tasks and recenters on business execution. All three pillars are informed and updated by the Viable Stepping Stones along the transformation journey.

## 3.1 Minimum Viable Product (MVP)

Eric Ries applied the concept of the Minimum Viable Product (MVP) to the testing of products and business ideas (Ries, 2011): The MVP is the iteration or status of a product or service which allows the maximum amount of validated learning about customers to be collected with the least effort. The Minimum Viable Product (MVP) provides the minimum of features that allows customers to assess its value and the benefits it offers. By definition, the MVP is anything from the mock-up of a product idea (e.g., a demo video or the visualization of the brand story) to the functional product the customer may want to use. The idea of the Viable Stepping Stone is based on the latter case, the functional iteration of the product or services that will be applied to, and by, the customer.

Unfortunately, the MVP is often misinterpreted as being the minimum set of required functionalities. A good summary of this misinterpretation and its consequences can be found in (Korolev, 2019). This interpretation of the MVP neglects other features of the product or service that are important to the customer. In the correct interpretation of the MVP, the user experience along the whole value chain is addressed. Functionality, usability, reliability, and design of the product or services are considered to be of equal importance. The Minimum Viable Product allows one to engage with and learn from the customer (Ries, 2011). The observation of customer behavior and the collation of customer feedback on the MVP inform the further development of the product or service.

The concept of the Viable Stepping Stones transfers the idea of the MVP from the development of products and services in start-ups to established organizations undergoing transformation. Instead of testing the customer's reaction to the MVP, the Viable Stepping Stones explore the fit of the sub-projects and their deliverables with the business execution. To allow for controlled testing of the different change solutions, the Viable Stepping Stone sets the timeline for the alignment of sub-projects. The preparation for the Viable Stepping Stone integrates deliverables from the sub-projects of the transformation and respectively adjusts the business processes to ensure viability of business execution.

## Comparing the Minimum Viable Product and the Viable Stepping Stone

The "Viable Stepping Stone" is not limited to the product or service offered to the customer. It includes the business processes and deliverables in preparation for the provision of the product or service to the customer. Alongside the perceived value offered by the product or service, the viability and experience of both customers and associates along the business process are considered. Providing a controlled high-performance scenario, the "Viable Stepping Stone" becomes the test platform for process steps of business execution and for the fit of deliverables from the sub-projects of the transformation initiative. Eric Ries pointed out the need for creating milestones for teams operating autonomously (Ries, 2017). The Viable Stepping Stones can be considered the tool to create such a milestone in the context of transformation in established operations (Table 1).

**Table 1** Characteristics of the MVP and the Viable Stepping Stone—Compared

| | Minimum Viable Product (MVP) | "Viable Stepping Stone" (VSS) |
|---|---|---|
| Definition | The iteration of the product with the minimum features allowing for engagement with and learning from the customer | Transient optimization of the business execution in adaptation to the progress of the transformation and the changes in the marketplace |
| Format | Anything from the nonfunctional prototype to the functional product or service | Business execution based on updated and optimized business processes |
| Purpose | Collate feedback and gain insights from customers | Collate feedback and gain insights from customers and associates |
| Targets | Inform product development, product commercialization, and leadership | Inform all functions involved in the business execution, transformation management, and leadership |
| Objectives | • Further iterate the design process and improve the product. | • Further optimize business execution.<br>• Mitigate the risk of business disruption due to upcoming deployments of change tasks.<br>• Further iterate the sub-projects of the transformation initiative.<br>• Adjust the transformation goal and journey. |
| Timing | • Progress of product or service development.<br>• Critical steps along the product or service development cycles. | • Business calendar.<br>• Critical steps along the business cycle.<br>• Important changes in the product or service portfolio.<br>• Relevant changes in the marketplace, e.g., changes in the competitive landscape, regulation, or deregulation of the market, disruptive market transformation.<br>• Progress of the transformation and milestones along the transformation journey. |

## 3.2 Design-Based Methodologies

Design Thinking and similar design-based methodologies are based on customer-focused processes that aim at the development of solutions and services. Instead of bringing the final solution to the customer, prototypes and early iterations of the product or service are tested on the customer for iterative learning and further improvement (Ries, 2011; Ries, 2017). The MVP is a snapshot of the developing product or service. In a similar way, the Viable Stepping Stone is the temporary alignment of the change tasks with the business execution along the transformation journey. The Viable Stepping Stone becomes the iteration of the business processes that will be tested and challenged by employees and customers in a controlled high-performance scenario. Insights from one Viable Stepping Stone will be implemented and tested at one of the subsequent stepping stones.

## 3.3 The Three-Pillar Model

With the Three-Pillar Model, Peter Wollmann, Frank Kühn, and Michael Kempf (Wollmann et al., 2020) establish the framework for the dynamic management of transformation in challenging environments. According to the Three-Pillar Model, the transformation management is built on the pillars of Sustainable Purpose, Connected Resources, and the Travelling Organization.

**Sustainable Purpose**

- Sets the direction of travel.
- Engages individuals and teams.
- Gives the transformation meaning.
- Ensures buy-in of associates.
- Defines the design and success criteria.

**Connected Resources**

- Sources the required competencies and capacities.
- Aligns and harmonizes tasks and activities.
- Ensures effectiveness and efficiency.

**Travelling Organization**

- Considers progress along the transformation journey.
- Updates transformation management based on applied change.

The Three-Pillar Model and the Viable Stepping Stones (VSS) are complementary concepts that inform and support each other (Table 2). Reto Püringer (2020) describes how the transformation management based on the Three Pillars can overcome the challenges rooted in the siloed structure of established organizations. As the organization characteristics tend to influence the setup of transformation

**Table 2** The Concept of the Viable Stepping Stones (VSS) Complements and Operationalizes the Three-Pillar Model—Interdependencies and bi-directional contribution of both concepts in driving business-focused transformation

| Three-Pillar Model (3 PM) | 3 PM informs/ supports the VSS | VSS informs/ supports the 3 PM |
|---|---|---|
| **Sustainable Purpose** | • Sets the goals and the direction for the change.<br>• Gives the change the required importance and meaning.<br>• Defines criteria for the design and management of the VSS process. | • Refocusses the transformation onto business execution.<br>• Engages associates and customers.<br>• Allows for the individual experience of change.<br>• Fine-tunes the change goals.<br>• Updates the sustainable purpose.<br>• Renews the commitment to the change. |
| **Connected Resources** | • Defines the quality criteria for the design and management of the VSS process. | • Refocusses the transformation onto business execution.<br>• Aligns and complements sub-projects. |
| **Travelling Organization** | • Transforms business execution.<br>• Offers and deploys change solutions.<br>• Adjusts the transformation based on the changes applied. | • Highlights critical milestones.<br>• Complements the change solutions, as appropriate.<br>• Ensures viability of the business processes.<br>• Offers a controlled test environment for change solutions.<br>• Adjusts the progress along the transformation journey. |

projects, his Three Pillars can be easily transferred to the management of diverse transformation projects.

The Viable Stepping Stones are embedded in the Three-Pillar Model. They (re-) center the organization and the transformation on the business execution. All aspects of the three pillars apply to the Viable Stepping Stone. The concept of the Viable Stepping Stones is rooted in the pillar of the Travelling Organization and applies the ideas of both the pillar of Connected Resources and the pillar of the Sustainable Purpose. In return, the Viable Stepping Stones offer the opportunity to update the three pillars for the progress of the transformation and for changes in the marketplace.

# 4 The Viable Stepping Stone Process

Preparing for the Viable Stepping Stone requires the extrapolation of the state of the transformation and the anticipation of the market environment on the respective time horizon set by the Viable Stepping Stone. Only if this analysis is carried out carefully and respective measures have been put in place to ensure the viability of the business execution will the required controlled high-performance environment be created. The Viable Stepping Stone process defines the critical steps that culminate in optimized business execution and the collation of meaningful feedback and insights for the further improvement of business processes and the adjustment of the transformation initiative.

## 4.1 The Viable Stepping Stone Process Step by Step

There are six sequential steps in the Viable Stepping Stone process:

1. **SCHEDULE** the Viable Stepping Stone.
2. **ANTICIPATE** the status of the sub-projects and the business scenario on the time horizon of the Viable Stepping Stone.
3. **ANALYZE** the interdependencies of the sub-projects and the fit with the business scenario.
4. **ENSURE** the viability of the business processes.
5. **OBSERVE** the business execution.
6. **IMPROVE** the business execution and adjust the transformation.

All the steps of the Viable Stepping Stone process aim for the alignment of all relevant factors and the optimization of the business processes to collate insights for the further improvement of business execution and the transformation initiative (Fig. 6).

Each of the six steps of the Viable Stepping Stone process is focused on a distinct and "mission-critical" task. In the following, these steps will be laid out in detail.

### Schedule

The Viable Stepping Stone sets the timeline for optimizing business execution. A variety of factors may be considered when scheduling the Viable Stepping Stone:

- Calendar (quarterly, half-yearly, yearly).
- Milestones of the transformation project (e.g., critical changes to important sub-projects or transition to new project phases).
- Business calendar (e.g., important steps and checkpoints along the business cycle).
- Objective setting and performance management cycles.
- Internal triggers (e.g., product launches, launches of new campaigns, changes to the customer engagement approach).

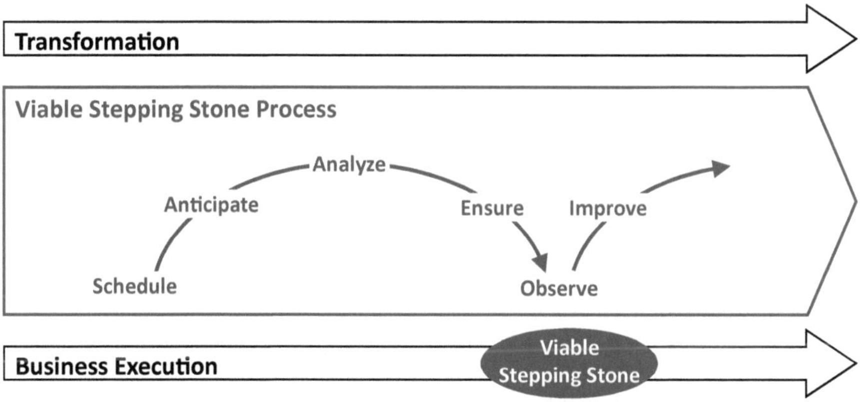


**Fig. 6** **The Viable Stepping Stone Process**—Synergistically matching and improving transformation and business execution with the structured design methodology-based process (Illustrated by the authors, used with permission, all rights reserved)

- External triggers (e.g., changes in the competitive landscape, regulation, or de-regulation of markets).

These factors give the Viable Stepping Stone its purpose and meaning in respect of both transformation and business execution. Ideally the Viable Stepping Stone marks the critical point in time when it is worth investing the effort to optimize the business execution, to adjust the transformation project, and to better prepare the organization for further changes.

## Anticipate

The optimization of business execution requires analysis of all business-relevant sub-projects for the estimated status on the time horizon of the Viable Stepping Stone.

- What will be the status of the sub-projects at the VSS?
- What will be the required input into the sub-projects at the VSS?
- What will be the output of the sub-projects at the VSS?
- What are the internal factors influencing business execution?
- What will be the external factors in the marketplace critical for successful business execution?

Only full understanding of the status, requirements, and contributions of all relevant elements (i.e., the status of the sub-projects, the internal factors not addressed by the transformation project, and the external factors shaping the market environment) allows for a thorough analysis of interdependencies.

### Analyze

At the Analyze step of the Viable Stepping Stone process, all the elements are assessed for interdependencies and fit along the business processes. This assessment of the sub-projects of the transformation initiative as well as of the internal and external factors impacting the business execution is carried out in anticipation of the time point of the Viable Stepping Stone.

- Will the elements be sufficiently informed and provided with input?
- Will the elements deliver the required output?
- Will there be redundancies?
- Will some elements conflict with others?
- Will there be gaps along the business processes?
- Will there be internal and/ or external factors disrupting the business processes?

The identification of gaps and conflicts along the business processes allows for corrective actions ensuring the viability of the business processes at the time point of the Viable Stepping Stone.

### Ensure

There is a variety of measures to close gaps in the business processes and to ensure the viability of business execution.

- Timing of the discontinuation of sub-projects.
- Timing of the initiation of sub-projects.
- Altered phasing of the progress of sub-projects.
- Interim solution to close gaps among the sub-projects.
- Temporary discontinuation of products and services.
- Manage expectations of associates and customers.

With each of the corrective measures, metrics will be defined to analyze their impact on the viability of the business execution.

### Observe

The tracking of metrics and the collation of insights on how the sub-projects of the transformation initiative and the corrective measures interact informs further improvement of both business execution and transformation.

- Viability of business processes.
- Technicalities.
- Quality of products and services, effectiveness, reliability, and efficacy.
- Utilization and management of resources.
- Employee satisfaction.
- Customer satisfaction.

With the right metrics, the Viable Stepping Stone can be used to test new and transformed solutions. Optimized and controlled business execution at the Viable Stepping Stone allows for analysis of its elements along the business processes.

**Improve Business Execution and Adjust Transformation**
The metrics tracked and the insights collated from the Viable Stepping Stone allow for the continuous improvement and iteration of tools, processes, products, and services.

- Medium to long-term: Adjust the direction of travel and the timing of the transformation project.
- Short to medium-term: Set goals for individuals and teams for business execution as well as for transformation.
- Short-term: Improve business execution at the Viable Stepping Stone.

While the learning from the Viable Stepping Stone will be fed back into the sub-projects of the transformation initiative and improvements of the business processes will be applied directly to ongoing business execution, implications on individual and team goals inform the objective setting and performance management processes of the organization.

## 4.2 Connecting Transformation Management with Business Execution

The Viable Stepping Stones process moderates exchange among transformation management and business execution. The sequential steps of the process facilitate the alignment and the crosstalk of both parallel dynamics within the organization (Fig. 7). Doing so, the Viable Stepping Stone process follows the general form of the Build-Measure-Learn Loop described by Ries (2017).

By providing clarity on the critical tasks to be completed, each of the Viable Stepping Stone processes becomes a powerful framework for the alignment of activities in transformation and business execution. The Viable Stepping Stone process aligns the different and sometimes conflicting perspectives on both sides, and it translates the required contribution into tangible tasks to be addressed by individuals and teams. Thus, the Viable Stepping Stone process operationalizes the optimization of business processes to the benefit of both business execution and further transformation of the organization.

For efficient management of the Viable Stepping Stone process, the steps preparing for the stepping-stone as well as the steps moving out of the Viable Stepping Stone require equal attention. The better the tasks are translated into tangible objectives for the sub-project teams of the transformation as well as for the business teams, the better the Viable Stepping Stone can be prepared, the higher the viability of the business execution will be, and the better the learning from the stepping stone will allow for improvement of business execution and transformation (Fig. 8).

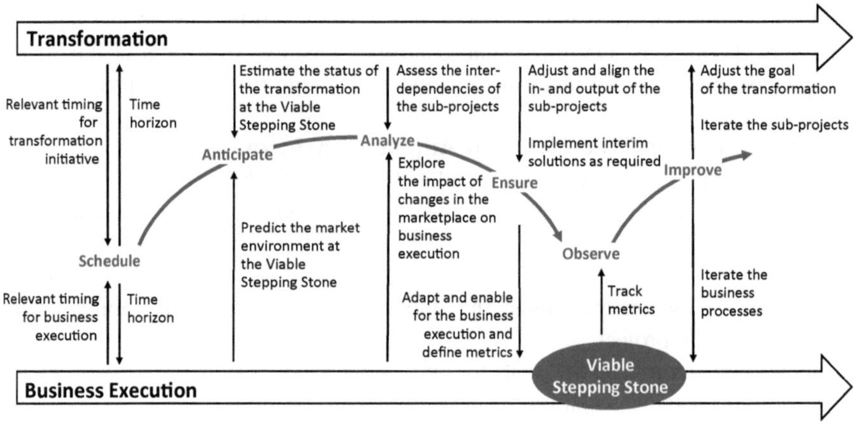


**Fig. 7** **The Phases of the Viable Stepping Stone Process**—Clear deliverables from the transformation and business management on each step of the process (Illustrated by the authors, used with permission, all rights reserved)

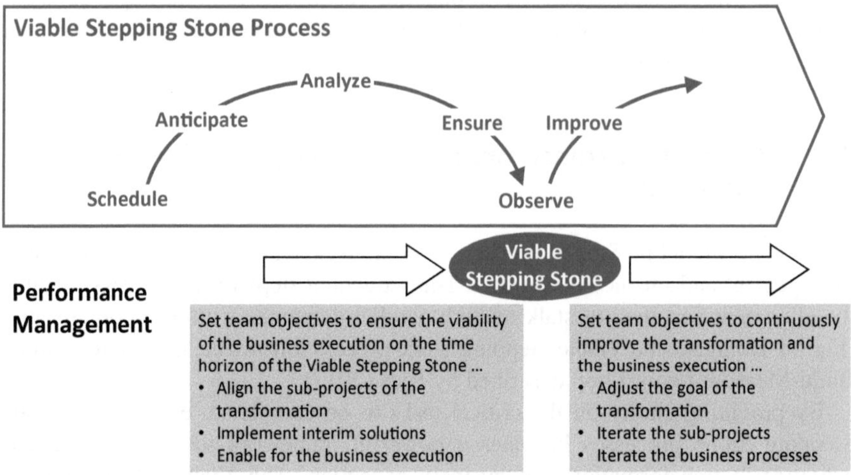


**Fig. 8** **Performance Management Tasks in Support of the Viable Stepping Stone Process**—Specific goals and task preparing for and moving out of the Viable Stepping Stone (Illustrated by the authors, used with permission, all rights reserved)

## 5 Viable Stepping Stones and OKRs

The Objectives and Key Results (OKR) framework was developed by Intel in the 1970s and became popular through Google and other companies in Silicon Valley implementing the concept. Currently, OKRs are the most widely applied strategy management framework across the world (Kalgovas & Glatz, 2020). OKR is an agile framework that supports companies from start-ups to large enterprises to execute their strategy successfully by bridging the gap between abstract strategic goals and specific tasks on an operational level. The framework embodies agile principles such as a participative and iterative approach, strict customer focus, and self-organization on team level, to name but a few. By interweaving these principles with objective setting and the operationalization of strategic goals, OKRs make agile principles feasible and relevant in daily business (for more information see, e.g., Doerr, 2018).

The basic ideas of the framework are:

- Iterative approach: Objectives and Key Results are set in quarterly cycles.
- Joint learning and improvement: In each cycle, reviews and retrospectives are held to learn and improve continuously.
- Outcome orientation: The formulation of OKRs is outcome-oriented, focusing on the generated value of actions rather than only on the things done.
- Top-down and bottom-up development of OKRs: Teams are asked to set their priorities based on operative challenges and strategic goals.
- Transparency and self-organization: OKRs are transparent and visible for everyone, making relevant information accessible for self-organized teams.

## 5.1 The OKR Cycle

The OKR cycle consists of three main phases that will be described briefly to demonstrate how the VSS and OKR can be integrated.

### Prepare

In this phase, Objectives and Key results are defined and aligned in a top-down and bottom-up approach. The top management sets the OKRs at the company level and provides this as an orientation for departments and teams. Meanwhile, departments and teams prepare themselves using OKR drafts based on operative priorities and customer needs. In the following alignment workshops, top-down and bottom-up OKRs are aligned and finalized.

### Execute

The Execution phase starts with an official kick-off of the OKR cycle. Now teams start executing projects and tasks to achieve the OKRs. To ensure alignment, transparency, and tracking of results, the teams hold short weekly or biweekly OKR check-ins.

### Learn

At the end of each cycle, teams conduct a review and a retrospective. The review has the goal to measure and evaluate the results and goal achievement in the cycle. The retrospective aims at improving the OKR process and collaboration within the team (Fig. 9).

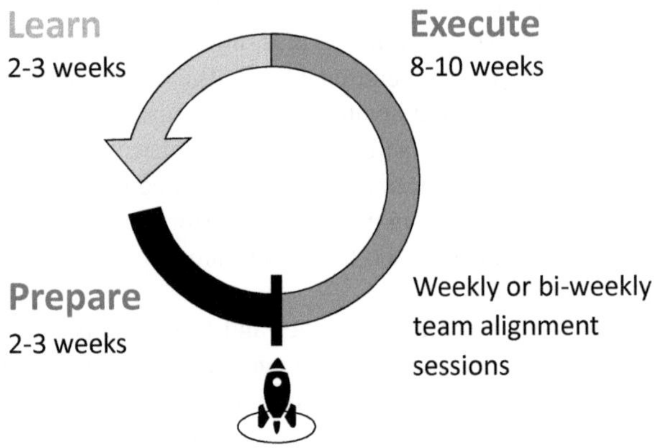


**Fig. 9** The Objectives and Key Results (OKR) Cycle—Three phases address the setting of objectives, the activities delivering against these objectives, and the learning for further improvement of the OKR cycles (Illustration: cidpartners 2021©)

## 5.2 Complementary Processes for Defining Goals and Tracking Results in Transformation Processes

Whether you are already working with one of the mentioned frameworks or not, when integrating OKRs and VSSs, it is important to clearly define the specific focus and value-added of each approach. The frameworks have similarities and overlaps. Therefore, you should define which specific problems need to be solved with each framework. As outlined above, the Viable Stepping Stone process is especially helpful to steer huge transformation processes in diverse organizations, whereas the OKR approach can be used to improve alignment and focus within and between teams. The complementary values added of the two approaches could be defined as follows:

<u>Objectives and Key Results (OKR) Cycle:</u>

- Answer to question: Which value do we offer to our customers?
- Focus on the operationalization of the Viable Stepping Stone process.
- Short-term perspective (e.g., three or four months).
- Outcome-oriented thinking.
- Based on agile principles.

<u>Viable Stepping Stone (VSS) Process:</u>

- Answer to question: How does the transformation affect the business?
- Focus on optimization of the business.
- Mid-term perspective (e.g., six to nine months) spanning two OKR cycles.
- MVP-oriented thinking.
- Based on agile principles.

### 5.3 OKR Cycles Supporting the Viable Stepping Stone Process

The Viable Stepping Stone process aligns with two OKR cycles: The first OKR cycle is preparing for the Viable Stepping Stone and the second supports the steps at and beyond the Viable Stepping Stone (Fig. 10 and Table 3).

The particularity of the Viable Stepping Stone process is the anticipation of the status of the transformation and the business execution at the time point of the Viable Stepping Stone. The first three steps of the Viable Stepping Stone process focus all activities at this time point and provide sufficient clarity and structure for the Prepare step of the OKR cycle.

Besides the differences and the complementary foci, it is important to stress that both approaches are based on agile principles. Using both frameworks will anchor agile principles (e.g., iterative approach and continuous learning) at different levels of the transformation process and the business.

## 6 Conclusion

The concept of Viable Stepping Stones provides a robust framework for the business-centered management of transformation in diverse organizations.

The idea of Viable Stepping Stones fully aligns with the Three Pillars of Organization and Leadership (Kühn et al., 2020). It aligns to the connectivity pillar, as the Viable Stepping Stones connect activities, resources, and people across the sub-projects of the transformation and the business teams. The Viable Stepping

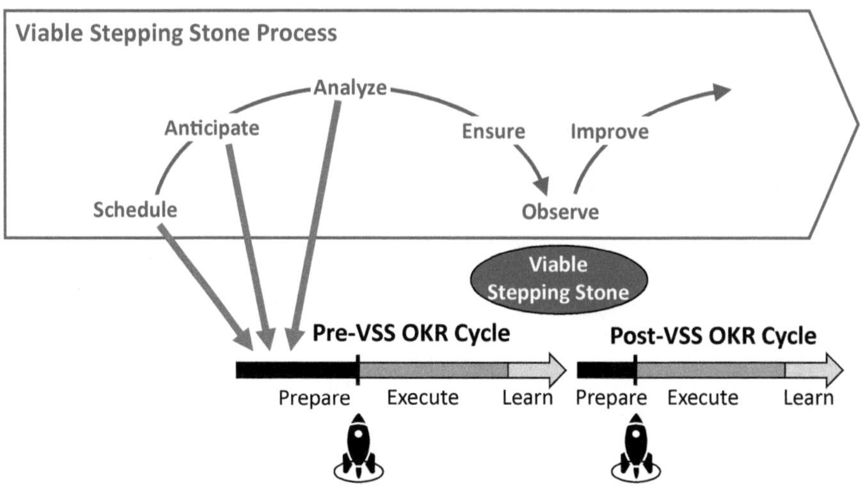


**Fig. 10 VSS and OKR: Two complementary approaches**—The Viable Stepping Stone process focuses the pre-VSS OKR cycle on ensuring the viability of business execution at the time point of the Viable Stepping Stone. The observations at the Viable Stepping Stone inform the post-VSS OKR cycle. (Illustrated by the authors, used with permission, all rights reserved)

**Table 3** **Alignment of the Viable Stepping Stone process with OKR cycles**—The pre- and post-VSS OKR cycles provide the framework for managing business and transformation goals and tasks along the Viable Stepping Stone process

| Pre-Viable Stepping Stone OKR Cycle | |
|---|---|
| **Viable stepping stone process (performance relevant topics)** | **OKR cycle** |
| **Schedule**<br>• Identify relevant internal and external triggers for the VSS.<br>• Schedule the VSS.<br>• Communicate the VSS and initiate the process. | **Prepare**<br>• Prepare phase of pre-viable stepping stone OKR cycle is a bit longer than normal prepare phase: The Schedule, Anticipate, and analyze steps of the viable stepping stone process require sufficient attention. |
| **Anticipate**<br>• Analyze the market environment.<br>• Extrapolate the competitive scenario to the time point of the VSS.<br>• Anticipate the status of the sub-projects. | |
| **Analyze**<br>• Analyze the fit and gaps of the sub-projects.<br>• Identify the need for corrective actions. | |
| **Ensure**<br>• Initiate corrective measures, complete corrective measures in time. | **Execute**<br>• Teams start projects and initiatives to achieve their OKRs. |
| **Observe**<br>• Analyze the business process.<br>• Identify synergies.<br>• Identify risk to the viability of the business process.<br>• Assess the fit of the status of the sub-projects. | **Learn**<br>• Teams conduct review (on goal achievement) and retrospective (on OKR process and collaboration). |
| **Post-viable stepping stone OKR cycle** | |
| **Viable stepping stone process (performance relevant topics)** | **OKR cycle** |
| **Observe**<br>• Identify opportunities for improving business execution.<br>• Identify required adjustments to the sub-projects/ transformation. | **Prepare**<br>• Prepare phase of post-viable stepping stone OKR cycle has usual length and integrates and operationalizes required adjustments from VSS. |
| **Improve**<br>• Optimize business execution.<br>• Adjust the transformation and its sub-projects. | **Execute**<br>• Teams start projects and initiatives to achieve their OKRs. |
| **Improve**<br>• Analyze the improved business processes.<br>• Assess the adjustments to the sub-projects of the transformation.<br>• Inform the subsequent viable stepping stone.<br>• Inform the subsequent OKR cycle. | **Learn**<br>• Teams conduct review (on goal achievement) and retrospective (on OKR process and collaboration). |

Stone defines a common goal to stress test both transformation and business execution. Derived and aligned short- and medium-term objectives, as well as the Viable Stepping Stone process itself, connect individuals and teams. The forward looking optimization of the fit of the status of the sub-projects of the transformation with the business realities at the time point of the Viable Stepping Stone considers the changes in business execution along the transformation journey. Thus, the Viable Stepping Stone takes into account the continuous change in the transforming organization according to the pillar of the Travelling Organization. The third pillar of the Three-Pillar Model is addressed with the Viable Stepping Stone itself: ensuring the viability of the business execution along the transformation journey, it offers the opportunity for continuous learning and improvement of business execution as well as adjustment of the sub-projects to the transforming organization and to changes in the competitive environment. In addition, the Viable Stepping Stone aims to allow for a positive employee and customer experience. This enables the updating of the Sustainable Purpose and the renewal of the commitment to the transformation. Achieving a higher degree of connectivity, considering the travelling organization, and continuous updating of the sustainable purpose helps to establish the “fail faster to succeed sooner” mindset required for an agile way of working and the improved adaptability within the organization (Sanabria, 2020). The Viable Stepping Stone concept applies this beyond established business to the management of transformation.

Especially in diverse organizations, the Viable Stepping Stones drive the continuous alignment of business functions and teams with the sub-projects of the transformation. To ensure the operationalization of business and change tasks, OKR cycles help bridge transformation goals and business strategy into tangible tasks. Each Viable Stepping Stone process aligns with two OKR cycles: The pre-VSS OKR cycle defines the objectives and tasks ensuring the viability of the business process at the Viable Stepping Stone. The Prepare phase of this OKR cycle is structured by the first steps of the Viable Stepping Stone process. As a consequence, the Prepare phase may be more intense and take longer than in regular OKR settings. The second and post-VSS OKR cycle is informed by the observations during the Viable Stepping Stone and sets the objectives and tasks to further improve business execution and adjust the transformation.

The combination of the Viable Stepping Stones with the OKR processes supports the Three-Pillar Model and complements the toolbox for agile and business-centered transformation not only in diverse organizations.

## References

Doerr, J. (2018). *Measure what matters—OKRs*. Penguin.

Hoenig de Locarnini, N., & Kühn, F. (2021). Emergent change: Embracing complexity as a key challenge in a travelling organization. In P. Wollmann, F. Kühn, M. Kempf, & R. Püringer (Eds.), *Organization and leadership in disruptive times—Design and implementation of the 3-P-model*. SpringerNature.

Kalgovas, B., & Glatz, J. (2020). *The state of OKRs—Global Enterprise report*. Detecon.

Kühn, F., Kempf, M., & Camberlain, J. (2020). The concept of purpose, travelling and connectivity: Three pillars of organization and leadership. In P. Wollmann, F. Kühn, & M. Kempf (Eds.), *Three pillars of organization and leadership in disruptive times—Navigating your company successfully through the 21st century business world*. SpringerNature.

Püringer, R. (2020). How established companies can moved to the next level by using the three-pillar model. In P. Wollmann, F. Kühn, & M. Kempf (Eds.), *(2020): Three pillars of organization and leadership in disruptive times—Navigating your company successfully through the 21st century business world* (Three pillars of organization and leadership). SpringerNature.

Ries, E. (2017). *The Startup way*. Currency.

Ries, E. (2011). *The lean Startup*. Penguin.

Sanabria, F. (2020). Purpose journey thinking and connectivity people to people in global companies. In P. Wollmann, F. Kühn, & M. Kempf (Eds.), *Three pillars of organization and leadership in disruptive times—Navigating your company successfully through the 21st century business world*. SpringerNature.

Sergey Korolev. (2019). *Minimum Viable Product: Common MVP misconceptions that may lead you off track*. Retrieved September 29, 2021, from https://railsware.com/blog/mvp-misconceptions/

Wollmann, P., Kühn, F., & Kempf, M. (2020). Three pillars of organization and leadership. In P. Wollmann, F. Kühn, & M. Kempf (Eds.), *Three pillars of organization and leadership in disruptive times—Navigating your company successfully through the 21st century business world*. SpringerNature.

Wollmann, P., Kühn, F., Kempf, M., & Püringer, R. (Eds.). (2021). *Organization and leadership in disruptive times—Design and implementation of the 3-P-model*. SpringerNature.

**Stefan Turnwald** is an experienced Functional Excellence and Learning & Development expert for more than 20 years in the pharmaceutical industry. He started his career as a commercial representative. After switching into the learning development function, he continuously grew his responsibilities and the geographic span of his activities. Stefan is driven by the continuous transformation and improvement of the interface of the pharmaceutical operation to external stakeholders. With his holistic approach, Stefan strives for the transformation of organizational structures, functions, business procedures for patient-centered and customer-focused way of working. He has managed and contributed to several change and business transformation projects at local, regional and global levels. His career has spanned roles and projects in established operations of various size as well as in start-up organizations. Stefan studied biology at the Friedrich-Alexander-University Erlangen-Nuremberg, Germany. Currently, he works and lives in Central Switzerland.

**Julia Zirn** is managing partner at cidpartners, a renowned organizational consultancy for the facilitation and implementation of strategy and change processes located in Bonn and Berlin. Julia has been advising companies, teams and executives from a wide range of industries, whereby "integrating perspectives" is always at the heart of her client projects. With curiosity about people and an analytical eye for processes and structures, Julia facilitates and advises on the development of powerful solutions for complex challenges. Julia studied international business, sociology and cultural studies in Frankfurt, London and at Zeppelin University in Friedrichshafen and has been published in the Journal for Organizational Development and 3 Pillars of Organization and Leadership Volume 1, among others.

# Agile and Design-Based Methodologies in Sales and Service Delivery: The Application of Design for Execution to Field Teams in the Pharmaceutical Industry

Stefan Turnwald, Toni-Anne Jennings, and Julia Zirn

**Abstract**

Agile and design-based methodologies are the trend in transformation management and organizational development. Methodologies such as Design Thinking are well established in the development of products and services. These approaches bear the potential for iteration and adaptation to the specific needs in the execution of the business and, in particular, engagement with customers. Rather than the design of products and services, the design of the delivery of these products and services will be the focus of this chapter.

Design for Execution provides the modular toolbox optimized for the needs, challenges, and dynamics of customer-facing and field teams in business execution. It allows for picking the right flow for the required task in the preparation, execution, and follow-up from customer touchpoints. With its robust, design-based structure it guides the team in agile and customer-focused thinking and working. The Design for Execution toolbox prepares field teams for the facilitator- or peer-led design sprints that continuously improve the interface to the customer. The different Design for Execution flows tailor and focus team activities on specific aspects and tasks while engaging and empowering the team members. They create the agile and solution-focused environment required for successful business execution in diverse organizations in volatile environments.

S. Turnwald (✉)
Zug, Switzerland
e-mail: stefan.turnwald@compski.onmicrosoft.com

T.-A. Jennings
Warwickshire, UK

J. Zirn
cidpartners, Bonn, Germany
e-mail: zirn@cidpartners.de

 
M. Kempf, F. Kühn (eds.), *Navigating a Travelling Organization*, Future of Business and Finance, https://doi.org/10.1007/978-3-030-95326-3_6

In the context of transformation initiatives, Design for Execution provides the engagement of the individuals and teams in a customer-facing organization in shaping part of their own future. This bottom-up updating and continuous improvement of the customer engagement approach helps in the deployment of change solutions and links change solutions into actual business execution. Consequently, the Design for Execution methodology becomes the tool for navigating the customer-facing organization within the travelling organization.

# 1 Introduction: The Need for Design-Based Methodologies in Sales and Customer Service

During the last two decades, Design Thinking and derived methodologies have been increasingly adopted across many industries. In the pharmaceutical industry, these customer-focused and design-based methodologies have been established in the design of customer and patient services, and in the creation of support tools for sales teams and other customer-facing roles. Despite the utilization of Design Thinking for back-end tasks by headquarters teams, its application to the tasks of the customer-facing organization is lagging somewhat.

## 1.1 What This Chapter Offers You

The authors explore the opportunity that design-based methodologies offer to a customer-facing organization in commercial operations. With the in-depth experience from within the pharmaceutical industry, Stefan Turnwald and Toni-Anne Jennings lay out the specifics of the sales and customer service function and its requirements for establishing a customer-focused and design-based way of working. The "Design for Execution" methodology will be introduced as a way of bringing design-based methodologies to the customer-facing organization. "Design for Execution" offers modular and highly flexible tools for an easy and sustainable implementation of the customer-focused and design-based way of working at the interface to the customer. The pharmaceutical industry will be used as an example of the impact of the "Design for Execution" methodology and tools for the development, transformation, and performance of customer-facing teams and individuals. Julia Zirn concludes the chapter with a discussion of complementary transformation, leadership, and management tools and their value in driving transformation in diverse organizations as well as in increasingly volatile business environments.

**Application of the Three-Pillar Model**

The Three Pillars (Wollmann et al., 2020, 2021) are defined as:

1. Sustainable Purpose—the raison d'être of an organization, bringing new orientation and certainty to the people for their joint endeavor and success
2. Travelling Organization—the mindset of an organization in a permanent state of flux, interacting with the market and customer journey, with rapid adaptivity
3. Connected Resources—interconnecting all needed resources inside and outside the silos, creating consistency between goals and concepts, strategies and processes, competencies, and roles.

This chapter focuses on how to engage and navigate the customer-facing organization along the continuous improvement process and along transformation journeys. The authors introduce the Design for Execution methodology that adapts the customer-focused and design-based way of working to the reality and needs of individuals and teams working at the interface to the customer. Next to the conceptual layout of the methodology, the chapter describes the Design for Execution Toolbox with its standardized and easy-to-manage task-specific Design for Execution Flows. These flows can be iterated and sequentially combined to address the relevant tasks along the brand or business cycles.

The introduction of the methodology with its tools is complemented by the discussion of its application to commercial customer-facing teams in the pharmaceutical industry.

## 2 The Particularities of the Customer-Facing Organization

The customer-facing part of the organization forms the interface to the customer. Bringing the marketable product to the customer, its tasks and responsibilities range from the transactional creation of leads, through tactical execution of product communication, account management, product-related pre-, peri-, and post-sales services, up to the establishment of strategic joint value creation or of initiating joint ventures with customer organizations. Another way of differentiation is to address roles and tasks at the interface to the customer as the front end and to consider all other roles and tasks supporting engagement with the customer as the back end.

Traditionally, research and development, product management, and support functions could be considered the back end supporting the sales and customer service function at the front end. In other words, the product is designed at the back end and promoted, sold, and delivered to the customer at the front end. This traditional scenario allows for a clear differentiation between the back end and the front end tasks and deliverables.

Often, the application of design-based methodologies is limited to back-end tasks and deliverables. The subsequent phases of the business cycle are often considered to be executed based on directions given by the back end: the production of the product, the enablement of the front end, the final deployment of the product and sales and service solutions, to the actual customer engagement, and beyond.

## 2.1 The Value of Design-Based Methodologies Applied to a Customer-Facing Organization

Especially in the relationship-based customer engagement approach, there are a lot of opportunities to leverage design-based processes to improve excellence in customer engagement. In relationship-based customer engagement, customers are offered a dedicated company representative and service teams with whom they will interact and can reach out to. The personal engagement allows for the building of relationships and trust. This requires the skillful and customer-focused adaptation of the product communication and the tailored delivery of product-related services.

In contrast to the back-end scenario, design-based methodologies do not address the design of the product and sales and service solutions. At the front end, design-based methodologies leverage the full creative potential of the customer-facing individuals and teams in finding the best and most efficient ways to connect with customers. Nor must we forget that customer-facing individuals and teams are instrumental in adding the additional level of individualization for customer engagement.

## 2.2 Transformation of the Customer-Facing Organization and COVID-19 Challenges

The business world is changing at an unprecedented speed. Some of the megatrends of this transformation are impacting customer-facing organizations.

- The **consolidation of markets** with customer organizations of increasing size and complexity shifts the focus from individual to institutional customer engagement. The focus shifts from business-to-consumer (B2C) to business-to-business **(B2B) relationships** with customers and from selling to individual customers to addressing groups of diverse decision-makers through **account management**.
- The **digitalization of the world of work** introduces new ways of working and adds new digital channels for engagement with the customer. At the same time, the availability of **remote engagement channels** facilitates the transfer from face-to-face customer visits to remote video and screen-sharing platforms. The implementation of new digital and non-personal engagement channels bears the risk that back-end functions may **defocus the support of the relationship-based customer engagement** at the front end.

- **COVID-19** and the measures put in place to control the spread of the pandemic have increased the speed of this transformation. **Social distancing and access limitations** to customer organizations have disrupted customer relationships and transferred engagement to remote and non-personal digital engagement channels. In addition, **customer organizations differ in their reaction** to the pandemic, and **official rules and policies change** over time.

The changes in the business world in combination with the pandemic may lead to more diverse and volatile market environments that will impose additional challenges on the business organization. The implementation of design-based methodologies at the interface to the customer will enable organizations to design solutions to these challenges.

### 2.3 Design Criteria for Design-Based Methodologies Suitable for a Customer-Facing Organization

The design-based methodology is tailored to the needs of the customer-facing organization:

- Link back-end and front-end tasks and responsibilities along the product or solution cycle
- Complete and close the loop of the product or solution cycle to allow for new iterations and continuous improvement
- Address all steps of the product or solution cycle with an agile, customer-focused, and design-based way of working
- Easy to integrate into the busy and customer-driven work schedule at the front end to the customer
- Feasible in face-to-face, remote and hybrid settings
- Standardized and simple processes, agendas, and formats
- Adaptable tools tailored for the specific tasks and challenges of the customer-facing organization
- Easy facilitation by managers or peers
- Sustainable deployment
- Empowering customer-facing individuals and teams and leveraging their competencies and creativity

## 3 Design for Execution

In the last decade, design-based methodologies became popular. The groundbreaking publications of Meinel et al. (2011), Liedtka and Ogilvie (2011), and Kumar (2012) familiarized the business world with the Design Thinking processes and toolboxes. Thereafter, the customer-focused and design-based way of working has been increasingly adopted in the design of products and solutions.

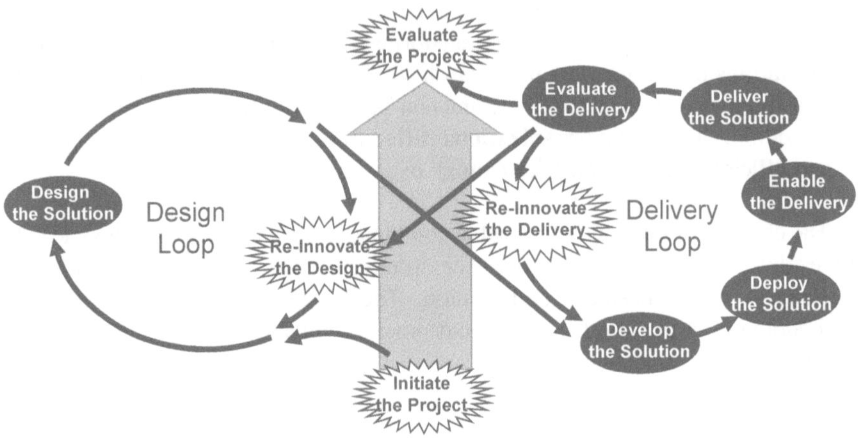


**Fig. 1** Design for execution. Two interlinked process loops cover the critical steps of the solution or business cycle starting with the design and deployment of the product or solution across the enablement of the delivery and the delivery of the product or solution, and beyond to the evaluation of the delivery. This last step closes the cycle into its new iteration and the refinement of the solution design or the development of new solutions. (Illustrated by the authors, used with permission, all rights reserved)

The authors introduced the Design for Execution methodology that expands the application of the design-based way of working beyond *design* to the *delivery* of products and solutions to the customer (Fig. 1).

Both the Design Loop and the Delivery Loop co-exist and complement each other along the iterative product or solution cycle as well as from the initiation to the evaluation of solution-focused projects. Consequently, Design for Execution can be applied to the management of rolling business cycles as well as to the management of single solution-focused projects (Table 1).

The Design for Execution methodology provides a robust framework for the integration and alignment of back-end tasks in the design of the product or solution with the front-end tasks in its delivery to the customer. The two loops of the Design for Execution Methodology allow for a new iteration within the single loop as well as cycling through completed product or solution cycles across both the Design Loop and the Delivery Loop. It addresses all the steps of the product or solution cycle in a highly flexible and dynamic manner thus establishing structured processes for the continuous improvement of product design and delivery.

## 4 The "Design the Solution" Flow

The common way to engage individuals or teams of the customer-facing organization in the design of products or solutions is to involve selected sales or customer service specialists in the back-end-driven and centered design process. Another approach is to apply the design process to specific roles in the customer-facing

**Table 1** Steps of the design for execution loops

| | |
|---|---|
| **Design loop** | |
| Design the solution | • Explore the opportunities to design new or to improve existing products or solutions<br>• Design, stress-test, and improve the product or solution<br>• Provide the design of the product or solution |
| *Transition* | • *Hand over the design of the product or solution into the Delivery Loop*<br>• *Re-enter the Design Loop to further improve the design of the product or solution* |
| **Delivery loop** | |
| Develop the solution | • Develop the functional and/or physical product or solution<br>• Upscale the development into the production of the product or solution<br>• Produce the product or solution |
| Enable the delivery | • Prepare the customer-facing organization for the delivery of the product or solution to the customer<br>• Transfer the relevant knowledge, skills, and know-how to the customer-facing organization<br>• Establish and activate processes, platforms, tools, and content in support of the customer-facing organization |
| Deploy the solution | • Hand the product or solution over to the customer-facing organization<br>• Familiarize the customer-facing organization with the product or solution |
| Deliver the solution | • Engage with the customer<br>• Communicate on the product or solution<br>• Drive the adoption of the product or solution |
| Evaluate the delivery | • Monitor the success of the delivery of the product or solution<br>• Assess the relevance of the product or solution for the customer<br>• Collate customer feedback and market insights |
| *Transition* | • *Re-enter the Delivery Loop to further improve the delivery of the product or solution*<br>• *Provide the customer feedback and market insights back into the Design Loop to inform the iterative improvement of the product or solution* |

The combination of both loops covers the steps of the product or solution cycle with Design Loop addressing the back-end tasks and the Delivery Loop focusing on the front-end task

organization, addressing them as the internal customers of sales or customer service solutions. In both cases, the setup, schedule, and dynamics of the design process are often optimized to the needs of the back-end roles and the respective office setting.

What would an agile and customer-focused design process that is adapted to the needs and reality of the customer-facing organization look like? How should one consider the combination of office- and field-based work settings? How should one accommodate the process given that work schedules are driven by the customer's agenda? How can we take into account the often-limited experience and expertise in agile and design-based methodologies and their facilitation? The "Design the Solution" Flow of the Design for Execution methodology offers the answer to these questions (Fig. 2).

The "Design the Flow" iterates and adapts the Design Thinking methodology to reality and the needs of the customer-facing organization. It aligns with phases 2–5

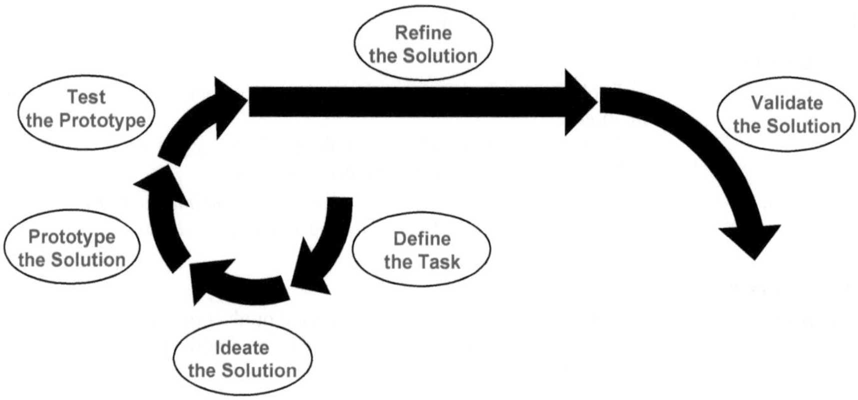


**Fig. 2** "Design the solution" flow. The "Design the Solution" Flow follows the standard phases of the Design Thinking process expanded by the additional refinement of the tested prototype and the second testing of the prototype to validate the design on the solution. (Illustrated by the authors, used with permission, all rights reserved)

of the Design Thinking process: Define, Ideate, Prototype, Test. The focus, dynamics, and objectives of the Design Thinking phases remain the same. The first phase of the Design Thinking process is omitted in the "Design the Solution" Flow as Design for Execution methodology allows for a wider range of tasks to be addressed: while the Design Thinking process always starts with customer immersion, the "Design the Solution" Flow may be triggered by outcomes from previous steps of the Design for Execution process. If the "Design the Solution" Flow is used with the Design Loop of Design for Execution methodology, the customer-focus of the design activity will be ensured with the dedicated Customer Immersion Flow preceding the Design the Execution Flow (see "The Design for Execution Toolbox" for details).

The second deviation from the Design Thinking process is the addition of the Refine the Solution and the Validate the Solution phases. It anchors the refinement of the prototyped solution and its retesting in the "Design the Solution" Flow in the process (Table 2).

The schedule of the "Design the Solution" Flow reflects the needs of customer-facing organizations to allow for the integration of the design process into daily work routines.

- The "Design the Solution" Flow is scheduled as the design sprint with the minimum time required in synchronous facilitator-led sessions and away from the customer
- The refinement and retesting of the prototype have been added to keep the effort and time for building the first prototype to the required minimum and to allow for best possible leveraging of the creative potential of customer-facing individuals and teams. The asynchronous setting of the Refine the Solution phase allows for the flexible integration of the design tasks into the busy and often customer-driven work schedule at the front end to the customer.

**Table 2** Schedule of the design the solution flow—Combination of synchronous, facilitator-led, and asynchronous, self-organized parts

| Phase | Tasks | Timing | Setting | Dynamics |
|---|---|---|---|---|
| **Design the solution flow** | | | | |
| Define the task | • Introduce the task for the design activity[a] | 10 min | • Facilitator-led<br>• Classroom, remote or hybrid setting<br>• Synchronous collaboration | Plenary group |
| Ideate the solution | • Collate and explore design options | 10 min | | Plenary group or breakout teams |
| Build the prototype | • Build the testable prototype of the prioritized design idea | 20 min | | Breakout teams |
| Test the prototype | • Challenge the design idea and collate feedback on the prototype | 15–20 min | | Plenary group |
| Refine the solution | • Improve the design idea based on the feedback provided<br>• Prepare the reiterated prototype for retesting | 30–120 min | • Self-guided<br>• Integrated into individual work schedule<br>• Individual work or team collaboration | Breakout teams and/or individual |
| Validate the solution | • Challenge the reiterated design idea<br>• Approve or reject the prototype | 25–30 min | • Facilitator-led<br>• Classroom, remote or hybrid setting<br>• Synchronous collaboration | Plenary group |
| *Transition options* | • *Approve the solution for execution in engagements with the customer*<br>• *Approve the solution to inform the next step of the Design for Execution methodology*<br>• *Reject the solution and re-enter the "Design the Solution" Flow for improvement*<br>• *Reject and retire the solution* | | | |

[a] To allow for the customer-focused design process, the "Design the Solution" Flow should be prepared and informed with the dedicated Customer Immersion Flow

## 5 Design for Execution Sessions

The "Design the Solution" Flow is characterized by its mix of synchronous, facilitator-led collaboration with the asynchronous self-organized activities in the Refine the Solution phase. This splits the synchronous, facilitator-led parts into sessions: the first session with the phases Define the Task, Ideate the Solution, Build the Prototype, and Test the Prototype, and the second, subsequent session with the Validate the Solution phase. In the sequence of different "Design the

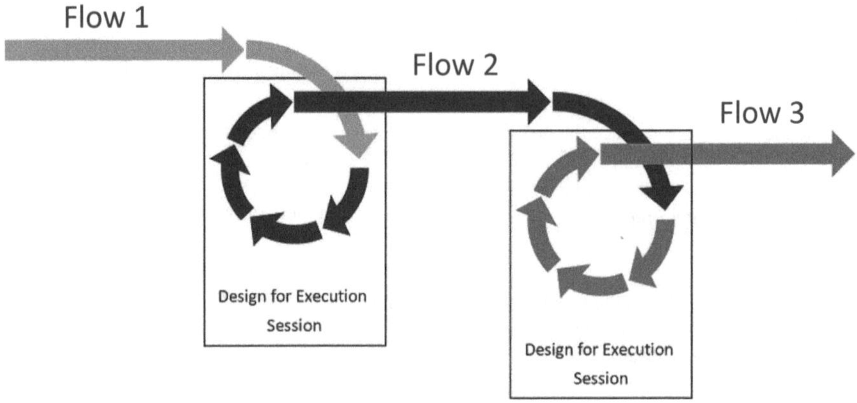


**Fig. 3** Sequencing of the design for execution flows. The Design for Execution Sessions cover the validation of the solution from the previous session (flow 1) with the first part of the next flow (flow 2) and so forth. (Illustrated by the authors, used with permission, all rights reserved)

Solution" Flows (Fig. 3), the second part of the preceding flow is combined with the first part of the other flow into one Design for Execution Session (Table 3).

The structure and the agenda of the Design for Execution Sessions allow for integration into the busy work schedule of a customer-facing organization.

- The combination of parts from two "Design the Solution" Flows reduces the number of sessions.
- Short synchronous, facilitator-led sessions based on the design sprint approach allow for easy integration into participants' calendars.
- With the support of digital solutions, i.e., virtual classrooms, virtual collaboration, and sharing platforms, virtual whiteboards and polling solutions, Design for Execution Sessions can be conducted in face-to-face, in remote, or hybrid (a combination of face-to-face and remote) settings.

## 6 The Design for Execution Toolbox

The "Design the Solution" Flow is the basic flow of the Design for Execution methodology. It is optimized for the improvement or design of new solutions. Every "Design the Solution" Flow starts with the definition of the task to be addressed with the design process. As described above, the Empathize phase of Design Thinking is purposefully left out to be able to use the Design the Solution Flow with a wider range of use cases. If the design task requires the customer's situation to be explored and understood, a customer-focused way of working will be ensured by preceding the "Design the Solution" Flow with a Customer Immersion Flow.

**Table 3** Design for execution session agenda—Short design sprint session linking subsequent "Design the Solution" Flows with the asynchronous, self-organized follow-up

| Timing | Agenda item | Flow/Task | Actions | Dynamics |
|---|---|---|---|---|
| 5 min 00:00–00:05 | Welcome | | • Welcome the participants | Plenary group |
| 25 min 00:05–00:30 | Validate the solution | Flow 1 (task from the previous session) | • Challenge the newly iterated design idea<br>• Approve or reject the prototype | Plenary group |
| 10 min 00:30–00:40 | Define the task | Flow 2 (new task introduced in the current session) | • Introduce the task for the design activity | Plenary group |
| 10 min 00:40–00:50 | Ideate the solution | | • Collate and explore design options | Plenary group or breakout teams |
| 20 min 00:50–01:10 | Build the prototype | | • Build the testable prototype of the prioritized design idea | Breakout teams |
| 15 min 01:10–01:25 | Test the prototype | | • Challenge the design idea and collate feedback on the prototype | Plenary group |
| 5 min 01:25–01:30 | Close | | • Hand out follow-up assignments<br>• Farewell | Plenary group |
| 30–120 min (based on the task) | Refine the solution | Flow 2 (new task introduced in the current session) | • Improve the design idea based on the feedback provided<br>• Prepare the newly iterated prototype for the retesting | Self-organized session follow-up Breakout teams and/or individual |

## 6.1 Customer Immersion Flow

The Customer Immersion Flow precedes and complements the "Design the Solution" Flow with observations of the customer to gain an understanding of the customer's business, challenges, and needs. The identification of opportunities to design new, or improve existing, products and services is the goal. At the end of the Customer Immersion Flow, the identified opportunities will be prioritized and fed as design tasks into the "Design the Solution" Flow (Table 4).

### Task-Specific Variations of the "Design the Solution" Flow

Both the Customer Immersion Flow and the "Design the Solution" Flow are task-specific adaptations of the generic phases 1–6 (Table 5). Like the Customer Immersion Flow and the Solution Design Flow, other task-focused flows can be derived

**Table 4** Customer immersion flow and "design the solution" flow

| | Customer immersion flow | Solution design flow |
|---|---|---|
| Phase 1<br>Introduce the task | Define the task<br>• Focus on the relevant part of the customer's business | Define the task<br>• Introduce the task for the design activity |
| Phase 2<br>Explore the task and align the direction of travel | Change to the customer's point of view<br>• Collate ideas on how the customer may see the focused part of the business | Ideate the solution<br>• Collate and explore design options |
| Phase 3<br>Build the testable solution | Build the guiding questions<br>• Formulate guiding questions aiming for a better understanding of the customer's needs | Build the prototype<br>• Build the testable prototype of the prioritized design idea |
| Phase 4<br>Stress test the solution and prepare to execute the task | Challenge the guiding questions<br>• Ensure all important aspects of the customer's business are addressed | Test the prototype<br>• Challenge the design idea and collate feedback on the prototype |
| Phase 5<br>Execute the task and prepare for presentation | Immerse with the customer<br>• Observe the customer in their business<br>• Collate answers to the guiding questions<br>• Derive design tasks | Refine the solution<br>• Improve the design idea based on the feedback provided<br>• Prepare the newly iterated prototype for retesting |
| Phase 6<br>Present the outcome and decide on next steps | Validate the design tasks<br>• Present and challenge the design tasks<br>• Approve or reject the design tasks | Validate the solution<br>• Challenge the newly iterated design idea<br>• Approve or reject the prototype |

The combination of the Customer Immersion Flow and the Design Solution Flow covers all steps of the Design Thinking process and ensure the customer focus on the design activities in the Design Loop of the Design for Execution methodology

from the generic phases 1–6. This modularization provides clarity of the assignments across all flows, thus simplifying the facilitation tasks.

## 6.2 Knowledge Management Flow

The Knowledge Management Flow defines the knowledge areas that are critical to success and assesses knowledge and knowledge gaps in the collaborative approach. The missing information is collated in teamwork and driven by guiding questions. The collated information is used to update knowledge and knowledge gaps across the knowledge areas.

**Table 5** Knowledge management flow

| | Knowledge management flow | Comments |
|---|---|---|
| Phase 1 | Define the knowledge areas<br>• Focus on the knowledge areas critical to success, e.g., knowledge of the product or service offered, of the customer, of the patient, and of the competitive environment | • "What are the areas we need to know about?" |
| Phase 2 | Check the knowledge<br>• Collate the available knowledge within the knowledge areas | • "What do we know?" |
| Phase 3 | Identify the knowledge needs<br>• Explore the knowledge gaps across the knowledge areas | • "What do we need to learn about?" |
| Phase 4 | Develop guiding questions<br>• Formulate questions to guide the knowledge gathering process<br>• Target available information sources to address the guiding questions | • "What are the questions that trigger the relevant answers?"<br>• "To whom should we address these questions?" |
| Phase 5 | Collate the information<br>• Engage with the information sources<br>• Probe for and gather information | • Reach out to the information sources and gather the answers |
| Phase 6 | Update the knowledge<br>• Add the collated answers and update the knowledge<br>• Revise the knowledge gap | • "What have we learned?"<br>• "What are the remaining knowledge gaps?"<br>• "What new knowledge gaps have we identified?" |
| *Transition* | • *Re-enter the Knowledge Management Flow to gather more information*<br>• *Progress and inform the subsequent flows with the information collated* | |

## 6.3 Insights Generation Flow

The Insights Generation Flow captures the current understanding of the aspects of the business that are critical to success and formulates the respective hypothesis in the collaborative approach (Table 6). The team collates insights to challenge the hypothesis driven by insightful questions. The collated insights are used to verify or refute the hypothesis.

The detailed breakdown of the Knowledge Management Flow, and the Insights Generation Flow showcase the opportunity to build task-specific flows based on the generic phases 1–6. This pattern can be applied to a variety of additional flows supporting the steps of the Delivery Loop of the Design for Execution Methodology. In the following, additional flows will be addressed in short summaries.

## 6.4 Solution Exploration Flow

The Solution Exploration Flow exposes the product or service offered to the customer-facing team.

**Table 6** Insights generation flow

| | Insights generation flow | Comments |
|---|---|---|
| Phase 1 | Define the insights task<br>• Focus on aspects of the product or service offered, of the customer, of the patient, and of the competitive environment that requires better understanding | • "What do we need to understand better?"<br>• "What perspective would we need to take?" |
| Phase 2 | Change to the customer's perspective<br>• Analyze the task from the customer's, patient's, or competitor's perspective | • "What does it look like from 'the other side'?" |
| Phase 3 | Build the hypothesis<br>• Agree on the current understanding of the situation<br>• Formulate the hypothesis | • "What is our current understanding?" |
| Phase 4 | Develop insightful questions<br>• Formulate questions challenging the hypothesis | • "What are the questions that improve our understanding?"<br>• "To whom should we address these questions?" |
| Phase 5 | Collate the insights<br>• Engage with the information sources<br>• Probe for and gather information | • Reach out to the information sources and gather the answers |
| Phase 6 | Challenge the hypothesis<br>• Verify or refute the hypothesis | • "Can we confirm the hypothesis?" |
| *Transition* | • *Re-enter the Insights Generation Flow to gather more insights*<br>• *Progress and inform the subsequent flows with the information collated* | |

## 6.5 Solution Challenge Flow

The Solution Challenge Flow stress tests the product or service offered from the point of view of the customer, the patient, or the competition.

## 6.6 Engagement Design Flow

The Engagement Design Flow plans and prepares meaningful touchpoints with the customer to offer the product or service.

## 6.7 Engagement Challenge Flow

The Engagement Challenge Flow stress tests the prepared touchpoint and collates feedback for the further improvement of engagement with the customer.

## 6.8 Engagement Feedback Flow

The Engagement Feedback Flow focuses on aspects of the delivered customer engagement to ask for customer feedback.

### Sequencing of Flows

The different flows of the Design for Execution Methodology can be sequenced based on the specific requirements of business execution and along the Design for Execution process (Fig. 4). If required, the flows are repeated until the outcome is suitable to progress to the next step of the Design for Execution process.

Based on the task for which the different flows are optimized, the different steps of the Design for Execution methodology are supported (Fig. 5).

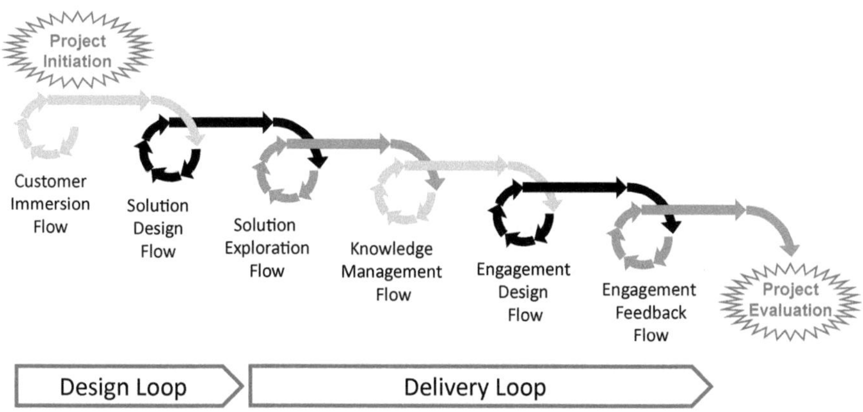


**Fig. 4** Sequencing of flows. The different flows of the Design for Execution Toolbox can be sequenced along the Design for Execution Loops. (Illustrated by the authors, used with permission, all rights reserved)

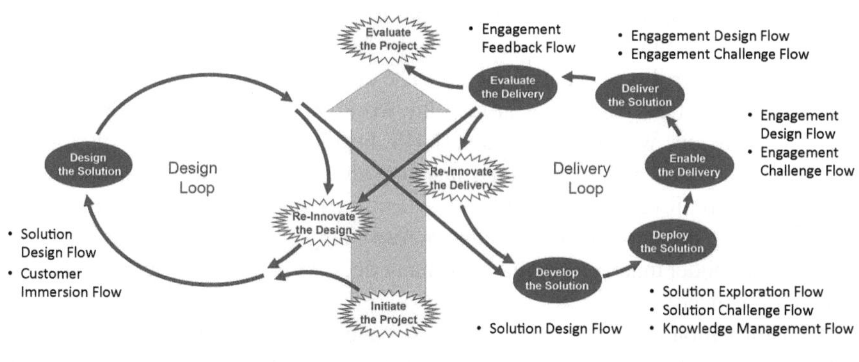


**Fig. 5** The design for execution flows align with the phases of the design for execution loops. The different flows of the Design for Execution Toolbox can be sequenced along the Design for Execution process. (Illustrated by the authors, used with permission, all rights reserved)

The suggested alignment in Fig. 5 may be adapted to the business challenge. New flows can be developed by adapting the generic steps of the flow to the new task to be addressed.

### Recommendations on the Facilitation and the Scheduling of Sessions

The reiterative structure of the flows ensures their flexible combination and easy facilitation by the managers of the field team or by team members in the peer facilitation approach. For the sustainable implementation of the agile and customer-focused way of working, a weekly to bi-weekly schedule of the Design for Execution sessions is recommended. The time between the sessions must allow for completion of the flow-specific tasks between the Design for Execution Sessions. The members of the field team should always feel capable, enabled, and empowered to integrate the Design for Execution process into their daily business and to collaboratively strive for the success of the team. It is the bottom-up dynamics and the collaborative approach of the Design for Execution methodology that empowers customer-facing individuals and leverages their competencies and creativity.

## 7 Design for Execution in Practice

As a senior leader with almost 30 years of pharmaceutical, commercial, customer-facing experience in the UK, Toni-Anne Jennings has seen many changes and challenges within her industry. Her role and that of the Field Force has changed substantially over the last three decades and never more so than in the last two years. The pharmaceutical industry has been on a road of transformation. One of the most significant developments is the increase of the various channels with which it interacts with its customers. No one expected that 100 % of customer-facing interactions would be via digital platforms for many months. The advancements in digital technology have accelerated beyond everyone's expectations. COVID-19 has brought unprecedented adaptation, powering innovation in the NHS forward 10 years.

These changes have created a burning platform in the pharmaceutical industry. To increase the willingness of our customers to be seen face to face requires more innovation and flexibility than ever before. The questions asked in the head offices of many pharmaceutical companies around the world is: "How will we manage field-based relationships with our customers (NHS, healthcare professionals and payers) in a fully integrated and value-added manner, given the limited access we have?" The industry employed and trained highly scientific, technical, and successful people who can have peer-to-peer discussions across many therapy areas; however, the face-to-face model that has worked over many decades is no longer as relevant, and adaptation is needed.

Transformation takes time, enabling and empowering customer-facing individuals to be included in the transformation greatly increases its chance of success. When you have an organization that designs and builds its strategic and tactical plans in a structured way using a traditional top-down brand planning process, they are at risk of missing the quickly changing needs of the customer. The organization must consider diversity across its internal and external customers to truly understand and mitigate the volatility often seen with the protocols and preferences of customers within the healthcare market

As a sales leader, the role in the evolution of the engagement model was to facilitate a multi-disciplinary team's involvement in the generation of ideas to build a solution that overcame the challenges we faced during COVID-19. There was a need to deploy a framework that engages the cross-functional team. Design for Execution was the toolkit we used to enable the team to generate a broad and diverse set of ideas to overcome the challenge we faced, which in turn would lead to more successful cross-functional decision-making. This would enable chosen solutions to be deployed quickly and with greater success.

## 7.1 Define the Task

To ensure a fully engaged team, it was important to determine how the task ahead would be deployed and to give clarity to the process, most importantly to set up the meeting as one with a fast-paced rhythm, to encourage less self-censorship, bringing higher levels of innovation and idea generation, something that can often be lacking in modern business planning cycles. Prior to the meeting, we defined the task as "increase engagement for the front-end team." A key lesson from this step was to define a task that was manageable, if the task agreed is too wide there is the risk that it will not be completed; we focused on the step of "access via multiple channels." Revisiting the task a few times narrowed it and prioritized what was the most important area of focus.

## 7.2 Ideate the Solution

The ideation element requires quality facilitation to generate manifold ideas and not encourage narrow thinking, also to fully engage all the participants, as often you can lose more reflective individuals in this fast-paced group session. Encouragement is needed to continue to develop the ideas further and not revert to "the norm" or, more often, what was believed by some to be impossible. Continuing to drive the idea generation developed the offering further and reduced the risk of repeating solutions from previous business cycles or applying filters that reduced the broad thinking of others

## 7.3 Build Prototype

By challenging individuals to think more laterally during the ideation phase, the move to building a prototype was high-energy and had increased creativity, incorporating all the feedback so far which is critical for refining the solution and understanding of how to build it so it can be deployed within the timeframe needed (i.e., COVID-19), therefore making it relevant for the current situation

The prototype stage allows you to create a model you can test in the next stage of the process. The prototype should not be too complicated to launch and easy to incorporate into your account and tactical plans. Why is this the case? Because, as discussed, there are time restraints that can slow things down, especially in a highly controlled environment such as pharmaceuticals; it can be refined if necessary when it is deployed. This reduces the "paralysis" that can often be seen within large organizations when creative ideas are launched that challenge the status quo. This further highlights the importance of building a solution with a team of multi-functional roles to enable champions of the solution to build the prototype in departments that have the expertise.

## 7.4 Test the Prototype

Facilitating the testing stage over the following week gave time to share and challenge the solution and be prepared to refine it. Testing with "live" situations uncovered further ideas and iterations that "flexed" the solution

## 7.5 Refine the Solution

Idea refinement happens concurrently with the development of the solution, and not just at the beginning of a project. It means revisiting the solution to take a fresh look. This enabled us to critically assess it against the original criteria to ensure the solution still met the goals originally set out. This fresh look at the most likely successful prototype avoids driving a solution that may not fully overcome the obstacles it was designed to overcome. It further informs our understanding of how it was received in testing, enabling us to work through alterations and refinements during this phase. Following the validation of the solution, Marketing was able to accelerate the assets needed to plan and execute the different touchpoints, testing the theories and rapidly eliminating tools that did not suit the focus agreed in the workshop.

## 7.6 Validate the Solution

Testing involved generating user feedback from the field tests on the prototypes we developed, as well as gaining a deeper understanding of the feedback from end users. This is a key stage: to assess how the solution worked in the customer's world and how it can be incorporated into the business, business plans, and the model of the organization.

Using the Design for Execution framework enabled my team to design and implement a continuous customer experience, with a strong focus on increasing access. The extended ideation team created an omni channel account plan, building multiple touchpoints with customers throughout an organization which laid the foundations of the new multiple channel focus. This approach enabled us to add value and increase access, aligned to the customer's preferred channel; relationships opened up virtually, and these became more open to resuming a face-to-face business relationship in the future.

It enabled the truly integrated approach that empowers a cross-functional team to co-create and co-own the next steps which, in turn, capture more of a pioneering view, enabling much-needed original thinking. It also created a more "activated" team, seeing them participate in a future-facing plan, something that was important during COVID-19 as they became more concerned about job losses and how relevant their roles were in these virtual interaction models.

It goes without saying that the industry will continue to transform in the coming years. How we evolve our business models and remain agile to respond to these changes depends on how quickly we adapt. By embedding *Design for Execution* into our business cycles, we can execute timely solutions and strategies that make the difference to our internal teams, our customers and, ultimately, to patient care.

## 8 Conclusion

The chapter shows in a comprehensive and practical way how design-based methodologies can improve the performance of sales and service delivery teams. By modular and iterative process design, the Design for Execution framework allows for flexibility and adaptability with respect to new learnings and changes in the market environment. Early prototyping and testing are an important part of each iteration and further strengthen learning and continuous improvement. The Design for Execution methodology adapts the concept of Micro Projects (Kühn & Kempf, 2014, 2021) to the reality and needs of customer-facing organizations. Micro Projects are a series of short workshops that address business-relevant tasks in the design-based approach. While the Design for Execution Sessions could be grouped into the format of Micro Projects, the methodology could also be applied in a recurring manner to drive the continuous improvement of the delivery of products and services to the customer.

The standardized structure and dynamics of the Design for Execution flows and the choice of task-focused methods simplify its delivery and allow for the facilitation of sessions by less experienced facilitators, e.g., the managers of customer-facing teams or assigned team members. The application of short and easy-to-handle interventions such as Micro Methods (Zirn & Allmers, 2018) allows for integration into daily business, and for producing results and positive employee experiences quickly. In addition, to Micro Methods, tools from Design Thinking toolkits can be used to create additional task-focused flows. The interested reader may like to consult the Design Thinking resources by Kumar (2012), Liedtka and Ogilvie (2011), or Doorley et al. (2018). Furthermore, Design for Execution constitutes a collaborative approach as prototype presentation and feedback is the service to the team. By combining synchronous and asynchronous elements, it meets the post-COVID-19 reality that has emerged in most organizations, namely a hybrid working culture. To sum up, Design for Execution is a highly practice-oriented and innovative approach to facilitating change in customer-facing organizations.

This design-based methodology also builds perfectly on the Three-Pillar Model (Wollmann et al., 2020, 2021). It focuses on the engagement of the customer-facing organization and leverages its full creative and customer-focused power. This aspect reflects the Pillar "Connected Resources" of the Three-Pillar Model. The "Sustainable Purpose" is mirrored in the collaborative and inclusive approach that allows for the continuous updating of the commitment of the customer-facing individuals and teams to the desired change. In respect of the "Travelling Organization," Design for Execution allows for the ongoing deployment of change solutions in customer-facing organizations. As such, it becomes the framework for the updating and optimization of the interface to the customer along the transformation journey.

## References

Doorley, S., Holcomb, S., Klebahn, P., Segovia, K., & Utley, J. (2018). *Design thinking bootleg*. Retrieved 18 October 2021 from https://dschool.stanford.edu/resources/design-thinking-bootleg

Kühn, F., & Kempf, M. (2014). *Time flies—Integrate timelines with commitment and results*. Integrated Consulting Group: Change.

Kühn, F., & Kempf, M. (2021). Transformation in the field of production: A five-day micro project. In P. Wollmann, F. Kühn, M. Kempf, & R. Püringer (Eds.), *Organization and leadership in disruptive times—Design and implementation of the 3-P-model*. SpringerNature.

Kumar, V. (2012). *101 design methods: A structured approach for driving innovation in your organization*. Wiley.

Liedtka, J., & Ogilvie, T. (2011). *Design for growth: A design thinking tool kit for managers*. Columbia University Press.

Meinel, C., Leifer, L., & Plattner, H. (2011). *Design thinking: understand—improve—apply*. SpringerNature.

Wollmann, P., Kühn, F., & Kempf, M. (Eds.). (2020). *Three pillars of organization and leadership in disruptive times—Navigating your company successfully through the 21st century business world*. SpringerNature.

Wollmann, P., Kühn, F., Kempf, M., & Püringer, R. (Eds.). (2021). *Organization and leadership in disruptive times—Design and implementation of the 3-P-model*. SpringerNature.

Zirn, J., & Allmers, S. (2018). *Micro methods for Agile projects*. Zeitschrift für Organisationsentwicklung.

**Stefan Turnwald** is an experienced Functional Excellence and Learning & Development expert for more than 20 years in the pharmaceutical industry. He started his career as a commercial representative. After switching into the learning development function, he continuously grew his responsibilities and the geographic span of his activities. Stefan is driven by the continuous transformation and improvement of the interface of the pharmaceutical operation to external stakeholders. With his holistic approach, Stefan strives for the transformation of organizational structures, functions, business procedures for patient-centered and customer-focused way of working. He has managed and contributed to several change and business transformation projects at local, regional and global levels. His career has spanned roles and projects in established operations of various size as well as in start-up organizations. Stefan studied biology at the Friedrich-Alexander-University Erlangen-Nuremberg, Germany. Currently, he works and lives in Central Switzerland.

**Toni-Anne Jennings** has a 30-year career in the UK Pharmaceutical Industry spanning diverse roles and across various Blue Chip Pharmaceutical companies. A leader through many organizational changes her interest has been how companies cultivate a culture of performance excellence. She has held varied positions within Sales, Marketing, and Market Access. Starting her career as a customer-facing representative and then specializing in Account Management and SFE through to senior leadership of Sales and Marketing. The last 10 years have focused on leading large sales forces and x functional teams. A visionary leader with a drive to help individuals excel in their chosen roles. Currently Vice President within a training and coaching organization, enabling to continue her work developing customer facing teams and increasing skills in execution of strategic plans.

**Julia Zirn** is managing partner at cidpartners, a renowned organizational consultancy for the facilitation and implementation of strategy and change processes located in Bonn and Berlin. Julia has been advising companies, teams and executives from a wide range of industries, whereby "integrating perspectives" is always at the heart of her client projects. With curiosity about people and an analytical eye for processes and structures, Julia facilitates and advises on the development of powerful solutions for complex challenges. Julia studied international business, sociology and cultural studies in Frankfurt, London and at Zeppelin University in Friedrichshafen and has been published in the Journal for Organizational Development and 3 Pillars of Organization and Leadership Volume 1, among others.

# The Leader's Personal Approach to Navigating a Travelling Organization

Heinz Peter Wallner and Kurt Völkl

**Abstract**

This chapter presents a holistic approach for leaders who want to be successful in today's organizations. This approach assumes that "navigating a travelling organization" is a form of learning exploration and that corresponding leadership development can only be an agile search process that moves iteratively toward a "virtuoso viability" under VUCA conditions. This framework has as its basic symbol a lemniscate—a figure-eight-shaped curve—that spans a developmental landscape with four domains: new thinking, new attitude, new action, and new insight.

## 1 Introduction to the Problem

In 1970, the phrase "Houston, we have a problem" became famous. Despite all plans and efforts to minimize risks for the Apollo 13 mission, an unexpected event arose and whipped the world into a frenzy. A group of NASA scientists had to confront the complex situation and, within a few hours, find a technical solution to a problem in the space capsule that seemed almost unsolvable. "The square peg had to go in the round hole." In extreme situations of this kind, we find two strategies in parallel integrative action: long-term, complicated planning for a great mission and an agile strategic solution for an immediate, totally surprising, and complex problem. It must be observed here that the long-term planning came first, so to speak, and therefore maintained the tension while assigning the agile solution to its place in the temporal

H. P. Wallner (✉)
St. Margarethen a.d.R, Austria
e-mail: wallner@trainthe8.com

K. Völkl
Graz, Austria



M. Kempf, F. Kühn (eds.), *Navigating a Travelling Organization*, Future of Business and Finance, https://doi.org/10.1007/978-3-030-95326-3_7

and spatial hierarchy. This kind of interplay between a planned approach and acute problem solving has long yielded good results in the world of organizations as well. Today, the agile search process needs to come more strongly into the foreground due to the rising complexity of the business world. Long-term planning, in contrast, is slipping into the background. It nevertheless remains important as the component that provides the tension for the development and serves to provide orientation.

Leaders in "travelling organizations" must always be able to incorporate both poles of this development. These organizations need both a stable, long-term framework for orientation that supports continual development and, at the same time, a flexible, agile problem-solving mode that makes it possible to search for new options in a sufficiently creative way. Under today's VUCA conditions (Bennis & Nanus, 1985), the agile mode has long outgrown its status as a temporary exception and is becoming the permanent mode of navigation.

Managers on all levels must simultaneously cultivate within themselves the skills for the long term—an element of patience, meaningfulness, and preservation—and for the short term: momentary turbulence in the face of unexpected events. To succeed in doing so, leaders need a new "personal approach" that makes their work in the emerging "world of hybrid organizations" easier.

**Application of the Three-Pillar Model**

The Three Pillars (Wollmann et al., 2020, 2021) are defined as:

1. Sustainable Purpose—The raison d'être of an organization, bringing new orientation and certainty to the people for their joint endeavor and success.
2. Travelling Organization—The mindset of an organization in a permanent state of flux, interacting with the market and customer journey, with rapid adaptivity.
3. Connected Resources—Interconnecting all needed resources inside and outside the silos, creating consistency between goals and concepts, strategies and processes, competencies and roles.

This chapter focuses on the aspect of the leader's navigation in travelling organizations. It is about a new basic attitude that is conducive to change and about a personal journey of exploration in self-leadership. This requires a personal approach for iterative, agile development: new thinking, new attitude, new action, and new insight. From this, a training and development program can be derived that offers leaders good opportunities to prove themselves under VUCA conditions and to navigate safely.

## 2 Navigating a Travelling Organization

Even if managers and team leaders no longer have a long-term navigation plan, and the goals of the journey cannot be specifically defined, a possible way of finding basic orientation is still needed. Here the sustainable purpose takes on the role of providing orientation toward a course of development that is meaningful and collectively understood. Principles are then derived from this purpose, within which an agile, flexible search process can be conducted in small stages. The organization draws the necessary degree of consistency from the decisions made by its leaders, who must always remain in harmony with the sustainable purpose. This results in a new way of staying on course. "Helmsmanship" is now being redefined. Leaders are faced with the challenge of co-creatively making the distant goal of the journey—which initially is not specifically known—accessible as an emotional image, a future toward which it is possible to steer intuitively. They must now slip into the role of "sense makers."

Navigating under VUCA conditions, however, also demands fast and flexible action in handling the many unexpected problems and challenges along the way. The travel takes on the character of a "step-by-step journey." Leaders are responsible for the skilled navigation that ensures the journey is not entirely left to "trial and error." If the old way of doing business went "*Big things on planned tracks can overcome obstacles through their robust inner dynamics*," today the motto has changed to "*Navigation is achieved by a permanent agile search process that can outrun chance through long-term orientation and meaning*."

## 3 Travelling Requires Self-Leadership

The first and most important step in continuing to survive in this VUCA world is to undergo a holistic development—of yourself as a person and in the role of a leader. The well-known term for this is **self-leadership**—provided this is interpreted more deeply and not focused on "self-management," which falls short in this context. An attempt at defining self-leadership reads as follows: "*Self-leadership is the conscious influencing of one's own intellectual world, inner attitudes and range of emotions, the entire spectrum of action, and the learning process to fully realize one's own creative potential*" (Wallner & Völkl, 2017, p. 35). To be aware of one's self and all one's vitality while giving way to a dynamic development, remaining in motion, exposing one's self to a vertical tension, and training daily: one could interpret Peter Sloterdijk (2009) in this way when he says: "You must change your life." Self-leadership and consistently working on oneself is a concept that makes a significant difference to a pampered life full of programmed tendencies and persistent habits. To make this state of vitality more accessible, we have developed the "train the eight" personal approach (Völkl & Wallner, 2008, 2013). It is this "mind-heart-movement-form-cycle" that allows people to tap into their inner powers of self-organization and provides sufficient developmental momentum for leadership life.

Navigating a travelling organization can only succeed to the extent that the organization's leaders understand how to empower themselves to deal with complex situations and to master open-ended search processes. In the complex problems space, Dave Snowden names the "probe-sense-respond" mode as the best possible point of approach alongside his CYNEFIN™ framework for decision-making (Snowden & Boone, 2007). Navigation under VUCA conditions can be understood as an iterative search process that always begins with "safe-to-fail" experimentation ("probe"). We provide the organization with a stimulus and wait for its reaction as well as for the results that appear ("sense"). In a joint reflection and learning loop, we evaluate what we have achieved and decide on the next steps ("respond"). Thanks to a long-term alignment with the sustainable purpose, every form of repetition is good repetition because it is also consistent with the purpose. In this way, the journey can stay on a meaningful course despite all of the agility.

## 4 Dealing with High Complexity

Navigating a travelling organization therefore fundamentally refers to finding effective ways of dealing with high complexity. The developmental pattern reveals a constant, agile search process that, through the "sense-making" mentioned above, is given a predefined direction. We also arrive at the probable conclusion that navigation must also follow these principles for the personal development process—i.e., self-leadership—as well. In this respect, the developmental patterns of the organization, the teams, and also the leaders can be described in a comparable way. On every level, mastering complexity is the fundamental prerequisite for navigation.

When leaders have access to a personal approach for their own development that familiarizes them with complexity and moves them to an attitude of "iteratively testing agility" (Kruse, 2010), it is much more likely that a new and robust agility will then become recognizable in the teams and subsequently at the organizational level as well. When leaders begin to take charge of navigating their own personal development journeys, a new fundamental attitude will develop, ultimately leading to the establishment of an agile mindset. What is important here is that leaders have the courage to subject themselves to the VUCA conditions and prove themselves time and again in this complex world. Only in this way can a pluralistic and resilient world continuously evolve, open to new insights, experiences, skills, and creativity to manage well the journey into the future (Sloterdijk, 2009, p. 246). In this kind of world, leaders who move and develop themselves on the basis of holistic training and practice and accept a "virtuoso" capacity to act under VUCA conditions as a challenge will be at a distinct advantage. With a little discipline (in the sense of being ready to practice), they can thus realign inner attitudes and open new, agile spectrums of possible action for navigation.

## 5 A New Personal Approach for Leaders

Any suitable personal approach that equips leaders to navigate in travelling organizations must be a holistic one. It is necessary to integrate the emotionally intuitive areas of the human being in the developmental model and focus on central success criteria for self-development, such as the "disinhibition to action" or the "decision for differentiated repetition." To this end, we have defined a development framework with four progressive domains that we call *mind*, *heart*, *motion*, and *form* (Fig. 1).

The framework spans a developmental landscape containing the four domains named above, which are connected by the powerful symbol of a "lemniscate of Bernoulli," a horizontal figure eight. Compared with a circle, a lemniscate is much better suited to describing developmental processes. In the agile organizational environment, the assignment of meanings is multifunctional and plays a supportive role. The primary meaning of the lemniscate is "infinity," which corresponds to the spirit of constant repetition, training, and practice. A lemniscate has an origin that can be defined as the point of decision. The origin is the place of new beginnings and decisions for positive repetition. The two focal points of the lemniscate symbolize the tension between the poles—or the energy field—that make development possible in the first place. If the lemniscate opens outwardly, increasing its loop space, this process symbolizes continuing development, the exploration and occupation of a new space, a journey in the holistic sense. Peter Kruse's concept of "iteratively testing agility" (Kruse, 2010) is brought into play by the constant repetition loops and the context of the four domains. We see this as an approach to navigating under high complexity.

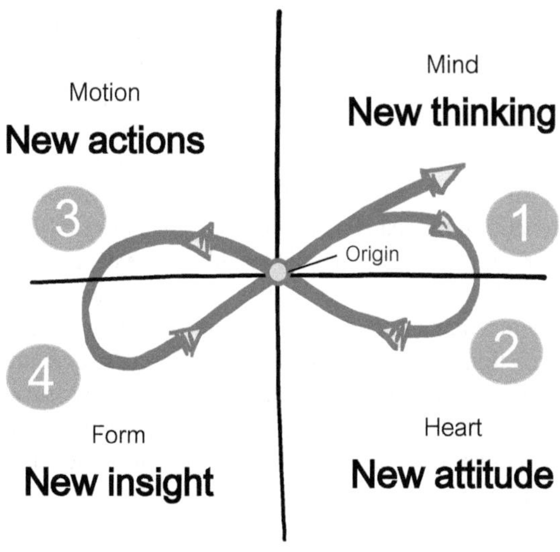


**Fig. 1** Development cycle to navigating a travelling organization (Illustrated by the authors, used with permission. All rights reserved)

## 6 The "Personal Approach to Navigating a Travelling Organization"

We begin our developmental journey along the lemniscate (horizontal figure eight) from the middle—initiated by the decision to start—toward the upper right, into the domain of the mind. Here, we find the new way of thinking (mind), and in this very place we decide whether the world will be open to us—to be recognized as a limitless field of potential—or whether it will remain narrow and closed. With a "growth mindset" (Dweck, 2006), we allow space for the idea that we can grow through the VUCA challenges, and that complexity is something that can be mastered. However, because thoughts without emotional energy remain irrelevant for our actions, we continue our developmental journey into the second domain. In this domain, that of the heart, we develop a new attitude that offers us an emotional, intuitive foundation for making decisions in complex situations. We begin to feel the possibilities we have mentally constructed and—through our self-leadership training program—develop the strength to start practicing. Development within our "inner space" has picked up speed. Before we enter the third domain, however, another decision is necessary. Strengthened inwardly, we need to develop the readiness to expose ourselves to a practice session, an experiment, an initial exploration in the external world—along with all the consequences. The beginning lies with the decision that we call the "disinhibition to action" after Peter Sloterdijk.

In the third domain of motion—a new form of action—(exclusively in the external space) we take on the task of navigating in a travelling organization. We dive into our field of practice, our experimentation space ("probe") and thus into the imperfect action that at first improves in stages—iteratively. In this domain, we open ourselves to the world of agility in small steps. In the fourth and last domain, that of form, we attain a new insight. This reflexive observation of our new action is where the aspect of learning and development first enters the cycle. Which of our experiments were successful? What parts of our new action are worth practicing and thus repeating? What do we have to change and improve? Rethink from the bottom up? Which spaces do we want to explore more extensively, and which do we prefer to leave behind? Are the results compatible with our sustainable purpose? This conscious reflection prepares us for the next decision. This time we make a "decision to positive repetition" and to a new, "improved" iteration of the "mind-heart-motion-form cycle" (we also refer to this cycle as the "train the eight cycle"). Positive repetition that carries within itself the aspect of development and is oriented toward our purpose is what enables us to create new habitual patterns and to develop ourselves seriously as human beings. Here we acquire new patterns of thinking, feeling, acting, and learning and thus new "forms" for successful navigation in travelling organizations. We consciously expand our mental horizons, develop new mindsets, conquer entirely new options for action with much higher variety, and develop to become learning, practicing human beings. Only this form of practice will open new worlds for us and allow us to develop skills for navigating in complex spaces.

## 6.1 The Domain of New Thinking ("MIND")

Every development that helps us advance begins with a creative thought (Fig. 2). At the beginning of the self-leadership process, the personal construction of reality finds itself in a process that is initially directed outwardly from within. Today, the realization that we construct our own reality through our thoughts is nothing new. This means that our development as leaders largely depends on how deeply we delve into the domain of new thinking. Our development is limited only by our thoughts. Therefore, in every second of our lives we determine the degree of our vitality. "Train the eight" is an invitation to leaders to think big and wide and to expand the space of the possible while firmly sticking with progressing in small, iterative steps. This skill will be a very useful one for the navigation of the organization and its teams.

Travelling organizations thus need leaders who are travellers themselves, who strive to expand the limits of their possibilities, who become curious discoverers. In the domain of new thinking (mind), an important principle applies: we find almost unlimited possibilities for shaping leadership and viable organizations. Added to this is a range of options that spreads out before us like a partially unknown landscape. Which areas we enter and open up for ourselves is less a question of ability than of conscious decision. It can be very helpful for leaders to have a first attempt for their own development. What are the future pictures for a viable organization and my successful contribution as a leader that I find attractive? This process is where the skill of "navigating in turbulent waters" begins to grow.

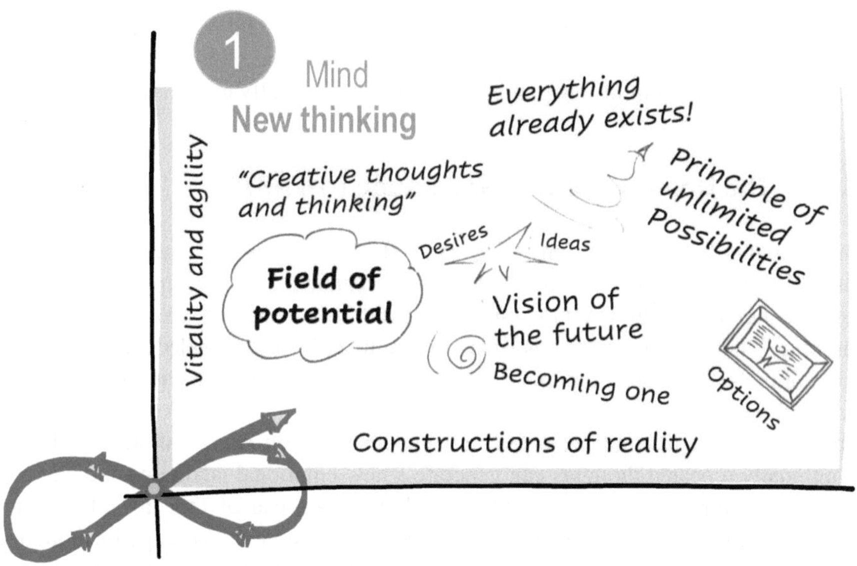


**Fig. 2** The first domain of the development cycle (Illustrated by the authors, used with permission. All rights reserved)

To make it easy to find initial answers, specific tools can be helpful. With the "Big Picture" tool, a few relevant questions are asked: What is the sustainable purpose of the organization in which I work and take on responsibility? What principles can I derive from this? What characterizes a leader who wants to contribute to the success of this kind of travelling organization? What behavior and what navigation skills make this leader a role model? What will employees particularly value here? What fundamental mindsets and skills will support an influential effectiveness in the complex spaces of the organization? Are there metaphors that describe this kind of leader (Wallner & Völkl, 2017)?

Our thinking is so conditioned that we often cannot appreciate the great treasures that lie before us. We "think past" our actual possibilities, so to speak, and overlook many valuable options in our inability to move outside familiar tracks (the attractors). And that has important consequences for everyday practice. It is not at all a matter of suddenly branching out into the great expanse. Rather, we should expand the limits of our possibilities gradually—to the limits of what we trust our own development to do and then a small extra, thoughtful step. Travelling is not only a "step-by-step" process on the organizational level, but also on the level of personal development. In this way, we can better utilize our personal field and realize more of our own possibilities at the end of the day. We expand the loop of the lemniscate outwardly.

A journey under VUCA conditions will require a new definition from leaders more frequently than before. What effective leadership means, and what abilities a person must develop to that end, is also—in the sense of "travelling"—undergoing a change. So it is wise to confront possible images of future leadership and compare them to one's own worldview. We have to become more flexible in our thinking and sound out new possibilities. The domain of the new way of thinking—the domain of the mind—is an invitation to broaden the spheres of one's thoughts and practice reinvention. This form of navigation allows us to constantly explore new spaces.

## 6.2 The Domain of the New Attitude ("HEART")

Our thoughts become emotions (Fig. 3). Today, we know that emotions are also rationalized narratives. Since the underlying algorithms are so complex, we cannot explain the origins of feelings—so we often label this entire area "emotionally intuitive." Ultimately, emotions also represent a deeper knowledge, since they conceal more "big data" than our conscious thoughts do. But we can use a correlation for our further development: emotions come continually out of our thoughts. This means that thoughts can also call up emotions on a very short-term level. Continually repeated thoughts can generate a new emotional landscape and characterize our entire being. We would do well to make use of this insight for our navigation in open-ended spaces. If we appropriate the new landscape of thoughts out of the domain of the mind and consistently pursue it with hovering attentiveness, our emotional landscape will follow after a while. Our feelings can do nothing else than form according to the pattern of our new way of thinking. In our personal

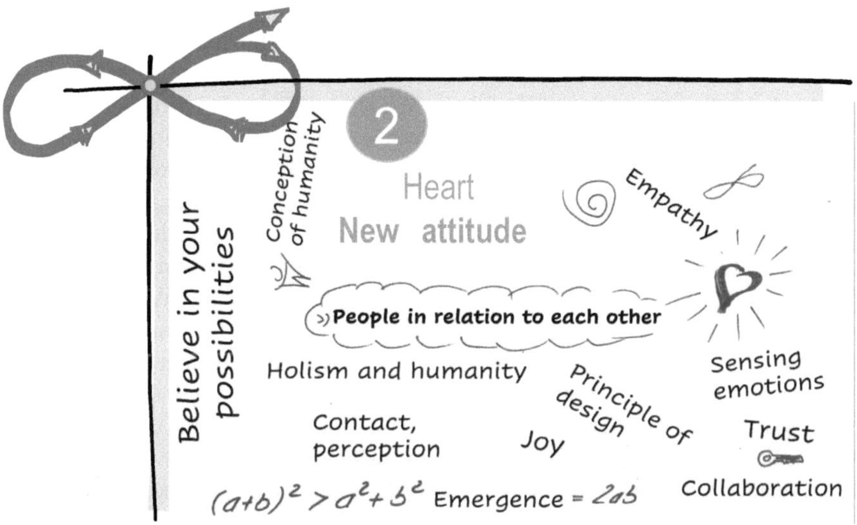


**Fig. 3** The second domain of the development cycle (Illustrated by the authors, used with permission. All rights reserved)

approach for leaders, we call this process mind-heart resonance (Wallner & Völkl, 2017).

If we have sketched our vision of the future as effective leaders in a travelling organization, an inner, intuitive processing will set in, and, after a while, we will be able to feel what we have "come up with." And therein arises the most important resource of change: willpower. This process then results in new attitudes. These attitudes are the foundation of our long-term decisions, and the true reason why we do things or refrain from doing them. So, we call the second domain the "new attitude" or the "heart quadrant."

The domain of attitude is also the source of a new authority. It requires leaders to subject themselves repeatedly to the VUCA conditions and learn. Only leaders who repeatedly prove themselves under complex conditions will develop this new authority. Travelling calls upon leaders to decisively "walk the talk."

Once we have developed sufficient mind-heart resonance, the "disinhibition to action" will follow. We adopted this phrase from Peter Sloterdijk since it seems particularly fitting. This disinhibition allows our ideas to leave the inner world and permeate reality—the outer world—in the form of experiments. This is where the mode of courageous exploration begins, a core aspect of navigating the travelling organization.

In order for the disinhibition to action to truly occur, we have to connect our resources (the third pillar of organization—connecting resources). We call it the "principle of correlation." We place ourselves in relationships: to ourselves, to other people, to resources, and to the environment. If meaning for us can be drawn from this, we can open a new path to the future—"**we are travelling**." Our personal worldview begins to mature and expand. We begin to believe in ourselves a little more, and in the people who will travel with us—we develop trust in the world, and, as if by magic, the necessary courage for disinhibition suddenly appears. Thus, we need only to allow the vision of the future we have constructed to permeate us so that we are emotionally touched by it. Visual methods—a collage, a vision of the future, or a moving story—often help to allow our image to flow down from our heads to our hearts.

The specific task of leaders is to "process" the new vision of the future. Some questions addressed to ourselves can be helpful here: What does being a leader mean for you in a deeper sense? What is your inner guiding principle? What values and attitudes do you prize the most in other leaders? What makes someone a role model for you? What internal images, passions, and values have you pursued all your life? What continually surfaces within you? When do you feel things start to "flow"? What stories do you want to be told about you by people who have worked under your leadership? Why is that important, and what do these stories trigger in you? What image would best express what you feel? What image puts your aspirations in a nutshell? What makes you a sustainable leader (Wallner & Völkl, 2017)?

## 6.3 The Domain of New Action ("MOTION")

The decision to disinhibit ourselves to act sets us in motion (Fig. 4), and sets the things in organizations in motion as well. By trying out something new, we interact with the environment in full complexity. In doing so, we come to the zone of

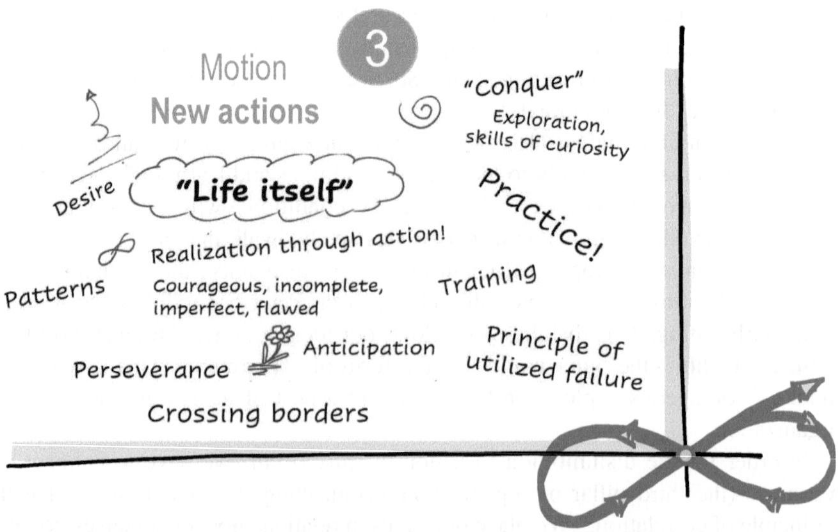


**Fig. 4** The third domain of the development cycle (Illustrated by the authors, used with permission. All rights reserved)

complexity as described in the CYNEFIN™ Framework. The three-step solution is described there as probe-sense-respond (Snowden & Boone, 2007; Snowden & Rancati, 2021).

Whenever we try something out that's meant to broaden our future scope of action, we must have the courage to take the first steps. Only our actions expose us to environmental feedback. Experiments have a few basic qualities: they produce side effects, and those side effects can be painful.

For navigation, it is important to take our first imperfect steps that bring us closer to our future pictures from the realm of "new attitude." Since we are now moving on the edge of our comfort zone, we will sense resistance. That resistance comes from at least two directions. An inner resistance can be observed, as well as resistance from other people whom our actions affect. However, a strong mind-heart resonance will enable us to overcome these inhibitions. Most people feel it is very liberating to try something new after a long time. In small steps, we practice moving forward. Without exaggerated expectations of success, we allow ourselves to make mistakes. Incomplete, flawed, imperfect action is what ultimately brings us forward when we declare our lives and leadership worlds to be a training ground. Every step—even one in a wrong direction—was and is an important step on our development path. We learn to navigate. Quite incidentally, we activate the "principle of deliberate failure." By doing so, we enable people to bring more awareness to every new attempt and thus develop authentic agility.

In the domain of motion, we will slip again and again into the role of the courageous conqueror, just like in the early days of globalization. Without great vision and inner conviction, it is unlikely that anyone would have ventured out to seek new worlds. We place our boot in the sand without knowing what awaits us in the new country. No matter how small and modest they might be, these conquests always represent the crossing of boundaries; they belong to us alone, and are more valuable than most great treasures. Every experience gained through practical activity strengthens us inwardly more than advice from the outside could ever do. Boundaries are at first a constriction, but also a form of protection. To approach them, we must expend courage and energy. If we follow the "train the eight" cycle of the horizontal figure eight, and if we have strengthened our willpower and developed adequate courage in the domain of the heart, we can risk stepping up to the border and going beyond it. In doing so, we sense the energy phenomenon of every border: we receive energy that gives us an impulse in the right direction. In nature, many exciting processes happen next to a border. But we humans have imposed on borders a daunting effect because we are focused on security.

In the domain of new action, we encounter a familiar discipline from Peter Senge and the learning organization. That discipline is "Personal Mastery" (Senge, 1990), for which the "train the eight" cycle offers a modus vivendi. What do we bring into our lives and our world of leadership for mastery? How can we attain a virtuoso viability under VUCA conditions?

Again, some questions addressed to ourselves can help here: From what do you recognize the excellence of your role models? What actions set them apart? Which actions create a living atmosphere, and what motivates people to develop their potential? What resources and which of your strengths can you apply? What generates energy in the team? Which of the many methods and tools from the agile world of the organization could you try out? Where do you sense resistance and how can you overcome it? What best fits you and your sustainable purpose (Wallner & Völkl, 2017)?

Today, leaders must develop a new, incredibly broad landscape of disciplines. All skills that can be trained are important. The "boxes and crates" mentality from dated management theories, according to which management's strategic knowledge is passed into the accumulated crates of the employees, must give way to agile, directly inclusive collaboration by all participants in the organization. This recognition in and of itself results in an inexhaustible training ground for leaders. How can I motivate passive observers to true participation? How can I best connect, facilitate and utilize human intelligence? How can we integrate artificial intelligence into the team and create successful interplay? The question of motivation can then be reduced: a motivated person is someone who is active along the lemniscate as initiator and implementer of an "agile practice process" and therefore establishes the "authority of a navigation trainer."

## 6.4 The Domain of New Insights ("FORM")

If we have bravely begun our "tests" in the world and tried out enough things at the same time, we must quickly process the feedback we receive and learn something from it. Therefore, the fourth domain in the "train the eight" approach is that of new insight (the quadrant of form, of new patterns) (Fig. 5). We must find out what is really worth improving and repeating. Only practiced action holds the potential for relevant growth. However, as is always the case in life, there are two sides to the coin here. Action that is practiced with total enthusiasm can also lead us astray. This enthusiasm frequently blinds us to the situations in which we find ourselves. Practiced action also needs a strong partner. At its core, this involves the reflection of the experienced. Every action brings an effect that we must examine. Only in this way can we experience reflected development. In the domain of form, we assure ourselves that we will remain on the course of our desired development, and we safeguard what we have already attained. But this also involves a new insight: what effect has our new action brought about? Has it strengthened us? Here we arrive at the core of navigation.

In the fourth domain, we conclude the holistic developmental cycle. An idea (mind) ultimately becomes a new form through the heart and motion. An idea has manifested itself in the world of organizations and leadership. In many cases, these forms will be actual things—if we have constructed and built something, for example. But in most cases involving our personal, holistic development, forms are new patterns that we bring into our lives. Every habit in our leadership lives is a form, because it represents a distinct, recognizable, repeating pattern of action. And here we latch onto a further principle of development: the wish for mastery and completion. Only that which strengthens us and truly benefits us and the world is

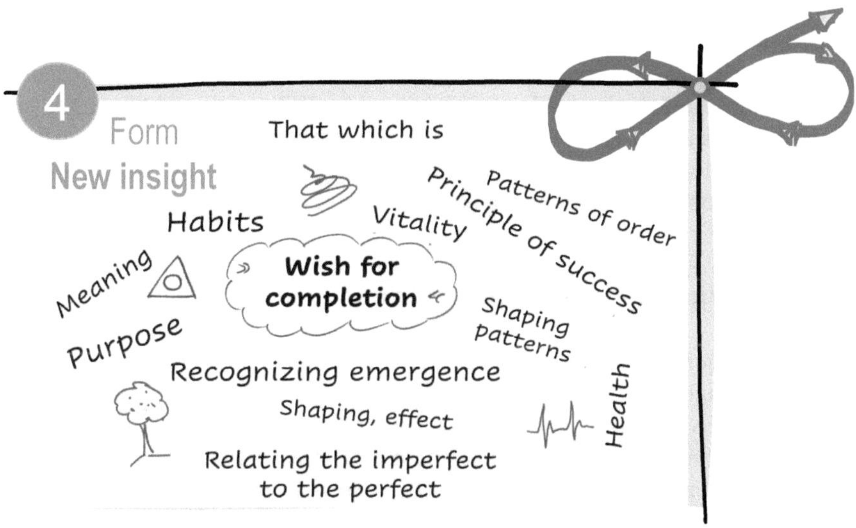


**Fig. 5** The fourth domain of the development cycle (Illustrated by the authors, used with permission. All rights reserved)

what we wish to expand. We want to leave behind and free ourselves from everything that inhibits us and fails to bring about the desired effect. This learning by doing is more than a simple "target vs. actual" comparison. In this domain, learning becomes a collective effort even if it involves self-leadership. Every person needs the network of a group for his or her development. The awareness of this connectivity brings us to the principle: "Pause until everyone has learned" (Wallner & Völkl, 2017). In the domain of form, we also create and deepen the meaning of the organization: its sustainable purpose. Strictly speaking, this is a form of the collective and continual construction of meaning.

Just as we created a mind-heart resonance in the first two domains, movement and form also bring about a synthesis of failure and success: It is a joyous success. It strengthens our belief in our possibilities and makes us braver for the next round.

And at the very end, a decision must be made so that we can really conclude the first round in the overall developmental cycle: what is required is the decision for repetition. But repetition isn't simply copying something. Positive repetition needs to make a difference: it represents a rejection of sameness. We, therefore, call this form of repetition "differentiated repetition."

To make it easier to open up the domain of insight—of form—for leaders, another set of useful questions can help. Which of your tests has proven itself and is therefore worth being incorporated into your training program? What will you reinforce? What will you do less of? What will you abandon? How will you keep your development going and decide to repeat something? What helps you develop a learning routine? What do your role models normally do? What details can you permanently include in your set of routines (Wallner & Völkl, 2017)?

The principle of differentiated repetition reminds us to be consistent. No change in leadership will benefit us if we are not prepared to practice. Only practice brings mastery. This makes every practice a good repetition. Self-leadership demands a repeated run through the "train the eight" cycle. With each repetition, we can broaden our vision of the future and put it into concrete terms, increase our inner commitment, disinhibit ourselves for action again, and start a new test to finally plan the next developmental phase in the domain of form (insight).

## 7 Navigation in Everyday Motion

Navigation requires openness to change, and that comes from having an attitude that embraces change. The "train the eight" approach is a tool for anyone who wants to subject themselves to holistic change and start out on their own developmental path of iterative testing. "Navigating a travelling organization" demands the capability to think long-term and holistically, to react with agility to everyday problems and to use the chances that lie before us. It is important to take the contradiction between preservation (the long cycle of development that steers us toward a sustainable purpose) and change (short-term problem solving under VUCA conditions, which requires agile practices) to the next level. In practical, day-to-day leadership, it looks like this: You make a "train the eight" canvas where you can enter your major, long-term, big-picture futures, your values, your new nourishing habits, and your learning routines. And every day, you complete a "My Daily" where you note your ideal day as a navigating leader. This is also a form of balance; to be specific, by following a great path of development with a certain ease, remaining in the basic attitude of day-to-day practice, and making small, consistent improvements. With our "train the eight" approach, we give the agile, iteratively testing development a face and a learning landscape. The four domains are connected in a horizontal figure eight, which symbolically shows the polarity of the development and visually represents the ever-recurring instances of decision: the disinhibition for action from the emotional-intuitive domain of the heart and the decision for differentiated repetition from the domain of the form.

## 8 With the Power of the Network

A travelling organization needs a living network of leaders who open up new thinking spaces together. The greatest challenge here is always conscious variation in the stabilizing structures of the organization. Here the organization's culture serves as a guardian against the whims of those who are all too enthusiastic about agility and who want unwaveringly to give innovation priority over tradition. This will also demand more than quickly sketched organizational models that surface in communities as fashions promising novel solutions. Travelling means opening creative spaces, keeping the options hovering, refusing to make hasty decisions, and waiting until everyone has learned. This is where the network comes into play.

The third pillar, connecting resources, fosters complexity and is a generator for new variants. Only in this synergy in newly created spaces can people mutually support and complement each other and courageously take the risks that are necessary for the navigation of the travelling organization.

## References and Further Readings


Bennis, W., & Nanus, B. (1985). *Leaders: The strategies for taking charge*. Harper & Row.

Dweck, C. S. (2006). *Mindset: The new psychology of success*. Random House.

Kruse, P. (2010). *Next practice—Erfolgreiches Management von Instabilität. Veränderung durch Vernetzung* (9th ed.). Gabal.

Senge, P. M. (1990). *The fifth discipline: The art and practice of the learning organization*. Doubleday and Currency.

Sloterdijk, P. (2009). *Du mußt dein Leben ändern. Über Anthropotechnik*. Suhrkamp.

Snowden, D., & Rancati, A. (2021). *Managing complexity (and chaos) in times of crises*. Publication Office of the European Union.

Snowden, D. J., & Boone, M. E. (2007). A leader's framework for decision making. *Harvard Business Review, 85*(11), 68–76, 149.

Völkl, K., & Wallner, H. P. (2008). *Das LILA Management Prinzip. Unternehmen neu denken und erfolgreich verändern*. Amalthea Signum.

Völkl, K., & Wallner, H. P. (2013). *Das innere Spiel. Wie Entscheidung und Veränderung spielerisch gelingen*. BusinessVillage.

Wallner, H. P., & Völkl, K. (2017). *Fokus Self-Leadership—Gesunde und wirkungsvolle Selbstführung in Zeiten hoher Komplexität*. Summerhill.

Wollmann, P., Kühn, F., & Kempf, M. (Eds.). (2020). *Three pillars of organization and leadership in disruptive times—navigating your company successfully through the 21st century business world*. SpringerNature.

Wollmann, P., Kühn, F., Kempf, M., & Püringer, R. (Eds.). (2021). *Organization and leadership in disruptive times—design and implementation of the 3-P-model*. SpringerNature.

**Heinz Peter Wallner** has been a management consultant since 1995. He devoted his interest and energy to questions of transformation and complex processes of change. As part of a research fellowship to work abroad, he conducted research on his topic "islands of sustainability" at the University of British Columbia, Vancouver, during his dissertation. This was followed by several EU research projects and numerous publications. In his consulting work, he focused on strategies for sustainable development and on complex change processes. Today, as an independent consultant, he contributes his skills as a creative conceptionist, facilitator and knowledge broker to leadership training, organizational consulting and teaching at universities and technical colleges. Heinz Peter is the author of numerous articles and books.

**Kurt Völkl** studied technical mathematics at the Graz University of Technology and completed high-level management training in St. Gallen. In 1992, he was appointed CEO of the Social Insurance of Mining Companies in Austria (VADÖB). In 2000, he assumed responsibility for controlling management at the Main Association of Austrian Social Insurance Institutions. This resulted in a coordinated Balanced Scorecard System for all social insurance organizations in Austria. He accompanied a major merger of two insurance organizations in a management capacity and was appointed CEO of the Insurance Institution for Railways and Mining (VAEB). Today Kurt is a professor at the University of Graz, at the Institute for Corporate Leadership and Entrepreneurship. He has published his research and development work in several books.

# Objectives and Key Results: How Navigating Travelling Organizations Might Succeed

Dominique Wirl and Sebastian Luge

**Abstract**

The need for travelling organizations is obvious, due to our volatile, uncertain, complex, and ambiguous environments. Thus, organizations have to explore new ways of navigation as long-term strategies and decisions do not fit these needs any longer. A new holistic agility is needed which enables organizations, leaders, and employees to succeed. Besides an agile mindset, new frameworks are needed. These have to answer actual needs in travelling organizations, e.g., orientation and flexibility at the same time. At this point, the OKR Framework (Objectives and Key Results) seems to be one way to meet these expectations. In this chapter, the framework and its answers to the needs of travelling organizations are described. First, a short overview of the framework itself is given. Second, there is a look at holistic agility. This is described in the first book of the series "Three Pillars of Organization and Leadership in Disruptive Times" (Wollmann et al., 2020)—as the DNA of travelling organizations. A proper look at how Objectives and Key Results cover and foster this concept will then be taken. At this point, four perspectives are relevant: agile mentality, self-reflection, readiness to embrace change, and willingness to deliver. Third, there is a deep dive into a concrete challenge regarding the implementation of Objectives and Key Results in a—more or less—traditional organization: In this case, Management by Objectives is one of the key leadership and controlling tools which is incorporated and covers an individual performance and compensation system. A shift from extrinsic to intrinsic motivation by fostering such a new (agile) culture is not enough to compensate, motivate, and retain high performers in teams. To get closer to a new way of individual compensation while using the Objectives and Key Result Framework and keep up motivation on a team level,

D. Wirl (✉) · S. Luge
Bonn, Germany
e-mail: wirl@cidpartners.de; luge_partner@cidpartners.de



M. Kempf, F. Kühn (eds.), *Navigating a Travelling Organization*, Future of Business and Finance, https://doi.org/10.1007/978-3-030-95326-3_8

new connections between team- and individual bonus systems are needed. The different steps of this change will be discussed: From a coexistence of a bonus system on an individual level and OKRs to an integration phase into a full transformation. Furthermore, some concrete take-aways for handling such challenges are given.

## 1 Short Overview of the OKR Framework

Objectives and Key Results are sometimes seen as "old wine in new bottles." Regarding the history of OKRs, this might not be that wrong. Still, it is more than that. It is a framework that not just helps to execute strategies in both ways—top-down and bottom-up—and to get better results, but also requires a new culture of leadership and collaboration. To get there, this chapter gives a short overview of the framework and its functionalities.

### 1.1 The Origins of OKR

Nowadays, "VUCA" seems to be quite a well-known term—which does not alter its importance and currency: We are living in a volatile, uncertain, complex, and ambiguous world, and OKRs describe a framework for organizations to handle these challenges. Most of the time, management teams create great ideas about the strategy that should help to navigate the company through the challenges given. But quite often, these strategies remain strategies and their execution fails (Kraaijenbrink, 2019). At this point, OKRs help to face these challenges and get strategies executed. OKRs were first used at Intel, introduced by Andy Grove as a collaborative framework for three levels of organization: The organization itself, teams, and individuals. Later on, they were also introduced in companies like Google, etc. (Doerr, 2018a). Their roots can be found in Drucker's process "Management by Objectives," Objectives and Key Results are seen as a development of it. They are a "survival tool" in a world that is getting faster and more and more complex (Doerr, 2018b). The core idea is quite simple: It is worth focusing on a few goals rather than trying to accomplish a lot of goals. This also helps to navigate travelling organizations in such disruptive goals.

### 1.2 What Are Objectives and Key Results?

Initially, we will take a look at the terms "Objectives," "Key Results," and "Initiatives"—also known as OKR Sets—before the whole cycle is introduced. Objectives describe where the team wants to go. They are ambitious, motivating, and describe a desired future state. Furthermore, they are qualitative and have a clear focus on the customer's value. Customers can be external or internal. Key Results are similar to a lever to achieve objectives and they help to measure whether the team is on its way to meet the objective. It is a crucial point to make results measurable and to find scales that are helpful. The third level in defining OKRs is initiatives. These are derived from the Key Results and contain single activities or desired outputs that pay into the Key Results.

## 1.3 The Typical OKR Cycle

To better understand how OKRs can be used, an example for a typical OKR cycle including the typical Meetings is demonstrated in the following. This process is as important as the drafting process of the described OKR sets (Fig. 1).

The illustration in Fig. 1 is an overview of the cycle, which is mostly 3–4 months long. Before teams can start to draft OKRs, it is important that organizational priorities are communicated. These priorities are like the north star, they might be the overall vision or strategy where the organization wants to go. After this communication, teams draft their OKR sets as described before. To demonstrate whether there are any conflicting or complementary goals, the alignment process, which can consist of one or more workshops, is crucial. These workshops are where teams present their OKR sets (derived from the organizational priorities previously communicated) and make intersections and overlaps, synergies and conflicts visible. The next step is to refine the OKRs. When this process of drafting, aligning, and refining is completed—which can be quite exhausting for teams and often shows up weak points in the cooperation—a kick-off workshop takes place. This is when the final commitment to the OKR sets for the starting cycle takes place. Everyone takes responsibility for achieving the defined goals. Weekly Check-Ins during the cycle help to support the teams to keep the OKRs in focus and to track progress. Furthermore, engagement and responsibility for the organizational goals are promoted. When the OKR cycle is completed after 3–4 months, a retrospective helps to learn from the past and to understand what could be done better in the future. This meeting is all about the co-working during the last cycle. This means that the process is rated as well as the emotions and individual perspectives of the team members. The final step of the OKR cycle is the review, which focuses on progress and results. It is a collective evaluation and identifies topics that should be included in the next cycle.

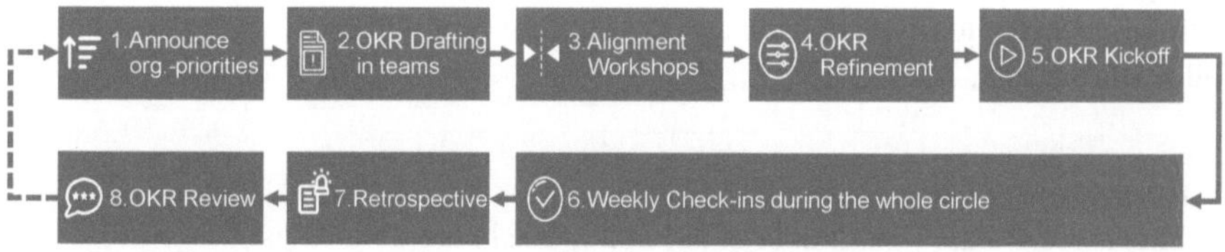


**Fig. 1** A typical OKR cycle (Workpath, 2021). (Illustrated by the authors, used with permission. All rights reserved)

On the one hand, this cycle of OKRs is a good way to navigate organizations and it might seem clear and easy. On the other hand, there are several pitfalls and challenges that might complicate the implementation of OKRs in teams. To name just some of them: Working in silos, leadership that is not part of the transformation, using key results as a to-do list, etc. However, a detailed description of these pitfalls and challenges is beyond the scope of this chapter.

# 2 How OKRs Meet New Ways of Navigation and Holistic Agility

## 2.1 The OKR Framework for Navigating Travelling Organizations

Travelling organizations open up new ways of navigation and agility in disruptive times. There are at least two perspectives on navigation and OKRs. First, OKRs are an instrument of navigation that face actual challenges. Unlike classic tools for leading organizations, the OKR framework opens up a more flexible and integrating way of leadership. Four main advantages of OKRs shall be pointed out here (Müller, 2020):

**Focus and discipline**: Goals are visible and measurable and are clearly communicated to the teams.

**Alignment**: At the beginning of every OKR cycle, all individuals and teams align to the goals and ensure that resources are used efficiently. This alignment takes place horizontally and vertically which ensures that divergent goals are identified.

**Motivation and employee engagement**: The objective setting is a combination of top-down- and bottom-up processes, which makes sure that individuals are involved in planning goals. This also strengthens commitment and motivation.

**Meaningful transparency**: Successes and past performance are more visible—this makes recognition of achievements and learning from the past easier.

Second, organizations might be on a bigger organizational journey to a travelling organization. To master this journey, OKRs can be helpful in several ways. They can be seen as an instrument to move the organization from a starting point to the north star of being a travelling organization by involving both perspectives: that of the top management as well as the employees. Additionally, the cultural shift that comes with OKRs helps to foster holistic agility. This concept will be shown in detail in the following section.

**Application of the Three-Pillar Model**

The Three Pillars (Wollmann et al., 2020, 2021) are defined as:

(continued)

(1) Sustainable Purpose—the raison d'être of an organization, bringing new orientation and certainty to the people for their joint endeavor and success
(2) Travelling Organization—the mindset of an organization in a permanent state of flux, interacting with the market and customer journey, with rapid adaptivity
(3) Connected Resources—interconnecting all needed resources inside and outside the silos, creating consistency between goals and concepts, strategies and processes, competencies, and roles

This chapter focuses on how to realize the navigation of a travelling organization from strategy to implementation by using the OKR framework. This fosters holistic agility in its four characteristics (agile mentality, self-reflection, readiness to embrace change, and willingness to deliver). Further, change in individual performance and bonus systems is needed: the organizational culture has to shift from an individual perspective to teams and common goals.

## 2.2 How OKRs Cover and Foster Holistic Agility

Looking for navigation in travelling organizations, holistic agility is a key factor. Four perspectives are relevant for holistic agility: agile mentality, self-reflection, readiness to embrace change, and willingness to deliver (Wollmann et al., 2020). This chapter will allow a proper look at how Objectives and Key Results cover and foster this concept.

**Agile mentality** represents a mindset of people as well as organizations that enables to them behave in a moving and changing world. In this world, development is not plannable (Hofert, 2018). Adaptation, reflection, and iteration play an important role in this context. To face the challenges of a moving world, adaptation and iteration are crucial. Regarding the OKR framework, there are several points that meet these expectations in an agile world. The idea of cycles, which last 3–4 months, allows teams to adapt their ways to implement the defined strategy or organizational priorities. The regular Check-Ins and review meetings show up any gaps between the desired future state and the goals achieved to date. Thanks to the short cycles there is enough space to adjust behaviors to achieve the announced organizational priorities or strategies. This shows that an agile mentality can take place at several points of the process—at the same time it needs to be lived and accepted on an emotional level by the people working together in the OKR cycles. Depending on the earlier organizational behaviors, this might be a quite big shift in organizational culture.

The same aspect as mentioned before applies to the perspective of **self-reflection**. This means that it is not just about reflection on processes, mistakes, and successes, but also about the self: What is my part in this? The OKR framework meets both perspectives of reflection: The review meeting enables the team to understand, which goals have been achieved and what part of the completed OKR cycle might be brought into the next cycle, whereas the retrospective focuses on the "working together." To bring this kind of reflection to a higher level, self-reflection is needed. Therefore, leaders should be aware of their important role in such processes: Not just time for retrospectives is needed, but also a mindset, that allows leaders and employees to talk about not knowing and deal with failures in a relaxed way. Therefore, "psychological safety" is needed (Hofert & Thonet, 2019). If this context is given, reflection enables real learning.

A further perspective of holistic agility is the **readiness to embrace change**. Therefore, the shortness of the cycles should be mentioned again. The readiness to adapt goals in such short cycles is proof of embracing change. Moreover, these cycles challenge management to think more often about organizational priorities—as they are an important input for each cycle. This enables organizations to stay in touch with changes in the market environment more intensely than before. Therefore, changes and adaptation become more and more familiar to everyone working within in the OKR cycle.

Finally, holistic agility is about the **willingness to deliver**. This perspective also aims at accountability, which is correlated with organizational success. Often, employees do not take on accountability and show low willingness to deliver because the goals, responsibilities, and roles are not transparent enough (DeRosa, 2018). OKRs help to clarify these pitfalls and uncover gaps that prevent people from delivering. The transparency of OKRs is one of the most important aspects of this perspective. Furthermore, alignment and a clear commitment during the Kick-Off support this willingness to deliver: Teams and individuals have the chance to discuss the ways they want to support the strategy's implementation. Moreover, OKRs are usually drafted in a rather ambitious way. This requires a stretch of teams and individuals to enable the goals to be achieved. At the same time, this has a motivating factor, because old solutions will most likely not deliver outstanding results.

In summary, OKRs offer many ways to support holistic agility in organizations—though mere implementation of the framework cannot yet be the solution: A shift of mindsets and behaviors is needed as well.

## 3 OKRs, Individual Performance, and Compensation Systems

While OKRs aim to maximize goals on a team basis, there are many companies that would like to maintain bonus systems on an individual level. The following describes these challenges. To show how to handle the challenges around individual and team bonus systems, several steps can be taken: First, Management by Objectives (MBO) and OKRs will be compared. Second, principles of the OKR framework are described to show how they call for another style of compensation systems. Third, a model for shifting from individual to team performance systems in several steps explains the inter-relations and possibilities. There will also be a brief look at the opportunities and limits of objective optimization.

## 3.1 Conceptual Differences Between MBO and OKRs

Quite a lot of companies use MBO to structure their goals, activities, and performance. When OKRs come up, there is a need to understand the differences between the two frameworks. Both frameworks, Management by Objectives (MBO) and Objectives and Key Results (OKRs) enable organizations, teams, and individuals to define their goals and measure their performance. At the same time, these two frameworks are based on different mindsets and ages of organizational development. OKR is often seen as a further development of MBO, which follows the general development and evolution of organizations in our dynamic and complex world. Before looking at these trends in greater detail, the comparison in Fig. 2 shows several criteria that exemplify the differences between the two frameworks:

This table shows the different perspectives of the frameworks on organizations and collaboration: While MBO is made in, and for, an environment that works well with a directive, top-down leadership approach, OKRs enable organizations to develop in a world where holistic agility—as described before—is needed. At the same time, MBO is usually linked to individual performance management, and the bonus system as its criteria—as shown before—aims at an individual approach (instead of a team view). Another relevant aspect is risk readiness: MBO focuses on goals that are achievable. If employees and leaders achieve their goals, they will receive their bonuses. The OKR framework assumes that people are even more motivated when goals are drafted ambitiously. But if OKRs and individual performance are linked, people will no longer draft ambitious goals and the new levels that might be achieved will decline. Furthermore, there is a trend to move away from traditional, individual bonus systems toward team bonuses. These aspects already show that the combination of OKRs and individual performance management creates some obstacles.

| Criterion | MBO | OKRs |
|---|---|---|
| **Motivation** | Extrinsic | Intrinsic |
| **Measurement** | Result | Process of achievement |
| **Duration of cycles** | One year | Three to four months |
| **Transparency** | Private - Between leader and employee | Public - Within the whole team / company |
| **Risk readiness** | Less pronounced | More pronounced |
| **Leadership style** | Command and Control | Coaching and servant leadership |
| **Vertical alignment** | Cascading goals | Top-down and bottom-up |
| **Horizontal alignment** | No | Yes |

**Fig. 2** Comparison of MBO versus OKR. (Illustrated by the authors, used with permission. All rights reserved)

## 3.2 How OKR Principles Influence Performance Management and Bonus Systems

### Working in Teams Versus Individual Performance

Assuming that organizations find themselves in a dynamic and complex world, agile frameworks are a way to face these challenges. As mentioned before, OKRs is a framework that helps to implement holistic agility in organizations. At the same time, self-organization in team collaboration and creativity are in demand. To meet these expectations, working in teams is essential, while working on individual goals is less beneficial. Furthermore, an image of employees and leaders prevails that puts intrinsic motivation in the foreground.

### Focus on Customers vs. Focus on Personal Development

Furthermore, there is an important difference between the two frameworks that must be pointed out: The purpose of OKRs is to focus on the outcome for customers and organizations; performance management is about the individual development of employees, which includes behavior, mindset, and further individual skills. At this point, three criteria are decisive: First, duration is a lot shorter within in the OKR framework than it is within MBO and/or individual performance systems. Assuming that we are living in a faster, more dynamic, and volatile world, it makes sense for goals to be adapted to shorter intervals. Second, transparency is—among other things—connected to the willingness to deliver: Assuming that everyone knows the goals that a team wants to achieve, there is more willingness to deliver, as a rule. At the same time, the more transparency exists, the easier it becomes to understand connections between goals. Third, leadership style—which is correlated to intrinsic versus extrinsic motivation—is one key factor that makes working with OKRs successful. If leaders are convinced that their teams are intrinsically motivated, a link between OKRs and individual bonus systems seems to become obsolete.

This explains why most people working with OKR recommend not mixing both approaches—in theory. In practice, there are organizations that work with an individual performance system using, e.g., MBO and want to implement OKRs to face the challenges in disruptive times. The way to meet this challenge will be shown in the following.

### From Individual Performance Management to Team Performance

As mentioned before, many organizations struggle when OKRs are implemented and an individual performance system is (still) in place. Based on experience with different companies, a model has been developed that shows a way from individual performance management to a focus on team performance.

## 3.3 Case: From MBO and Individual Bonus to OKRs

The case focuses on managers and leaders, not on employees. In a small, rather traditional organization with around 140 employees, MBO is incorporated and covers a core function regarding goal setting and an individual performance system. The management recognizes that increasingly disruptive times and market challenges require other ways of leading, motivating, and compensating. Furthermore, keeping their customers' needs in mind, focusing on the really important challenges, and implementing their strategy in a sustainable manner are reasons to implement OKRs. In short: OKRs are seen as a framework for navigating the organization that is starting to travel due to current challenges. At the same time, the leadership team is aware of the big shift in leading, collaborating, and compensating. Regarding the bonus system, change is needed: away from bonus for individual performance toward bonuses awarded on a team basis. The following illustration shows this shift over time—while the individual part of the bonus is getting smaller and smaller, the team perspective is taking over more and more parts of the bonus.

## Step-by-Step Transition within the OKR Framework

To design this way and change the bonus system, three steps are taken (Fig. 3):

1. *Side by side*: The two systems are both in place alongside one another.
2. *Integration*: First components of a team-based bonus are integrated into the existing bonus system, which consists mainly of individual aspects.
3. *Full transformation*: Parts of the individual performance system are increasingly removed; team aspects take over—up to an overall bonus depending on the success of the company.

Especially the transition between Phases 2 and 3 needs to be prepared carefully and it depends on the organization how far and how fast the individual part of the bonus will ultimately be removed. For this reason, we will show what kind of challenges organizations might encounter in different phases transforming from old legacy performance management to OKRs.

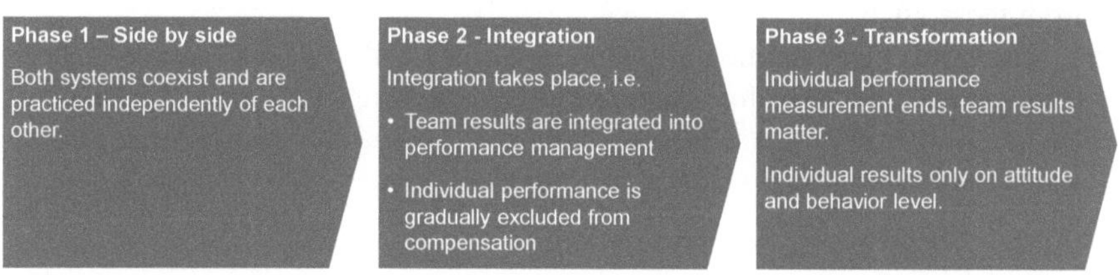


**Fig. 3** 3 phases from MBO and individual bonus to OKRs. (Illustrated by the authors, used with permission. All rights reserved)

**Phase 1: MBO and OKR side by side**

**High Tolerance for Ambiguity**

A big challenge arises when both systems exist side by side. The question for team members and for managers is which system is most important for me and my work, and what guides me in my decisions? With two systems in place, a high tolerance for ambiguity is needed. The difference of both systems needs to be clear to everyone and OKRs should not copy the goals that were defined in the individual performance management system.

**Takeaway:** Both systems must not conflict with each other. The most important step is to make managers' targets transparent to the team.

**Planning Cycles Do Not Fit**

Another challenge arises when MBO rhythms do not match the often-shorter OKR cycles. If individual performance targets are agreed on a yearly basis, this might corrupt the agile short-term and flexible principles that come with OKRs. One solution is to break down managers' goals into quarterly Objectives and Key Results, making use of the collective intelligence of the team. The planning fallacy bias might occur resulting in OKRs that are too small in the first quarter. That might result in high pressure on results in the following quarters. It is recommended that managers make their goals transparent and discuss with the team how these could be integrated into the OKRs. Additionally, if a manager's goals are set on a yearly basis, these goals cannot react to a VUCA world as quickly as OKRs can.

**Takeaway:** Shorter cycles for managers' goals can help to overcome this obstacle.

**Mindset Shift**

MBO typically comes from the mindset that what needs to be achieved is broken down from the top of the organization to the lower levels. The underlying assumption is that managers and top management know better about the right direction than their employees. This shows another source of ambiguity and complexity. If the team does not agree that the manager's goals are the right ones, there will not be a commitment on OKRs that are derived from those goals.

**Takeaway:** One solution is to make use of the collective intelligence of the team to create OKRs before the manager's targets are fixed.

**Phase 2: Integration of Team Aspects Into MBO System**

So far, we have assumed that managers use their individually set goals to guide the work of their teams in the right direction. The team is led by the manager, and the capacity to lead is limited in the manager's skills and resources. When the goals are not tied to the manager but to the whole team, there are many motivational and transformative effects that can occur. In other words: when the teams are led by goals that they have defined in a participative process instead of being led managers, their buy-in and commitment will be higher. Unfortunately, there might be some forces of inertia in place:

**Individual Bonus vs. Ambitious Goals**

If the manager's bonus is partially determined by what the team decides upon, he or she will try to influence the OKRs into a direction that is beneficial and safe for him.

**Takeaway:** OKRs need to be checked for their ambition level as well as for the team's capability to influence the goals autonomously.

**Alignment Requires New Skills**

Another big shift is that teams become more and more responsible for aligning their goals with those of other teams. With MBO, this alignment is negotiated between managers, now managers lose a certain degree of influence. Managers need to learn to trust the process of OKR goal-setting and inter-team alignment, especially in the first OKR cycles, because the teams need to gain new capabilities, which takes time. Following this, leadership training and OKR coaching are important since managers need to gain new skills and adopt another mindset to make OKR a successful framework. One aspect of this is the way that the success of metrics is measured. Most MBO systems focus on "lag measures." These are measures that only show performance with a time delay. To have a good steering effect in self-organized teams, OKRs need to focus on lead measures. These are metrics that can be influenced directly without a time delay. For many organizations, this is a massive shift in mindset and leadership practices.

**Takeaway:** If managers are asked to help their teams to come up with meaningful measures, they need to have a skill advantage. Another big shift for managers might be to step back from managing or micro-managing the work of their teams but to "guide from the side"; to coach and support their teams to be fully accountable for their performance. This is especially true when your remuneration depends on what your team does. In the integration phase, when team aspects have more and more relevance in the performance management systems of an organization, this is a crucial balancing act.

**Phase 3: Full Transformation: Team Aspects Take Over**

We have now come to a situation in which the organization realizes that individual performance management systems no longer make sense. Team aspects take over, paving the way for agile, self-organized teams with managers that support them to define, align and reach ambitious goals. But still, there are some forces of inertial that drag toward the legacy MBO systems and leadership behavior. Teams are now intrinsically motivated, but the compensation of managers is still tied to specific targets. To cut off old ropes it is important to remove extrinsic motivation systems.

**Focus on the Organization's Overall Success**

One way would be to convert the average bonus payments into an additional element of the fixed salary. There can be a bonus element that is still tied to success, but the best way would be to focus on the organization's overall success rather than on success in parts of the organization. The latter would hinder the alignment process to reach solutions that are beneficial to the overall company. It could even be beneficial to widen the idea of a variable compensation based on the overall success of the company to all employees, not only managers, to display trust and to strengthen accountability.

**Takeaway:** Focus on the overall success and not only on the success of units, departments, or teams.

**Recognizing Outstanding Performance**

Since bonuses are usually also used to recognize outstanding performance, other tools to do so need to be put in place. Motivation and recognition can be achieved by visible appreciation or constant developmental feedback.

**Takeaway:** No matter what you choose, it must be separated from the process and content of OKRs.

**New Onboarding Challenges**

A last challenge should be addressed in this section. When a company has made the shift from MBO to team performance systems like OKR, people that are new to the organization need to be onboarded thoroughly. This is true for both employees and managers. If they lack the competencies or the mindset needed, this needs to be addressed early in the onboarding process. For managers, this could even be checked in the recruiting process.

**Takeaway:** Make sure that new hires (especially in leadership positions) do not jeopardize OKR principles.

In this section, we only had the chance to address some of the aspects that occur during the step-by-step transformational process from individual performance management systems to OKRs that, by design, focus more on team aspects. Travelling organizations that are on this journey need to consciously address all phenomena that come to light in such a process and need to create a protected space for managers to address their questions and fears.

## 4 Conclusion

Travelling organizations need to live holistic agility as well as frameworks that make navigation possible in disruptive times. The OKR framework is a way to meet these challenges. Quite often, OKRs make underlying challenges visible that have been reducing companies' ability to perform and adapt. This means a big cultural shift for most of the leaders and employees in organizations. The comparison of MBO and OKR has shown many aspects that make this cultural shift tangible. One of the main challenges is the journey from an extrinsic, individual performance system to a team perspective. This includes cultural aspects as well as practical issues. At the same time, it represents the main differences between "classic" management and agile frameworks like OKR. We are moving away from hierarchical, top-down management, driven by strategies that are set for the years to come. In the focus there is a mix of top-down- and bottom-up perspectives, strategies are adopted in shorter cycles. Furthermore, the focus is on customers and driving collective intelligence by focusing on team and organizational performance. This means that a shift in performance systems is needed—as long as it is implemented in a whole cultural change in the tradition of holistic agility.

## References


DeRosa, D. (2018, December 25). *How to increase the willingness of employees to deliver* (B. 2. Community, Ed.) Retrieved April 25, 2021, from https://www.business2community.com/leadership/how-to-increase-the-willingness-of-employees-to-deliver-02152444

Doerr, J. (2018a). *Measure what matters. How google, bono, and the gates foundation rock the world with OKRs*. Penguin Random House.

Doerr, J. (2018b). *OKR: Objectives & Key Results. Wie Sie Ziele, auf die es wirklich ankommt, entwickeln, messen und umsetzen*. Franz Vahlen.

Hofert, S. (2018). *Das agile Mindset. Mitarbeiter entwickeln, Zukunft der Arbeit gestalten*. Springer Fachmedien.

Hofert, S., & Thonet, C. (2019). *Der agile Kulturwandel. 33 Lösungen für Veränderungen in Organisationen*. Springer Fachmedien.

Kraaijenbrink, J. (2019, September 10). 20 reasons why strategy execution fails. *Forbes Media LLC*. Retrieved April 09, 2021, from https://www.forbes.com/sites/jeroenkraaijenbrink/2019/09/10/20-reasons-why-strategy-execution-fails/?sh=383ef02d1ebe

Müller, J. (2020, July 17). Objectives and key results (OKR) — Eine Definition. *Workpath GmbH*, Munich. Retrieved April 09, 2021, from https://www.workpath.com/magazin/okr-definition

Wollmann, P., Kühn, F., & Kempf, M. (Eds.). (2020). *Three pillars of organization and leadership in disruptive times—navigating your company successfully through the 21st century business world*. SpringerNature.

Wollmann, P., Kühn, F., Kempf, M., & Püringer, R. (Eds.). (2021). *Organization and leadership in disruptive times—design and implementation of the 3-P-model*. SpringerNature.

Workpath GmbH. (2021, April 24). *Die OKR Methode: Was sind Objectives und Key Results.* https://www.workpath.com/de/okr

**Dominique Wirl** is a senior consultant in organizational transformation, change and development. Her focus is on leaders and teams and their development to better ways of leading, communicating and working together. For this she falls back on agile frameworks, mindset and integrating, co-creative methods. This is based on several years of experience as consultant and trainer and roots back in tourism and PR with leadership roles. Her work spans among others companies and organizations within the IT sector, energy sector, tax and law firms, manufacturing producing industries and NGOs. Various certifications around working with teams and individuals complement her degrees in business administration, cultural anthropology and organizational development.

**Sebastian Luge** is a senior consultant in organizational transformation and change projects. He focusses on designing structures and frameworks for collaboration that give organizations the capabilities to perform in volatile and uncertain environments. His key topics include self-organization, agile, strategy execution and leadership. He works pragmatically with lots of different agile frameworks like Objectives and Key Results and adapts them co-creatively with his clients to serve their organizational development as best as possible. He has worked in a wide range of industries as well as in NGOs and the public sector. He has a degree in Business Administration and has added various other certificates in agile topics, systems theory and organizational culture analysis and has 15 years of experience in consulting, team coaching, training and facilitation.

# Decision-Making in Travelling Organizations—How to-Principles and Practices

Detlev Trapp

**Abstract**

Decision-making as a basic operation of any organization requires special attention in the context of the concept of the "Travelling Organization" of the Three-Pillar Approach (Wollmann et al., *Three pillars of organization and leadership in disruptive times—Navigating your company successfully through the 21st century business world*, Springer Nature, 2020, *Organization and leadership in disruptive times—Design and implementation of the 3-P-Model*, Springer Nature, 2021). The less predictability and stability there is, the more it is important to set out in short iterative steps, supported by an agile mindset. If you want to be adaptable on the road, then a coordinated approach to decision-making premises and practices plays an important role. In this sense, navigation is nothing more than decision-making enabling you to stay on course.

## 1 Decision-Making in a VUCA Context

In times in which business models, as recently in the context of the coronavirus, have suddenly had to be fundamentally changed, and new working models and technologies are increasingly making it necessary to redesign existing processes and services, traditional decision-making processes no longer fit. To the extent that the speed of information and the dynamics of change increase and organizations can no longer process them, it is worth looking at the way decisions are made. Because even though decisions in organizations must be made more and more often in the face of growing uncertainty, the conscious examination of the question of how and

D. Trapp (✉)
Bonn, Germany
e-mail: trapp@cidpartners.de



M. Kempf, F. Kühn (eds.), *Navigating a Travelling Organization*, Future of Business and Finance, https://doi.org/10.1007/978-3-030-95326-3_9

where decisions are made often does not take place at all, or, if it does, only inadequately.

In many management boards, decisions continue to be made on the basis of classic patterns and routines. And even in supposedly more agile organizations, decision-making practices have evolved little, and the difference in the way things were done in hierarchical organizations can rarely be seen. The growing complexity behind individual decisions is met with the reduction and condensation of information. In some companies, there are clear guidelines regarding the scope of decision documents, which, for example, may not be longer than five pages, must have a fixed format, and must have a predefined structure and decision options with their respective implications. A considerable amount of time and effort often goes into preparing these documents. All of this is intended to help facilitate a mock objectification of decisions and conserve top management's precious time. As a framework for jointly addressing an issue, this may well make sense, but it is certainly not an adequate response to complexity and dynamics. The focus in these cases is on the quality of the decision that is made together and measured by the extent to which the desired outcome is achieved. However, this is only one possible perspective. The paradigm at the heart of this is a model of thinking that is based on planning and control. This rarely does justice to the complexity and dynamics of a VUCA world.

A different perspective on the quality of decisions is more appropriate for the changed framework conditions. The focus here lies on the acceptance of the decision. For "a good decision can be measured with a certain degree of certainty already at the time of the decision, namely by the number of process participants who jointly support the decision and do not merely agree to it" (Graf, 2018).

Decision-making as a basic operation of any organization requires special attention in the context of the concept of the "Travelling Organization" of the Three-Pillar Approach (Wollmann et al., 2020, 2021). The less predictability and stability there is, the more it is important to set out in short iterative steps, supported by an agile mindset. If you want to be adaptable on the road, then a coordinated approach to decision-making premises and practices plays an important role. In this understanding, navigation is nothing more than decision-making enabling you to stay on course.

## 2 Decisions as the Basic Operation of any Organization

The importance of decisions in a dynamic environment is underlined by their core. From a systemic point of view, decisions are determinations that transform the indeterminate into the determinate. Thus they are the basic operations of organizations. In other words, every action is preceded by a decision, be it a conscious or an unconscious decision. Even a decision that is ***not*** made can be a decision in this sense because it, too, leads to action (Boos & Buzanich-Pöltl, 2020).

In this sense, decisions are a central building block to transform the indeterminate into the determinate in the sense of the idea of the Travelling Organization and thus to support navigation. At the same time, every decision also implies a risk. In this sense, the decision-making culture of an organization always shows how it deals with risk (Sutrich, 2006).

The examination of decision-making practices in organizations starts at varying levels.

## 3 Clarify Decision Premises on a Map

The Three-Pillar Model, with its fundamental dimensions, provides a good map of premises for decisions.

The common reassurance related to the basic understanding of the crucial premises that serve the understanding of the organization plays an important role insofar as a fundamentally different understanding of these central dimensions will inevitably lead to misunderstandings, tensions and to different outcomes in decision-making processes. The clearer the shared map, the more efficient decision-making and the planning of interventions based on the decisions can serve the central purpose.

The Three Pillars (Wollmann et al., 2020, 2021) are defined as:

(1) Sustainable Purpose—The raison d'être of an organization, bringing new orientation and certainty to the people for their joint endeavor and success.
(2) Travelling Organization—The mindset of an organization in a permanent state of flux, interacting with the market and customer journey, with rapid adaptivity.
(3) Connected Resources—Interconnecting all needed resources inside and outside the silos, creating consistency between goals and concepts, strategies and processes, competencies, and roles.

This chapter focuses on how decision-making and the clarity around the understanding of what is important to build a decision-making culture that really supports the idea of Travelling Organizations is key for its success. This requires the willingness of management to invest time in designing and dealing with the practices, principles, and processes for decision-making. Navigating implies decision-making. In a dynamic and complex environment, it is important to understand how decision-making as a basic process in organizations can support the organization's adaptability and success.

A fundamental dimension in the Three-Pillar Model, as explained above, is purpose orientation in terms of decisions; this implies orienting decisions to the purpose of the organization. The more uncertain the future is, the more the purpose of an organization can serve as a "north star," as a point of orientation that also guides decisions.

## 4 Clarify Decision Categories

For further development in the direction of Travelling Organizations, a conscious approach to the distribution of decisions in an organization is essential. Connected to this is the question of which decisions are assigned to which roles. Many organizations have already gained experience in this area. Authority and responsibility have been distributed more throughout the system. Many organizations have become flatter, less hierarchical, and have moved operational decisions to the periphery and thus to where the knowledge needed for the decision is located. At the same time, they have also optimized the speed of decision-making and ensured that many decisions no longer have to be made at the top (Doering, 2021).

On the other hand, in many organizations that have introduced agile approaches, areas of tension arise in relation to decisions. The scaling of agile approaches reaches its limits at the point where classic decision-making processes and patterns come together with agile approaches, because this is where classic and agile mindsets collide.

A requirement for the distribution of authority is an examination of the types of decisions and the decision-making framework that is assigned to each role. In the best case, this discussion does not only take place once, but is regularly reviewed and adjusted. Agile organizations rely on so-called steering or governance meetings in which rules and roles are regularly reviewed and updated.

In order to avoid classic system–subsystem conflicts in a system with distributed authority that lead to decisions that are good for the subsystem making the decision, but not for the overall system, much transparency is needed about where the overall organization stands together with leadership that is always aligned with the purpose. Regular synchronization meetings can provide the necessary transparency of information.

The question of the degree of distribution of authority is always a question of what issues are involved. In this respect, it can be important to differentiate between centralization and decentralization of decision-making. A helpful sorting for this is provided by Vantrappen and Wirtz (2017) (Fig. 1).

## 5 Decision-Making Principles as Guiding Principles

Closely related to thoughts around the location of decisions are principles, understood here to mean principles that guide decisions. These have changed for many organizations in the current context of VUCA. The background here is also the reduced ability to plan and the increased relevance of rapid adaptability. In practice, we often experience—like the categories—a coexistence of principles that are based on more classical basic patterns alongside others that are based on agile approaches. The main principles are:

- The evolution from centralized to decentralized decision-making.
- The evolution away from a few big decisions to many small ones.

| When it is important to have… | Responsiveness | Reliability | Efficiency | Perennity |
|---|---|---|---|---|
| … it is usually advantageous to veer toward … | Decentralization | Centralization | Centralization | Centralization |
| … as that solution enables and stimulates … | Immediacy | Compliance | Syndication | Detachment |

**Fig. 1** "It too depends on your goals": When to decentralize decision-making, and when not to (Vantrappen & Wirtz, 2017). (cidpartners, 2021, all rights reserved by the author, used with permission)

- Orientation toward progress metrics in the sense of "lead measures" rather than "lag measures" (especially in the context of OKRs).
- The inclusion of a variety of perspectives (up to and including the use of artificial intelligence).
- A move away from linear to circular and iterative approaches.
- Waiting for the last possible moment to decide.

## 6 The Design of Decision-Making Processes and Practices

The question remains how the development toward an understanding of Travelling Organizations can be adequately supported by changing decision-making processes and practices. Here, a look at the concrete processes and individual practices is appropriate (Fig. 2).

Ultimately, it is also true that there is no "one-size-fits-all"—model that is fundamentally suitable for every organization. From our point of view, it is a matter of being aware of the principles behind the practices and whether they fit into the desired overall approach (Fig. 2). In the context of Travelling Organizations, we focus on selected recent decision-making practices and processes that map the aspect of including different perspectives.

In order to integrate different perspectives and at the same time avoid endless discussions to reach a consensus, a consent-driven approach, applied in organizations from a sociocratic and holacratic background, is a concept that helps to strengthen the idea of adaptability. The so-called iterative decision-making process, provides an example of how this could also work for Travelling Organizations (Robertson, 2015). It follows a very clear basic process and rules (Fig. 3).

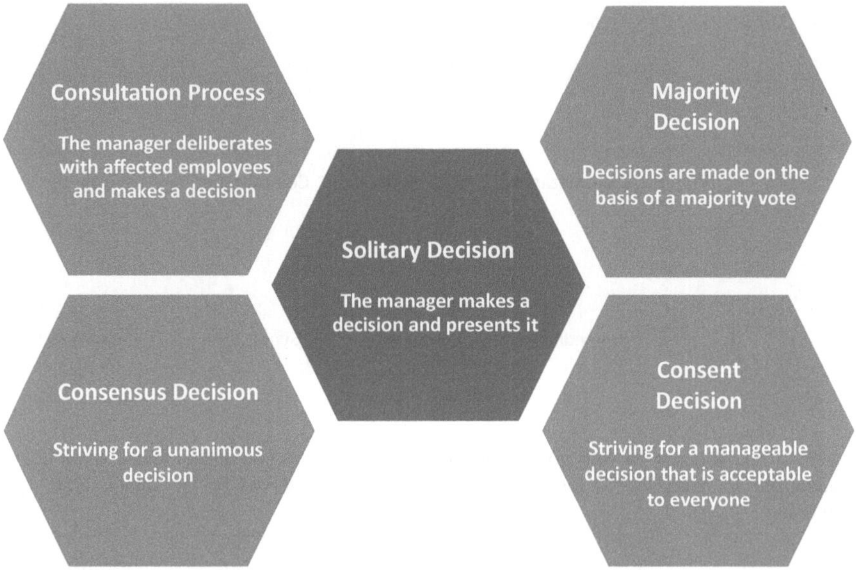


**Fig. 2** Decision-making: concrete processes and individual practices (cidpartners, 2021, all rights reserved by the author, used with permission)

Each step in the process (Fig. 3) is designed to align a group decision-making process with a "consent"-based decision. Unlike a consensus decision, this is a decision focusses on an outcome without serious objections from part of the group. In the process, everything is geared toward moving one step forward and moving the issue forward based on a proposed solution that everyone can agree on. Discussions and power play have no place in the process, as long as it is well facilitated.

The process uses energy that arises from tensions and transforms them constructively into solutions that need not claim to be perfect. Should it become apparent that new tensions arise as a result of the proposal or that the old ones are not eliminated, the issue can always be brought back for a new decision. In the Travelling Organization, the process thus supports the basic idea of decision-making as a central practice of navigation. If the environment changes or new insights are gained, then decisions are made again so as to stay on course.

## 7 Cidpartners Case Study: Redesigning the Decision-Making Culture in a Technology Company

In the context of organizational development of a large department (250 employees) of an international technology group, the examination of decision-making processes was a central aspect.

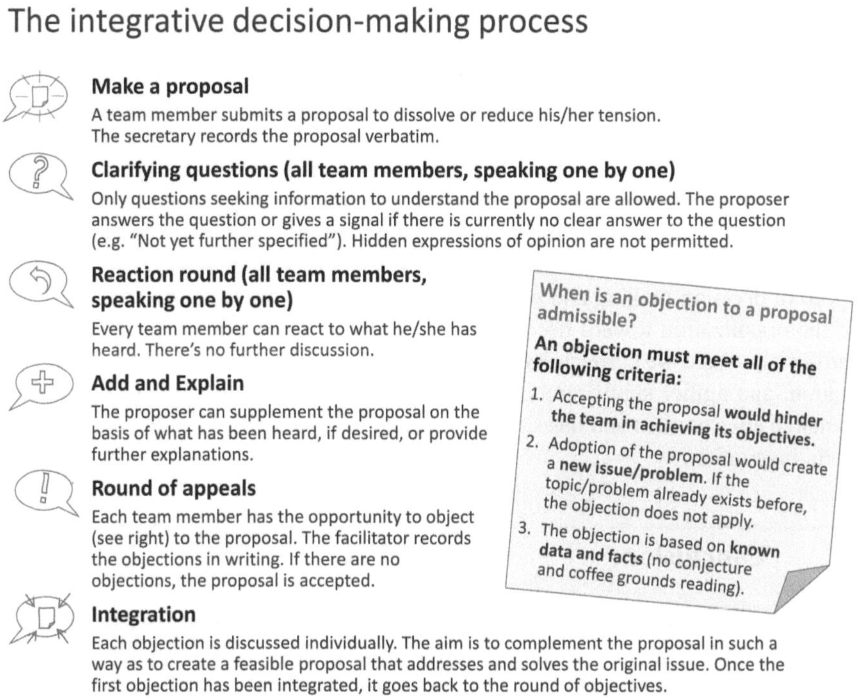


**Fig. 3** The integrative decision-making process (On the basis of https://www.holacracy.org/governance-meetings). (cidpartners, 2021, all rights reserved by the author, used with permission)

The division was characterized by high environmental dynamics, and the leadership had decided to switch to a role-based and dynamic-collaboration model in which responsibility was to be strongly distributed throughout the entire organization. Instead of a hierarchical decision-making cascade, which had previously been in use for years, most decisions were to be decentralized. The goal was to establish a highly flexible, issue-centered pool organization.

In the first step, existing decision-making structures and processes were examined and made transparent. In many places, there was little clarity about where decisions were made nor about ***how*** these decisions should be made.

As part of the organizational change, new structures were used as a basis to jointly determine, within the management circle, which decisions should remain centralized and which should be decentralized in the future. Next, a distinction was made between decisions that could be assigned to individual roles and others that were to be made jointly.

Starting from this basis, an essential step in the further operationalization consisted in the introduction of steering meetings in which work on the system could take place continuously. A slightly adapted variant of the holacratic integrative decision-making process served as a process for the joint decisions.

In the introductory phase, supported by agile coaches, challenges emerged on two levels. One concerned the general learning process of making more decentralized decisions, which was new for both managers and employees. In this context, the building of trust was essential. Wherever there was sufficient psychological security on the part of management, adjustment was easy. The second challenge was the introduction of what was initially perceived as a rigid decision-making process for joint decisions, which broke with existing patterns and was mostly perceived as difficult by those who could more easily assert their influence with the old practice.

In sum, the process bore fruit both at the level of clarification and in terms of speed of decision-making and was an essential element that supported the evolution of the organization toward becoming a Travelling Organization. The alignment of the decisions and the corresponding processes toward multi-perspectivity, decentralization, and agility significantly changed the navigation of the organization in the dynamic environment and has since been adopted by other areas of the organization as an inspiration.

## 8 Conclusion

- Decisions are, in the sense of the prerequisite for navigating as a basic operation of any organization, a central building block to support the concept of the Travelling Organization.
- To actively change a decision-making culture, different dimensions need to be considered:
  - Purpose
  - Decision premises
  - Decision categories
  - Decision principles
  - Decision-making processes
- For decisions to be made in a decentralized way in the interests of the organization as a whole, transparency about how the organization is progressing is an important prerequisite.
- Psychological safety is a key success factor for the implementation of a decentralized decision-making culture.

## References

Boos, F., & Buzanich-Pöltl. (2020). *Moving Organizations. Wie Sie sich durch agile Transformation krisenfest aufstellen*. Schäfer Poeschel.

cidpartners. (2021). *Graphics*. https://www.holacracy.org/governance-meetings

Doering, K. (2021). Komplexität in Entscheidungssituationen—Einführung von Entscheidungsprozessen in selbstorganisierten, agilen Organisationen. In M. A. Pfannstiel, W. Siedl, & P. F. J. Steinhoff (Eds.), *Agilität in Unternehmen*. Springer Gabler.

Graf, R. (2018). *Die neue Entscheidungskultur. Mit gemeinsam getragenen Entscheidungen zum Erfolg*. Hanser.

Robertson, B. (2015). *Holacracy: The new management system for a rapidly changing world.* Henry Holt.
Sutrich, O. (2006). *Besser entscheiden in Organisationen* (Vol. 3, pp. 4–9). Hernsteiner.
Vantrappen, H., & Wirtz, F. (2017). *When to decentralize decision making, and when not to.* Harvard Business Review. https://hbr.org/2017/12/when-to-decentralize-decision-making-and-when-not-to
Wollmann, P., Kühn, F., & Kempf, M. (Eds.). (2020). *Three pillars of organization and leadership in disruptive times—Navigating your company successfully through the 21st century business world.* Springer Nature.
Wollmann, P., Kühn, F., Kempf, M., & Püringer, R. (Eds.). (2021). *Organization and leadership in disruptive times—Design and implementation of the 3-P-model.* Springer Nature.

**Detlev Trapp** is passionate about helping organizations and leaders to build the capabilities and transform into better versions of themselves. He has been working with executive teams of large and medium-sized organizations as a transformation coach and facilitator for 20 years. Before that he worked as lecturer at the university, in a leading communications agency and as head of agency for one of the largest European New Media Networks. He is founder of the organizational development and transformation consultancy consulting cidpartners and co-founder of the GTD® training company Next Action and strongly believes in the power of self-organization and integrating perspectives. Additionally, he works as a lecturer for different universities.

# Navigating Investments for Transformation in a Travelling Organization

Reto Püringer and Frank Kühn

**Abstract**

Previous patent remedies are no longer sufficient to manage the investment portfolios of companies. In addition to the dynamics and scaling of new topics (such as artificial intelligence and data science) and the diversity of the appropriate management formats (sequential or spiral project models, iterative, and agile models, crisis interventions, strategic programs, etc.), it is the required speed of development, the rapid succession of updates, the consideration of different ways of working and interests from organizational hybridity which place new demands on management. The simple hierarchy can no longer do this in an ideal fashion.

For the development of a future-proof concept for a new navigation of transformation portfolios that can cope with this diversity, a framework of practices, criteria, and principles for joint evaluation and development is needed that is accepted and agreed upon by all stakeholders. These principles include ensuring that the decision-making process from the purpose and objectives of the enterprise to implementation in rapid projects has end-to-end agility, i.e., from recognizing the need for transformation to strategies, from these strategies to rapidly transformable projects to deliver benefit with corresponding continuous and end-to-end feedback processes. This must be the core of the traveling organization's navigation in terms of tools, practices, and mindset.

The chapter ends with a look at the challenges of transforming from the current to a new, significantly more effective, investment portfolio navigation system. The capabilities for future navigation need to be built into the transition from the outset. Therefore, a rapid, iterative approach with portfolio prototyping is

R. Püringer
Ebertswil, Switzerland

F. Kühn (✉)
Dortmund, Germany
e-mail: frank@kuehn-cp.com

 
M. Kempf, F. Kühn (eds.), *Navigating a Travelling Organization*, Future of Business and Finance, https://doi.org/10.1007/978-3-030-95326-3_10

suggested. The transformation of the portfolio process is itself an investment. Do we want to invest in it? Is this investment a priority for us?

## 1 A New Way to Navigate Investments Is Required

### 1.1 Be Fast or Be out

In which change projects should you invest money in the next strategic cycle? How much? In which topics should you invest (e.g., customers and efficiency)? What do you want to get out of this investment as a business outcome? A lot of organizations find it very hard to answer these questions.

Answering them is hard as it is difficult to predict what is available and what will be called for in the market 6–18 months from now, and it might be that a new startup or a competitor has just launched a new product on the market while you were just starting to invest in the same thing.

Traditional companies have always had a very forward-looking, standardized planning cycle: Every year company planning started to around Quarter 2 with the aim of planning budgets and investments for the following year. Based on these budgets, projects started their planning and resource plans were drafted as a result. But this planning approach no longer works (or only works in a very limited fashion) in the world we live in today, as we need to react much faster to market changes, and long-term planning is only relevant at the strategic level of an organization—for the planning for the next 6–18 months we need something new. Project prioritization that goes beyond 12 months is already outdated the day after the plan is made.

On the other side, we can all see how fast new digital capabilities have evolved and today, artificial intelligence (AI), data science, and cloud computing are available at a price that makes it possible to enter markets at a fraction of the previous cost. Thousands of start-ups are now on that playing field: they are focusing on the value chain of different industries and trying to figure out where in the value chain they can "break in" by applying digital solutions supported by data and AI. Organizations are at risk if they are not able to ensure that their future projects can cope with the skills and capabilities that these startups can bring to the table; and organizations need not wonder why the projects they plan are not the ones that will succeed in the marketplace.

The customer of today has also changed. Digital solutions are the new normal and the expectation is to have products and services available online or as "apps." If you do not have these and you are suddenly competing with a "new kid on the block" then your customers have the ability to switch to this competitor with just a few clicks. Your customers do not wait for a new "big bang" product every year; they expect to have frequent releases that upgrade existing products and services. A new "big bang" launch of a product once or twice a year is no longer enough—customers expect you to provide them with value all the time.

To answer the questions at the start of this paragraph it is clear: you cannot know! The world is changing too fast. You need to establish a new way where investments are "travelling," where you focus less on what will be in 18 months' time, but much more on what is needed today: deliver to the customer and learn and adapt your plans.

**Application of the Three-Pillar Model**
The Three Pillars (Wollmann et al. 2020, 2021) are defined as:

1. Sustainable Purpose—The raison d'être of an organization, bringing new orientation and certainty to the people for their joint endeavor and success
2. Travelling Organization—The mindset of an organization in a permanent state of flux, interacting with the market and customer journey, with rapid adaptivity.
3. Connected Resources—Interconnecting all resources needed inside and outside the silos, creating consistency between goals and concepts, strategies and processes, competencies, and roles.

This chapter focuses on how to realize the navigation of a travelling organization that needs to invest in the right projects for its journey. This requires an agile end-to-end portfolio process: From purpose to strategy to project work—and, feedback loops that constantly align ambition and realization. This must be based on a common orientation, provided by a sustainable purpose, and a connectivity between strategical thinking and practical implementation which must be realized with the right key people and teams in a consistent decision-making process.

## 1.2 Organizations Need to Change

In most traditional organizations, the planning of change portfolios and related investments are driven by a line organization (except for organizations where projects are their core business, such as consulting or some types of engineering company). The complication with line organization-driven planning of change investments is that the demand they see for change is related to the problem and incentives in their "silos." But nowadays customers demand solutions that work "end to end"; so simply planning from the point of view of one department will not be sufficient and may even be ineffective.

What this means is that organizations need to move away from "line-centric" change investment planning to a model that shapes the investments from a pure outcome perspective so that "end to end" solutions to customers can be delivered. The trick with this approach is that opinions of traditional management layers are not important for success in a first instance, as the "proof is in the pudding" of change

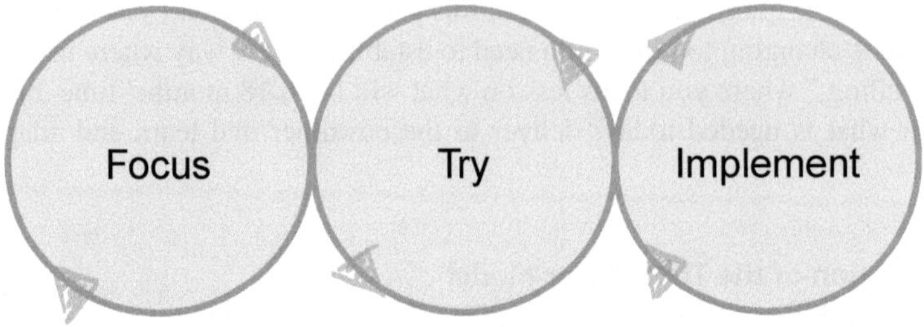


**Fig. 1** From illusion of stability to highly effective iterative practices (Illustrated by the authors, used with permission. All rights reserved)

investments cannot be predicted well. You need change from "anecdotal" project prioritization to an approach where you constantly deliver value to the customer, measure how this value has been perceived by the customer and then define again what the next value is that will be delivered in a second iteration.

The implication of this is that traditional organizational paradigms are reaching their limits. To cope with today's requirements, organizations need fast, and criteria-based decision-making (based upon shared transparency, data, and knowledge). It is no longer enough to have endless coordination meetings between departments where, at the end, the decisions taken appear to be a compromise to please everybody.

And we need to move away from the thinking that the "perfect" project needs to be defined upfront, a project that is then scoped in detail and can be delivered all at once. Of course, you need to know what outcome you want to achieve with your investment but you will need to deliver it by "travelling" step by step to the outcome to which you aspire: first with a "minimum viable product" that you can ship to customers and users followed by further iterations (based on customer and user feedback) until the business outcome has been achieved and no further iterations are required.

Along this journey, new market conditions and technical possibilities may arise that challenge the outcome itself. The outcome must be right at the time it is realized. This means that it can deviate from the initially agreed idea of what the outcome should be. This requires both courage and discipline to clearly focus, review and implement activities with a continuous feedback loop (Fig. 1).

It might already be obvious that the task to prioritize investments is moving from providing multi-year roadmaps and pre-defined portfolios on all levels to more continuously prioritized and measured iterations. This means that Portfolio Managers not only need to understand Portfolio Processes but they also need to be able to measure business cases and their assumptions on an ongoing basis based on a deep data-driven understanding of the business—with the focus on the here and now and not on which projects might be required 12 months from now.

All this has a fundamental impact on resource planning in quantitative and qualitative terms: with this new dynamism in delivering change, with more focus on iterations, the configuration of project teams and decision-making practices also needs a new paradigm. Rebalancing capacity based on iterations may result in chaos and instead of cross-functional project teams that are formed each time a project arises, you need "fixed" delivery resources over a longer period of time for dedicated "outcomes" (e.g., per product and per channel). This ensures that the focus of the resources is on delivering value and less involvement in coordination is required. The adjustment to the delivery capacity is then done more on an outcome level and can be adjusted when priorities of the organization shift. This also allows more strategic perspective on skills that are required but not yet available (e.g., AI and data science), so that those skills can be proactively procured externally or built up internally.

To apply these changes is not simple. But you will certainly need to change if you want to meet the requirements of today's world.

### 1.3 How to Do it?

Traditional Project Portfolio Management (PPM) approaches do not work any longer or, if they do, only in a very limited way (PMI 2017). Therefore, changes in management behavior regarding how to plan and execute change investments are required. Roles and responsibilities might need to change, and popular processes might have to be abandoned.

As always there are frameworks and standards available (e.g., SAFe) (Knaster and Leffingwell 2018) but they describe solutions that are hard to apply to specific situations and they have a heavy focus on how to execute development in detail (e.g., Agile Release Trains and Scrum Teams). They lack a practical and easy explanation of what is required to manage a portfolio of change in a world where constant change is the new normal.

What organizations need is a simple way to navigate investments in a travelling organization that can be understood across the organization and can be followed without needing to attend a training session lasting several days.

## 2 The Iterative Approach from Strategy to Implementation

### 2.1 The Approach

We have summarized the essential ideas in a map for the navigation of the travelling organization, with which we can follow the path from strategy to implementation (Fig. 2). This map provides clarity at all times about the connectivity between strategies, strategic project clusters and the projects themselves, and the decisions needed to adjust objectives, change priorities, and reallocate resources.

The particular challenge is timing. In traditional organizations, it is often of little use to have agile projects because the higher-level decision-making processes are not fast enough. A weekly working cycle is of no use if necessary, decisions are made on a monthly or quarterly basis. Fast feedback loops for the implementation of

| Step | Sustainable Purpose and Corporate Goals | Strategies | Strategic Clusters | Project Backlog and Project Practices | Project Execution | Operation |
|---|---|---|---|---|---|---|
| Example | We provide the world with resilient transformation models<br><br>Preferred partner for medium-sized global players by end of 2022 | We cooperate with well positioned consultancies and first movers | Eco-system development and co-creation | □ Collaboration project w/ consultancy X&Y<br>□ Customer Projects with A, B, and C | □ Tool K development, v2<br>□ Collaborative Strategy with customer Z | □ Tool K v1 in practice in chemical industries |
| | | We offer the models via online platforms with open access | IT-platforms and applications | □ Learning platform<br>□ IT-models for diff. industries | □ Tool with customer Z<br>□ Value chains w/ IT-providers | □ App for K-tool as Beta-version<br>□ Navigation prototype v0.6 |
| | | We offer facilitation for practical application – here we make our competitive advantage | Human resources and learning processes | □ HR Expansion strategy<br>□ Learning strategies for various customers | □ Learning & development customer Z<br>□ Recruitment process | □ On-the-job learning models |
| Circles | Strategic Review Circle | Strategic Navigation Circle | Cluster Circle | Project or Product Owner Circle | Project Teams with customers | |

**Fig. 2** Portfolio process from strategies to implementation and possible feedback loops. The example shows a service provider who builds and offers prototypes for management processes. (Illustrated by the authors, used with permission. All rights reserved)

strategies are of little help if the strategy meeting is only held once a year. So, there is a need to synchronize timelines to draw benefits from agile and familiar approaches.

The portfolio navigation map proposed in Fig. 2 consists of the following elements, which are connected via different decision circles:

- The fundamental decision about the purpose and objectives of the company.
- The strategies to implement the purpose and objectives.
- Based on the strategies: Strategic clusters to implement objectives for which projects can be defined.
- The listed projects are in a cluster backlog, from which the projects are selected, started, and managed with the appropriate procedure.
- The execution of the projects with regular reviews and retrospectives.
- The rapid implementation into operational practice.

This process takes place end-to-end from strategy to implementation in practice. Conversely, feedback loops take place on feasibility, results and key lessons learned. It is important that the feedback loops between the different steps can be asynchronous to ensure that decisions and corrections when travelling toward business outcomes can be made when needed.

## 2.2 The Design Principles

This approach combines several "design principles" (Kühn et al. 2011; Nagel 2017) that we know from current agile and familiar approaches. In the evaluation, however, we did not follow the concepts or "recipes" to the letter but examined their success factors and applied them as design principles to the approach presented here.

*Iteration*: This starts with iterative decision processes for dealing with complexity (Dörner 1997): Shorter decisions have been shown to lead to better results and less waste. This approach can also be found later in the "Cynefin" model in the "Probe—sense—respond" approach (Snowdon and Boone 2007). The displayed model is open to this based on its feedback loops at any stage.

*Collaboration*: Connected with these approaches, the principles for agility can be found in the Agile Manifesto (Beck et al. 2001). These include collaboration over contracting. This means to prefer joint work on the solution to the formality of any legal agreement. We provided this in the management circles of the displayed model.

*Pull*: In the practical implementation on Scrum projects (Sutherland and Schwaber 2020), it is then a matter of selecting from a backlog of functionalities those that the development team commits itself to implementing in the next sprint. The management principle is called pull (instead of push), based on confidence and trust (instead of command and control). Such backlogs can also be related to projects with a view to the portfolio: Which projects are important to us, where are they on our ranking list? And which projects do we think we are able to implement? This decision would then be made by a cluster team.

*Clarity*: The Objectives and Key Results (OKR) model is based on the dynamics of business development, technical possibilities, and new findings (Doerr 2018): Although the model is about goals, it is not about the formal fulfillment of goals but rather about regular, trusting exchange of experience within the team about what has been achieved so far and how it makes sense to proceed further. The focus is on this exchange; in this way, it differs significantly from, for example, Management by Objective (MBO) concepts.

*Team*: This trusting exchange in the team presupposes what was once again highlighted in the Aristotle study by Google: it requires "psychological safety" with which it is possible to bring everything openly to the table without having to fear personal disadvantage (Duhigg 2016; Edmondson 2018).

*Nesting*: Teams are interconnected and networked. A similar approach can be found in the Holocracy model (Robertson 2015). We provided this basic idea along the portfolio process.

*Delegation*: The decisions to be made are distributed among the different circles and teams along the process. Decision-making practices should also be considered: Are decisions tied to roles in the team? Are decision-making powers delegated on a case-by-case basis? Do decisions take place by consensus or consent? (e.g., Cumps 2019).

These basic principles make the challenge clear. The key is to apply these exemplary approaches consistently throughout the process described. This not only means that the projects are managed accordingly, but also that the practices and terminologies of the entire process and its navigation follow agreed principles. Not only do the project teams navigate themselves according to these principles, but so do the cluster teams, which navigate the investment across projects, and the top management team, which has the confidence to set up and navigate strategic clusters based on the company's goals and strategies.

## 2.3 The Practical Navigation of the Travelling Organization

If we understand the navigation of the travelling organization as a journey into the future of the company (and not only as steering along previously trodden paths), then the portfolio process is a key navigation tool, based upon iterative, quick communication loops.

Based on the above principles, practical implementation can look very different. For example, we can create a calendar for the various meetings (Fig. 3). In it, we define the types of meeting, circle, date/time, topics. The easiest way to schedule meetings is with the help of jours fixes; nevertheless, the meetings must be flexible enough to allow so that any necessary decisions to be made as quickly as possible.

In smaller companies, we often see a number of different roles in one person: The same person determines strategies and clusters, and often they are also the project owner. In such cases it can be helpful to distinguish these roles explicitly.

***Case: The Personalized Approach***

| Circles | Strategic Review | Strategic Navi - gation Circle | Cluster Circles | Project/ Product Owner Circle | Project Teams w/ Customers | In addition: Project Forum |
|---|---|---|---|---|---|---|
| Goals | □ To review and update strategies<br>□ To get overall feedback about the clarity, feasibility and implementation of strategies<br>□ To get information about the need of strategic resource development in quantitative and qualitative terms | □ To transfer strategies into clusters<br>□ To align and coordinate clusters<br>□ To allocate resources to clusters<br>□ To learn from clusters and projects (general) | □ To transfer strategic cluster requirements to the projects, their definition, missions and scopes<br>□ To keep the backlog of such projects up-to-date<br>□ To prioritize projects and create project roadmap<br>□ To get feedback on strategic feasibility and formulate feedback on the navigation circle | □ To align, coordinate and synergize projects in terms of content, timing, allocation of resources<br>□ To coordinate exchange knowhow between projects and with other experts<br>□ To get feedback on strategic feasibility | □ To share and agree requirements<br>□ To develop solutions<br>□ To transfer solutions into customers' operation and evaluate feedback | □ To support transparency and broad acceptance in the company<br>□ To show the effective implementation of strategic ambitions<br>□ To get feedback |
| Participants | □ Top Management<br>□ Members of Strategic Navigation Circle | □ Managers responsible for strategies<br>□ Members Strategic Navigation Circle<br>□ Cluster Managers | □ Cluster managers<br>□ Project managers | □ Project/product Owners<br>□ Project managers | □ Project Managers and teams<br>□ Customers | □ Participants in the portfolio process and the involved projects<br>□ All staff of the company |
| Freq. | □ Quarterly | □ Monthly | □ Every two weeks | □ Weekly | □ Continuously<br>□ Jours fixes | □ Continuously<br>□ Events |

**Fig. 3** Meeting Calendar with some examples (Illustrated by the authors, used with permission. All rights reserved)

*The company—a medium-sized global player in the metal industry—always does the right technical projects. How do they manage that? The COO allows so many technical projects in the strategic portfolio and in the implementation pipeline that he thinks he can navigate the situation. He attends important project meetings from different perspectives: as COO, as owner of a strategic cluster, as project owner. He listens to the discussion, communicates his impressions, balances them with strategic directions and knowledge from other projects and latest strategy meetings, explains why he is making which proposals and in which role. In this way, he not only reveals his criteria, but also inspires entrepreneurial thinking and acceptance in the teams. He encourages the teams to exchange ideas, creates the space for this and contributes the framework. Thus, their experience is that deviating developments are limited to a risk of 2–3 weeks.*

In this model, the decision-making process is not distributed among different events, but is brought into the projects by the attendance of a key manager. In this way, the company is highly agile; however, this advantage is tied to one person. This jeopardizes the resilience of the process. Personal redundancy (rules of representation) should have to be arranged here.

# 3 Relevant Criteria for Investments in the Travelling Organization

## 3.1 Investing in Performance Improvement and Future Resilience

In the complex situation described above, it is important to apply the "right" criteria to the portfolio and the portfolio process: How do we know we have the right issues in the portfolio? How do we deal with them appropriately? These questions apply equally to classic project portfolio management (e.g., Hirzel et al. 2009) and to portfolios that are planned and managed more iteratively according to agile principles such as displayed in SAFe (Knaster and Leffingwell 2018). In our approach (Fig. 2), we have concretized the strategic reference to the projects with the help of strategic clusters.

What topics are we referring to? To all topics that, in addition to the regular business, steering, and support processes, are to be addressed due to a special initiative and require a special investment and decisions to do so. For this reason, we use the term "investment": We "invest" money in performance improvement and future resilience.

This includes investment in material resources as well as personnel expenses. Following this definition, it covers all plans, programs, projects of any kind, epics and workshops for current problem solutions, innovations, and changes. To simplify the wording here, we will simply use the term "projects" here.

This does not include contract projects, for example, in engineering companies because these projects represent their business activities and are agreed and scheduled according to their resource situations; in these companies, however, internal organizational projects would be relevant. This does not include improvement measures that are part of the company's routine, e.g., work hacks or innovation days, for which the effort is regularly planned; if such sessions result in investment requirements, however, these must also be considered here.

However, the development of the criteria and especially their weighting is never finished. It must follow market requirements and the company's own strategy process.

***The Entrance Door to the Portfolio***

*The company, which operates in the mobile communications sector, has installed an evaluation step before the broader discussion of investments, and implemented this process in an evaluation tool. Each initiator can use it to determine whether his or her idea meets both the company's strategic criteria and, in particular, the clusters' criteria which also involve criteria of urgency, risk and priorities. The corporate criteria may change, for example, if the strategy changes from expansion to a focus on quality customers. Or, from a cluster perspective, there are new dynamics around minimum viable products, additional resource availability, gaps, or niches of needed content. Then an investment that previously seemed attractive may no longer be worthwhile, or other initiatives may suddenly be more attractive. This practice leads to the right questions about the investments, their prioritization, cancelling, reconfiguration, or tailoring. The practice is very well accepted: It requires a commitment to strategic, economic, and risk-oriented criteria for the corporate portfolio; it operationalizes them directly in an investment selection tool; and the application by project initiators and regular reassessments require little effort.*

## 3.2 Criteria along the Portfolio Process

In Fig. 2 we have described the portfolio process from strategy to implementation, and in Fig. 3 we have illustrated the associated communication circles and navigation topics. What are the criteria to be considered in each phase of the iterative process with its continuous feedback loops? What are the stars that we can use to guide the navigation of the ship? Such items must be specifically defined and tested in each company. Here are some examples.

1. Defining strategies.
   - Sufficient understanding of markets, ecosystem, customer dynamics.
   - Rapid adaptability to uncertain development in the ecosystem.
   - Focus on the right topics for the travelling organization and its future fitness.
2. Tailoring and aligning the cluster.
   - Feasible and manageable volume (no overload of the cluster portfolio and roadmap).
   - Balancing the cluster: Between opportunities and risks, strategic and operational needs.
   - Synergies among projects in terms of content, resources, knowledge, and measurability.
   - Consistent, compatible, and pragmatic set of models, methods, and tools.
3. Managing the cluster.
   - Meeting the time pattern of the journey (roadmap, pipeline).
   - Coordination of internal and external resources and partnerships.

   - Flexibility in terms of scoping, minimum viable products (MVPs), timing, allocation of resources.
   - Taking benefit from learning opportunities in the cluster.
4. Managing the investment.
   - Adequate procedure model for clear, complicated, or complex investments (Snowdon and Boone 2007), especially a well-timed iteration process.
   - Achievable and adaptable project targets, e.g., working with product backlogs and MVPs (Sutherland and Schwaber 2020).
   - Competent and committed project owners and teams, realizing their roles and responsibilities reliably.
   - Continuous measurement of targets and requirements—with regular review and updating.

And then there are overarching behavioral aspects linked to the corporate and leadership culture, which are a prerequisite for the effective implementation of the portfolio process as a whole in the same way as required for the joint journey and navigation to succeed. Here are three that have often proven highly critical in travelling organizations: (1) Keeping to committed priorities, processes, practices, and decisions, (2) Being open to addressing and coping with conflicts and impediments, immediate communication, (3) Caring for leadership culture: supporting, enabling, empowering, and encouraging the teams and their success.

## 3.3 From Anecdotal Criteria to Data-Driven Portfolio Decisions

The criteria described above are a good indication but if you have ever attended Portfolio Management Meetings, then you will have surely seen that the decision as to which projects are prioritized, and which ones are not, results in a challenging discussion. The issue is that portfolio decisions are forward-looking based on a variety of assumptions underpinning the investment case. Every assumption in the investment case has a confidence interval, and it is often impossible to come up with a single view as to what is right and what is wrong. Therefore, the decision made in portfolio prioritization is based on the estimation and opinion of the individuals in the meeting. But when individuals in organizations make decisions then this is not fully rational and cognitive biases (e.g., confirmation bias, loss aversion, anchoring, and bandwagon effect) come into play. As a result, the configuration of the project portfolio might not fully reflect its full potential due to trade-offs made during portfolio discussions.

To overcome this challenge, it is important that the 6 steps in Fig. 2 are taken using a consistent set of criteria across all the 6 steps, including a limited number of quantitative indicators that can be reviewed independently of individual opinions. As an example: A retail company has defined customer and utilization KPIs as the basis for their application portfolio decisions (number of new customers, daily or monthly usage of an app, payback, etc.); every project was required to provide target KPIs and the path until target KPI levels are achieved. Regular reviews of the KPIs during execution has been done and KPIs such as number of new customers have been followed using customer feedback rather than opinions. This has significantly simplified portfolio discussions and helped to understand which KPIs were achieved, which ones not, and why—across the whole organization.

To achieve this more data-driven approach projects must first focus on a minimum viable product (MVP) that can be brought to the market as fast as possible in order to obtain customer feedback. Clear KPIs help to steer the direction of the MVP and, based on the success of the MVP, more iterations can be made to scale it up—if the MVP is not successful then it can either be stopped or put on hold; this frees up money and resources for other ideas that again are built, tested—and, if worthwhile, ultimately scaled up.

Therefore, to fully exploit the power of the approach and its agility (Figs. 1 and 2) it is suggested to loop investments forward and back quickly and include market feedback to fully capture the value of all relevant portfolio ideas.

## 4 Conclusion

Keeping to agreements and promises is crucial. Managers from many organizations report that they are increasingly confronted with the situation that decisions are not made consistently or are then not implemented reliably. This finding also affects portfolio processes and the selected procedures for individual measures.

***Conflict about Procedures***

*In a company where industrial equipment for the global market is manufactured, the SCRUM method is tried out. The IT department serves as a pilot area and all conditions for self-organized and creative work are created. The employees are very happy with the approach, work progresses well, performance is outstanding. One day they are visited by an established manager who asks them to stop their current work to prioritize his order, which he wants completed in the next few days. This order has nothing to do with their project, nor with the strategic cluster of which the project is an important part. The Scrum Master is not able to handle this situation, the top-down hierarchical mindset wins, and the current Sprint can no longer be rescued. The conflict escalates but remains unresolved due to hesitation at board level, themselves struggling with the consistency required by the portfolio process. Some very talented team members leave the company because they not only find the practical situation frustrating for the project, but also fear that the agile mindset in the company will not be sustainably supported.*

For the implementation of a portfolio process, especially with increasingly scarce resources, we need a goal-oriented culture of discipline and consistency, otherwise, we waste resources and lose good people. Decisions must stand as long as they are not superseded by new decisions. This can happen quickly in the dynamics of our time, but this is not a contradiction.

## 5 Takeaways

We have presented a portfolio process designed to align the navigation of the travelling organization and to ensure successful investments in both performance improvement and future resilience. What does such a portfolio process need? A first step is to commit to the expected advantages:

- Effective focus and iterative decision-making practices to use the resources in the best way possible and minimize waste of scarce resources.
- A repertoire of management approaches that are appropriate to the diversity of strategic projects and that reduce risk even for highly innovative projects.
- Enabling quick successes both on the market and in the financial goals of the company.
- Flexible and rapid interaction in the ecosystem, advancing the organization's ability to transform and the staff's travelling mindset.
- Improving employee engagement through fast tangible success, also making the organization attractive on the challenging and competitive labor market.

From our investment, portfolio management and navigation experiences, we have learned that an effective portfolio process challenges the organizational system, its culture and/or capabilities:

- Change in organizational culture must support the navigation process, including consistency in process discipline, decision-making, and implementation.
- This needs a good knowledge of the toolset and repertoire of practices appropriate to the investment at hand, and effective implementation of that knowledge along the portfolio process.
- This is based on appropriate communication and decision-making practices in the process, using cross-structural communication circles and distributing decisions to where the expertise is based.

And finally, an effective approach for the implementation of the future portfolio process is key. Waiting does not help. You have to start and learn immediately. This can also happen iteratively, with planned loops in which new practices are tried out. To limit risk, implementation can initially be limited to one strategy bundle or a single portfolio cluster.

This covers the strategic part of the portfolio process. At the same time, in the implementation part, it will make sense to immediately learn and apply the appropriate practices in the projects themselves. These can be classic stage-gate procedures in individual projects or agile practices in other projects.

This two-pronged, strategic-operational approach quickly results in a development that creates benefits for the business. Navigation is then also a double challenge: It concerns the introduction of the new process and, at the same time, its first practical application.

## References

Beck, K. et al. (2001). *Manifesto for Agile Software Development*. Retrieved September 11, 2021, from https://agilemanifesto.org/iso/en/manifesto.html

Cumps, J. (2019). *Sociocracy 3.0—The novel: Unleash the full potential of people and organizations*. Lannoo Campus.

Doerr, J. (2018). *Measure what matters—OKRs*. Penguin.

Dörner, D. (1997). *The logic of failure: Recognizing and avoiding error in complex situations* (4th ed.). Perseus.

Duhigg, C. (2016, March 25). What Google learned from its quest to build the perfect team. *New York Times*.

Edmondson, A. C. (2018). *The fearless organization*. Wiley.

Hirzel, M., Kühn, F., & Wollmann, P. (Eds.). (2009). *Projektportfolio-Management* (2nd ed.). Gabler.

Knaster, R., & Leffingwell, D. (2018). *SAFe 4.5 distilled: Applying the scaled agile framework for lean enterprises*. Addison Wesley.

Kühn, F., Bodingbauer, D., & Dolleschal, H. (2011). Organisation der Zukunft. *ICG Change* 1/2011.

Nagel, R. (2017). *Organisationsdesign*. Schaeffer-Poeschel.

PMI. (2017). *The standard for portfolio management* (4th ed.). Project Management Institute (PMI).

Robertson, B. J. (2015). *Holacracy*. Henry Holt.

Snowdon, D. J., & Boone, M. E. (2007). A leader's framework for decision making. *Harvard Business Review* 11/2007.

Sutherland, K., & Schwaber, J. (2020). *The 2020 scrum guide*. Retrieved September 11, 2021, from https://scrumguides.org/scrum-guide.html

Wollmann, P., Kühn, F., & Kempf, M. (Eds.). (2020). *Three pillars of organization and leadership in disruptive times—Navigating your company successfully through the 21st century business world*. SpringerNature.

Wollmann, P., Kühn, F., Kempf, M., & Püringer, R. (Eds.). (2021). *Organization and leadership in disruptive times—Design and implementation of the 3-P-model*. SpringerNature.

**Reto Püringer** has worked for more than 20 years in the banking and insurance industry. He has held various senior positions in global companies. His practical experience ranges from Strategy Development, Business Model Design, Product/Proposition Development/Management, Enterprise-wide Portfolio Management, Program/Project Management, Operations/IT Management, Large Scale Change Program Delivery to Financial/Actuarial Management over different geographies and time zones, hierarchies and units, cultures and systems. Reto has managed multinational and multicultural change and transformation endeavors across the globe and managed teams of various sizes both on site and remotely. Reto holds a degree in Economical Informatics and Marketing and completed an Executive MBA at the University of Zurich.

**Frank Kühn** has been supporting companies and institutions in the areas of transformation, organization, and leadership for many years. His clients involve him as a development partner for both their urgent change projects and sustainable future concepts. Frank has a degree in engineering and a doctorate in work science. In leading positions in research and industry, he was responsible for labor management, production strategies, and project management. In the early 1990s, he joined HLP Hirzel Leder & Partners in Frankfurt and later co-founded the ICG Integrated Consulting Group Germany in Berlin and was a partner in the European group in Graz. Today, he is an independent consultant, business partner of ICG and is associated with other project partners and think tanks. He brings his experience to the development of methodologies such as the Three-Pillar Model and has published numerous articles in management journals and books.

# Part III

# Application and Experiences

# Navigating the Ivory Tower

Melusine Reimers

**Abstract**

The chapter provides an overview of the travelling of universities being particularly relevant in the area of start-up support. Based on a case description from the Excellence Start-up Center of the Ruhr-University Bochum, the chapter shows how and where challenges and new potentials can arise when such a project extends organizationally across all units of the university. Based on the "Three Pillars," concrete solutions will be proposed as to how universities can become fit for the future without simply running after the market. Universities must learn to better connect their (human) resources and implement holistic agility in their mindset—especially that of their employees. Temporary project teams across units and hierarchical boundaries, connectivity of competences, and time and space for individual relationships can help.

## 1 Introduction

In recent years, the public mission of universities in Germany has been supplemented by a field of activity widely known as "transfer." While research and teaching were originally the central activities of a university, now there should also be a direct exchange with the surrounding reality. Transfer means taking up impulses from the economy and civil society and having an impact in these areas. A specific position within the framework of transfer strategies relates to the promotion of spin-offs from research. Here, the people who developed them are transferring results developed within research or even during studies into entrepreneurial activity. This could also be described as an immediate further development of applied research. This entails some challenges and fundamental changes not only legally

M. Reimers (✉)
Bochum, Germany



M. Kempf, F. Kühn (eds.), *Navigating a Travelling Organization*, Future of Business and Finance, https://doi.org/10.1007/978-3-030-95326-3_11

but also organizationally. A university as a (usually) decentralized form consisting of two parallel organizational units (academia and administration), diverse economic and noneconomic activities as well as direct dependence on external and internal politics is in itself a prime example of a hybrid organization. Due to the new task of integrating both in-house and external start-ups into the university's own organizational forms of research and teaching using the university's own start-up funding, classic market changes and requirements are now also having a direct influence on universities and their diverse units. The ivory tower is no longer stable; instead, the entire organization must cope with navigating between academia, business, and administration.

## 2 Situation

A university is a strongly hierarchical organization, sometimes with several thousand employees, and its internal structure has often grown historically. In particular, the implementation of externally funded projects extends the "organization" beyond the university, insofar as hierarchical levels, as well as cultures of public project sponsors or ministries, are included in the organizational forms of the projects. Depending on the age and orientation of the university, there are differences in its internal navigation, but important principles are nevertheless mostly decentralization, participation, and the autonomy of the faculty. Decentralization becomes evident, for example, in the autonomous use and management of budgets, infrastructure, or personnel holding chairs and in administrative units. Various committees are designed to ensure the participation of all university members and, examination regulations aside, researchers are independent in the design of their research and teaching. Universities in Germany are also part of the public administration and resemble public

**Application of the Three-Pillar Model**
The Three Pillars (Wollmann et al., 2020, 2021) are defined as:

(1) Sustainable Purpose—The organizational why, giving orientation and a critical basic attitude.
(2) Travelling Organization—An agile mindset in which activities and circumstances are treated as flexible and fluid.
(3) Connected Resources—An active network between all needed resources inside and outside the organization.

The 3-P model represents a way for public institutions such as universities to get a grip on their challenge of successful collaboration with startups. Navigating along the three pillars not only helps to operate closer to reality

(continued)

in a sustainable way, but also helps to counteract the overload of leaders as well as employees and thus no longer focus the organization's performance on individual employees only.

## 2.1 The Peter Principle

In this respect, the "Peter Principle," prominently framed by Laurence J. Peter and Raymond Hull in the 1970s (Peter & Hull, 2014), is partly applicable to universities with external funding and their extremely high hierarchies: "In a hierarchy every employee tends to rise to his level of incompetence."

When employing the Peter Principle, one should be aware of the fact that, among other things, it ignores structural discrimination against women, and the concept of "incompetence" initially appears essentialist. At German universities, the share of women among the entire staff is just 54%, among academic staff around 40%, while major inequalities are evident among professors, with only 25% (Statistisches Bundesamt, 2020). These figures show that German universities are by no means spaces free of discrimination, but they do allow for the careful application of the Peter Principle to nonacademic personnel. Careful application, in that the reader is urged to allow for countervailing effects of structural discrimination at all times. Moreover, this application does not use the concept of "incompetence" in an essentialist way, which is why it will be replaced by "overstrain" in the following. Overstraining can be countered by providing individuals with targeted training for their jobs. The time factor also plays a role in this way, as any excessive demands can be overcome.

So let us carefully note: In a university adapting structures from its additional organization forms such as ministries or agencies executing projects, many employees arrive at the level of their own overstrain sooner or later. Those who have not yet reached these levels, or who permanently deny them due to structural discrimination, thus deliver the performance of the organization (keyword: glass ceiling). This tendency is forced by the disparate modes of employment of senior administrators/professors and so-called "mid-level staff": the former are usually civil servants and/or at least employed with fixed-term contracts, whereas the mid-level staff are employed precariously (employment relationships that entail particularly low wages, low social security due to fixed-term contracts and an uncertain future for the employee). The goal of the mid-level staff is therefore to eventually achieve a permanent, safe position, for which massive workloads are taken on and an enormous willingness to perform is developed. Even within a fixed-term appointment, it is, of course, possible to climb further hierarchical levels or even salary grades, which is why a de-fixed-term appointment of a professor does not directly mean a drop in performance. A similar picture emerges in the natural partners of universities: Ministries and agencies executing public projects are, hierarchically, also highly differentiated, stable organizations in which employees are repeatedly promoted to positions that overtax them in terms of content or form. In this respect, the hierarchies of the universities are "extended" even further by the close cooperation with ministries and project sponsors, especially in the area of third-party funding. Mirroring their structures, the differentiation of hierarchies in individual organizational units or project contexts at a university can thus be immensely increased (from student employees to ministers). A practical example of this extension of hierarchies in a project context could be the following: The project office receives an e-mail from the project sponsor with a short-term deadline for the feedback of information to the ministry and the request to confirm it. The responsible colleague is on leave, but the office receives an additional note that feedback on the deadline is nevertheless expected by the next day. This is actually a detailed and direct instruction with an influence on the internal work organization, which would be expected from a manager. In this case, however, it comes from an external institution, but it must still be followed.

Another aspect of why the Peter Principle can be applied to universities and their organizational units is that universities are so-called "expert organizations" (Rybnicek et al., 2015) or "professional bureaucracies" (Mintzberg, 1979). Such organizations primarily employ highly qualified experts who apply their knowledge to changing problems with a high level of autonomy and willingness to achieve. Experience and status in the specialized field are much more important than any goals the organization may have. Managers must themselves demonstrate professional expertise; otherwise, they may run into problems of recognition. Promotions are therefore based on professional expertise rather than on suitability for the activities of the position. In other words, an outstanding academic does not necessarily have to be able to develop and implement solid project plans, monitor financials, or lead a team. So if this outstanding scholar has made it to a high position in the hierarchy because he or she brings technical expertise, he or she may be completely overwhelmed by the demands of the job.

## 2.2 The Principle of Delay

State institutions such as universities and ministries are based on bureaucratic and democratic processes for a reason: Among other things, this is to avoid corruption and inequalities. The purpose of public institutions is to implement political decisions in all areas of society and to guarantee legal certainty and equality. They are organizations maintained in the public interest and therefore must, at all times, consider public interest in form of committees or bureaucracy. In addition to the Peter Principle, another principle can therefore be observed for public institutions—that of delay: Reality appears in public institutions with a time lag. Public institutions react to problems that have been raised in democratic processes and for which a solution must be found in the public interest. Therefore, they do not respond to reality immediately, but only in a mediated way. This is also, or even especially, true for research, since time is a key factor in developing research designs and verifying hypotheses—quite apart from the time that elapses before research is funded and published. In concrete terms, the delay principle means, for example, that public funding and support programs for research are designed on the basis of problems or circumstances in which they are needed. In their development, however, they must pass through certain committees and evaluations in order to be democratically legitimized and secure in their application. Reality, however, does not wait. Until the described processes of implementation and evaluation are completed and the funding instruments can be used, the circumstances and issues in society are likely to have changed again. An absolute overload of public institutions according to this principle became obvious in 2020 with the outbreak of the COVID-19 pandemic. Ever new realizations of reality, as well as emerging problems, ran almost simultaneously with the permanent need to respond.

### 2.3 Start-ups and the Peter-Delay-Fail

Taking both principles together results in a picture of public institutions that is certainly problematic. As a rule, overburdened employees develop measures and make decisions on the basis of outdated views of reality. Within the ivory tower that is academia itself, this would possibly not be particularly noticeable, since being in touch with reality is limited by political committees anyway and is actually reserved exclusively for research (here also with a time delay). However, as soon as transfer activities take place, universities come into direct confrontation with reality or want to exert a direct influence on it. A further culmination arises through the cooperation with start-ups, which belong to a completely different and significantly faster reality. In order to achieve scaling growth, start-ups have to run ahead of the problems, so to speak, and in this respect demand top performance from every single employee. Permanently overstrained employees, according to the Peter Principle, are rare in start-ups, as they can be quickly replaced on the basis of precarious working conditions. Start-ups also encounter and demand permanent "in-time" reactions from the partnerships surrounding them, since, otherwise, market advantages and thus, possibly, the entire start-up could be lost. Thus, if public institutions want to collaborate with startups, massive cultural differences must be overcome and all organizational units involved must be navigated sensitively. Otherwise, either a cleverly navigating start-up will use state institutions for its own economic purposes, or innovations from research will miss their opportunities for implementation and thus, ultimately, miss their goal.

## 3 Case-Study "Start-up Project at the Ruhr University Bochum"

Missed opportunities for implementation and unused patents tend to lie unseen in German universities—something a new funding line from the state of North-Rhine-Westphalia (NRW) has been seeking to remedy since 2019. Within the framework of "Excellence Start-up Centers" (ESCs), six NRW universities are supported in the

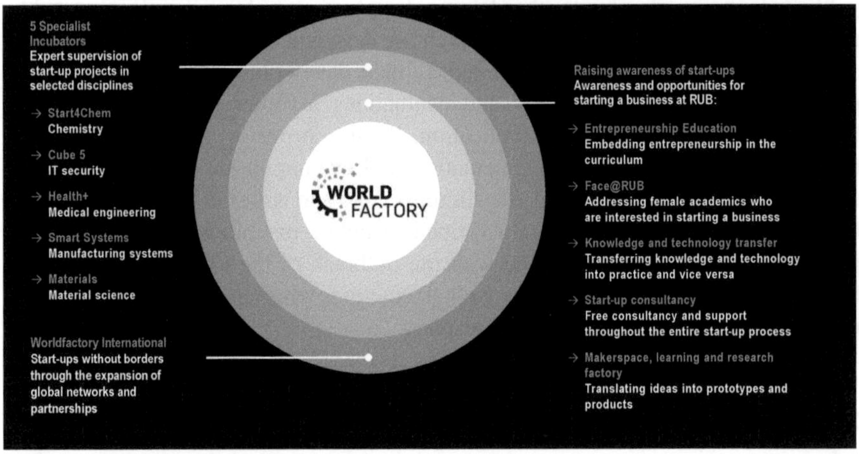


**Fig. 1** Layers of **WORLD**FACTORY Start-up Center (© **WSC** 2021, *used with permission. All rights reserved*)

promotion of start-ups with a total of EUR 150 million. Although the centers are structured differently, they all follow the same funding line and try to encourage "their" universities to be more start-up friendly. In the following, the project "**WORLD**FACTORY Start-up Center" (WSC) at the Ruhr University Bochum (RUB) will serve as a case study.

Parts of the project already existed prior to the funding; these are now being expanded and extended with the help of EUR 21 million over five years. Following the example of the successful "Cube 5" hub for IT security, four additional specialized hubs were developed in the RUB's top research areas in order to sustainably increase transfer potential. At the same time, the amplitude of the full-scale university (unlike a technical university) was to be taken on board and a comprehensive sensitization for the topic of start-ups had to take place (Fig. 1).

The WSC differs from other universities' start-up centers in the way that the chosen approach and the offers designed according to it can be tailored individually and holistically to the needs of those interested in starting up (along the lines of the Entre Comp model of the EU). Events, courses, and workshops are not linear but modular in structure and should, thus, also be able to respond to the constantly changing (market) requirements for start-ups and their founders in the long term. At RUB, founding a start-up is not understood as a sprint, but as an enduring marathon, which is why the start-up teams are accompanied in their processes until they are able to establish themselves on the market in a stable and long-term manner. During the sometimes long development phases, especially in high-tech areas, students, teachers, and researchers should continue to be involved so that a start-up idea can have an overall effect on the surrounding research areas.

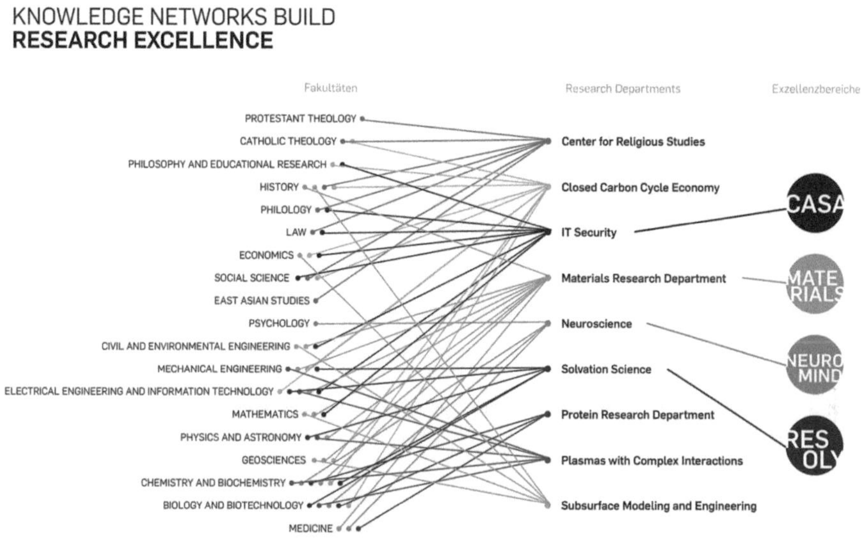


**Fig. 2** Knowledge Networks of the Ruhr-University Bochum (© **WSC** 2021, *used with permission. All rights reserved*)

> **The approach of the WSC:**
> 1. The development of five specialized hubs in the university's top research areas.
> 2. The decentralized structure of the project within the university.
> 3. The promotion of social and sustainable start-up ideas in order to contribute to the structural change in the Ruhr region with start-ups.

With the WSC, the RUB is pursuing two strategic development paths politically that are closely linked. Embedded in the measures of the Excellence Strategy, basic research is to be interlinked via innovative start-up approaches in order to further develop the transfer potential from top-level research. Oriented toward NRW's lead markets and on the basis of its interdisciplinary research departments established through proven research strength, the RUB has already developed specialist unique selling points via four areas of excellence (Fig. 2). On the other hand, the WSC aims to tap the transfer potential in the disciplinary amplitude of the RUB with its 20 faculties and around 47,000 university members across all phases of the start-up process.

The decentralized integration of the WSC is supposed to work as a breeding ground for the sustainable penetration and mobilization of all the university structures by establishing and professionalizing founding start-ups as a university field of activity. As a full-scale university, the Ruhr-University's departments range from those typically known for knowledge-based start-ups to large departments in

**Fig. 3** Environment of **WORLD**FACTORY Start-up Center (© **WSC** 2021, *used with permission. All rights reserved*)

the humanities and social sciences which are also essential for successful start-up teams.

Due to this complexity of the project and the risk of the Peter-Delay-Fail, there is an increased demand for the navigation of the various organizational units over which the project spans (Fig. 3).

Structurally, the project is located directly in the Rector's Department under the leadership of the Pro-Rector for Research and Transfer. He is supported by a project office which, like the so-called central WSC team and the "Makerspace," is embedded in Department 1: Strategy and Development, Section 4: Transfer and Entrepreneurship (a total of 15 staff positions). In addition to 9 project employees in other administrative units such as Department 1, Section 2: Development and Committees, Department 8: Communication, there are also members in the fundraising unit. Further, there are 28 other project members located in different chairs performing cutting-edge research aimed at the implementation of the incubators, and the Maria Jahoda Center for International Gender Studies with the goal of implementing support for female start-up founders as well as within the Department of Economics with the idea of implementing entrepreneurship education and project evaluation. Stakeholders from the business community are also directly involved in the project set-up with their own personnel spend to fund several positions. For example, Bochum Economic Development is responsible for the implementation and execution of ideas competitions as well as an annual business plan competition, in which a special prize is awarded by the RUB. The RUB Academy is involved with the qualification of female start-up founders by providing specialized expert advice and further training as well as with the design of an event center on Mark 51°7, the former Opel site in Bochum. In addition, the WSC works with local hubs, companies, and already spun-out start-ups to provide mentoring networks, access to finance or project partners. In this respect, the WSC's 56 employees and leaders belong to very diverse organizational units, both internally and externally.

"Above" the university, there are also additional hierarchical levels, since the project is politically accompanied by NRW's Ministry of Economic Affairs, Innovation, Digitalization and Energy and is administered by an agency (especially in terms of financial management and reporting). Therefore, just like the other ESC projects the WSC spans over 15 hierarchical levels. With regard to the 3-Ps, the following challenges arise for the management of the ESC projects as well as for the embedding of university start-up support in general:

**Sustainable Purpose**

- A university's goal is, so to speak, "pre-defined" (by the state's educational, research, and transfer mandate). Especially with regard to start-up support, however, it is unclear what the actual purpose of start-up support is both as a whole and for each organizational unit involved: Is it to produce unicorns? Is it to produce a mass of start-ups? Is it not to produce start-ups at all but rather raise awareness of founding start-ups throughout the university?
- The project proposals provide metrics and milestones, but these were defined before the project started and they are inevitably based on a past reality as well as the requirements of the funding line, which are also based on a past reality.

**Travelling Organization**

- To the extent that the projects are subject to constant changes from the ministry, university management, economic stakeholders, professors, and the project sponsor, ESC projects must remain flexible in dealing with change. Working with start-ups also requires a high degree of flexibility. Decisions are often made using opaque agreements or situations due to the hierarchical gradient.
- The daily university routine hardly allows for further development, there is hardly any error culture and agile project understanding is limited to the decentralized structure of the university. Employees of the various ESC projects therefore sometimes find themselves in a kind of defensive state alternating with complete excessive demands.

**Connecting Resources**

- The projects span several units, hierarchical levels, and institutions; in this respect, there are neither uniform structures or processes nor a common IT infrastructure. The exchange of information and project progress is regulated via jour fixe meetings in the respective units or reporting systems.
- The various units and institutions each have very slow decision-making structures for testing and implementing new processes.

Collaboration between start-ups and universities, as in the WSC or other ESC projects, means that both leaders and all other staff involved are constantly faced with questions of appropriate navigation: How do I navigate this tension between administration, academia, and entrepreneurship? What paradigms shape the different areas? What journey is each of them on? And: What does this mean for the common journey of university start-up funding?

## 4 One Possible Way Out

The 3-P model represents a way for public institutions such as universities to get a grip on their challenge of successful collaboration with startups. Navigating along the three pillars not only helps them to operate closer to reality in a sustainable way, but also helps to counteract the overload of leaders as well as employees and thus no longer focuses the organization's performance on individual employees alone:

- Sustainable Purpose helps to promote a critical attitude within the organizational units involved by keeping the question of one's area of responsibility and all activities constantly present. Representations of reality by external parties, such as founders or investors, can thus be questioned more critically and confidently by employees.
- Travelling Organization counters, above all, the delay principle by promoting the agility and speed of the public institution. Rapid testing, preliminary decisions, or short iteration loops lead to the organization itself developing a more accurate picture of reality and empower employees to process information independently.
- The promotion of Connecting Resources, i.e., trusting connections internally and externally, leads to employees knowing how they can counteract excessive demands or where they can turn for support in finding solutions. In addition, information from outside comes into the institution, passes through it more quickly and is processed in a way that is comprehensible to all employees.

The 3-Ps also respond to the hybrid nature of universities, particularly in complexly structured transfer projects that span diverse organizational units with a wide variety of forms of autonomy, participation, and decentralization and which are characterized by lateral leadership. In the Ruhr-University's 2019 Digital Strategy for the Administration, under the point "Potential of Employees," the issue that employees should be further trained in agile project work, in particular, was addressed ("Communication, information and further training measures, especially on project work, support employees in change processes and strengthen their skills."). This was intended to promote the culture of innovation in the administration, since innovative science must be accompanied by an administration that is at least up to date. The formulation in fact addresses the risk of the Peter Delay fail, since precisely this form of employee empowerment can promote both. Insofar as a section on innovative project work would not be absolutely necessary for the digital strategy, it seems relevant here. Below you will find an interview with Christina Reinhard, the acting chancellor of RUB, about the background and effects of the digital strategy.

**The Following are Some Excerpts from a Conversation with Christina Reinhard about Navigating the RUB Within the Area of Tension between Administration, Business, and Science:**

*As the central leader of the administration, how do you specifically go about realizing a sustainable change, for example, in the direction of "innovation culture"?*

There are different levels when wanting to strengthen innovation culture: on the one hand the cultural, and on the other hand, the more technical level related to measures. On the more technical side, the "Process orientation and digitization in administration" program was launched in 2019 to provide a framework for various activities in the direction of innovation. New change and innovation culture units were to tackle and implement concrete projects in this regard. The factors that had an impact at the cultural level also included my own actions—which often had much more influence than long speeches. But I also had to take into account the fact that there are different types of employees in the administration. On the one hand, change agents and, on the other, preservationists. I probably belong to the first, i.e., I definitely stress and challenge the organization. The preservers, however, cannot be ignored here, as they are also important, especially in a university administration. In certain departments, the two often meet; I therefore try, again and again, to form mixed working groups from these types and to demand exchange. In this context, error culture is not insignificant, in the way that an important function of the administration lies in the legal safeguarding of processes. In particular, mixed teams and leaders who admit their own mistakes can support this process. And, as a final point, I see freedom as a central aspect for a successful culture of innovation. We still have some catching up to do in this regard, I am sure—my vision would be something like: One day a week, all employees are given free time to work on their individual projects.

*What challenges does the management of a project like the WSC pose for the administration, the various project staff, and the management levels of the units involved? How do you deal with them?*

What strikes me most are the different cultures of the organizational units involved—even when considering the ones from within the university they are very different. In the WSC, there are also external people involved. I mainly deal with the externals and step up in cases of conflict. In such a case, I try to hold individual conversations at management level in order to achieve an understanding of the different cultures—if unsuccessful, the next level is involved. I take these cultural conflicts very seriously and try to reflect on them thoroughly, but I also realize that, usually, there is not enough time for this during working hours. Sometimes, we take these issues home with us or even with us on annual leave. There shouldn't only be the opportunity for

(continued)

times of reflection in cases of conflict, but, in principle, opportunities should be created for employees to step out of work, reflect on priorities, and refocus.

*When, and on the basis of which aspects, would you define the RUB's Digital Strategy Bochum administration as successfully implemented?*

That's quite difficult to answer because it's constantly changing. When I started setting up the PDV program, I thought it would be a very long-term project with major goals and a comprehensive organizational development over ten years. Then the COVID pandemic hit us and, lo and behold, it becomes sink or swim! It seems that people are not quite as resistant to change after all, since, if they have to, they can implement and shape quite a bit of change. In parallel, I have realized that we have got a completely different kettle of fish to tackle about the legal framework for digitizing universities. And lastly, I realized that the expectations from our new employees and also our "customers" are much higher, which is why we definitely cannot take a comfortable ten years to implement a digitization strategy. So, we are now backing up the measures with significantly more resources. That is why I would say today that I will only open the first bottle of champagne when the four central projects of the program have been implemented: identity management, document management, digitization of procurement, and the entire HR process. I expect this to take another 2–3 years.

*In your opinion, how do the organizational development and structure of the administration relate to the innovativeness of the university as a whole?*

One should not underestimate the contribution that a well-functioning and service-oriented administration can make to the overarching goals of universities: namely research, transfer, and teaching. In contrast, a so-called "administrative brake," i.e., an administration in which the entire innovative dynamic of a university is blocked, would work in the exact opposite way. In particular, the Departments of Human Resources and Finance are inherently risk-averse, as special legal safeguards have to be put in place there. Scientists and students like to rail against this attitude, especially at international conferences, and demand that we, as an administration, should be different. My goal would be that, at some point, we could overcome this. Of course, we have to protect academics legally, but I would certainly like it if we could trust people as well; also, administrators should make use of their room to maneuver. In the worst case, innovative professors and employees can be lost due to an overly obstructive administration which has to be avoided as a matter of urgency. I see us more as shaping and enabling administration.

## 4.1 Navigational Development in a University Project

To take the paragraph for agile project work training from the digital strategy seriously, one and a half years after the start, the WSC has embarked on the journey of developing 3-P and a navigation with which the promotion of spin-offs at the RUB can be successfully implemented in the long term. The WSC project coordination, with the support of the coordination group (consisting of professors and nonacademic managers), decided to improve navigation by giving the project a period of time, with the support of external consultants, in which the strategic setup is given a higher priority than direct implementation. This gives staff the opportunity to evolve and learn new behaviors to overcome temporary or fundamental overwhelm. A circle consisting of external consultants as well as the project coordinator navigates the process of organizational development, prepares the monthly meetings of the overall project and moderates working groups on various topics. At a monthly WSC workshop, thematic input is given and impulses are set in the direction of the 3-P, while the results of the working groups are also presented.

The topics for the working groups result from a previous survey of employees on where they see a need for processes and clarification. During these workshops, the working groups can approach other employees for queries or feedback, and each employee can also provide feedback on the content of each working group. The organization of the topics of the working groups as well as their composition is also coordinated in these workshops. The working groups work with methodological support and have the task of defining clear processes and responsibilities for their topics. If conflicts or even individual challenges arise for individual employees during development, there is the option of resorting to individual coaching. Regular feedback to the coordination circle as well as in the general reporting system of the respective organizational units is also intended to stay in touch with the various management personnel involved (Fig. 4).

The process of development will not have been completed by the time this case study is finished, but the following effects can already be observed after three months:

- Dealing with the Purpose has led to a steadily increasing questioning of one's own (partly superfluous) activities. In addition, a common understanding of the overall project is developing, with a corresponding strengthening of confidence and mutual trust.
- By being organized in flexible working groups and connecting interests, knowledge, and experiences across structures, employees develop an understanding of the perspectives, approaches, and resources of other organizational units. External moderation promotes a habitual approach to methodical procedures in appointments.
- Initial overarching processes and responsibilities have been developed and negotiated. Implementation is still being approached hesitantly.
- The employees' motivation to improve their own work processes and practices significantly to create an impact could be overcome by committing to the

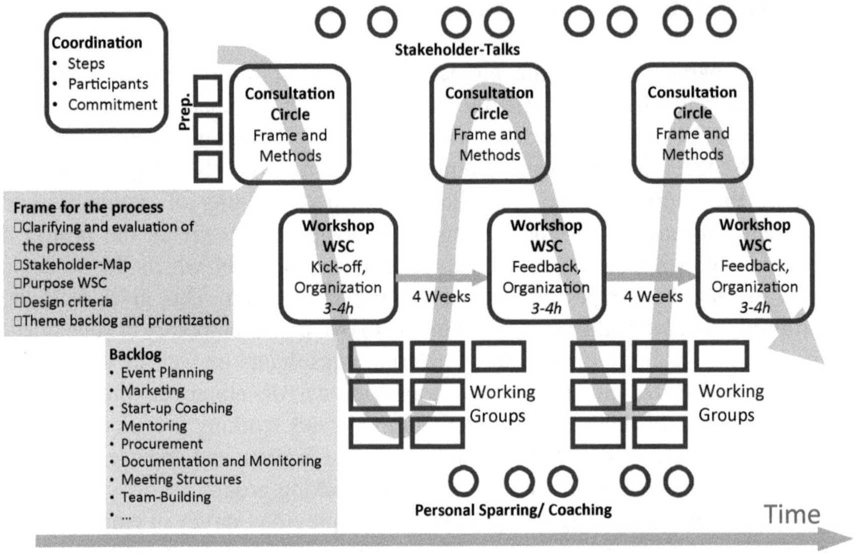


**Fig. 4** Description of the navigational development process at **WORLD**FACTORY Start-up Center (*Illustrated by the author, used with permission. All rights reserved*)

priorities of the project. The feeling of being permanently overburdened could be countered among individual employees.

## 5 Takeaways

When you try to navigate a tanker like a university, you can pull on the steering wheel with all your might, but the tanker still keeps going in the same direction. You might keep thinking: You are not going to be able to steer it around, nothing is moving here—but when you look back after a while and see the ship's course, you realize that you are actually heading in a different direction now. (*Christina Reinhard, Chancellor of the RUB*)

## References

Mintzberg, H. (1979). The professional bureaucracy. In H. Mintzberg (Ed.), *The structuring of organisations*. Prentice-Hall.

Peter, L. J., & Hull, R. (2014). *The Peter principle: Why things always go wrong* (Reprint Ed.). : Harper Business.

Rybnicek, R., Bergner, S., & Suk, K. (2015). *Führung in Expertenorganisationen*. In R. van Dick & J. Felfe (Eds.), *Handbuch Mitarbeiterführung: Wirtschaftspsychologisches Praxiswissen für Fach- und Führungskräfte*. Springer NachschlageWissen.

Statistisches Bundesamt. (2020). *Frauenanteile an Hochschulen in Deutschland nach akademischer Laufbahn in den Jahren 2017 bis 2019*, zitiert nach de.statista.com. Retrieved October 17, 2021, 5:12 pm, from https://de.statista.com/statistik/daten/studie/249318/umfrage/frauenanteile-an-hochschulen-in-deutschland/

Wollmann, P., Kühn, F., & Kempf, M. (Eds.). (2020). *Three pillars of organization and leadership in disruptive times—Navigating your company successfully through the 21st century business world*. SpringerNature.

Wollmann, P., Kühn, F., Kempf, M., & Püringer, R. (Eds.). (2021). *Organization and leadership in disruptive times—Design and implementation of the 3-P-model*. SpringerNature.

**Melusine Reimers** has been working at Ruhr-University Bochum since 2019 as start-up consultant and project manager of the university's own Start-up Center, where she can contribute her own experience from the start-up world. While still a student, she founded academic experience Worldwide e.V., a non-profit organization for highly qualified refugees. Afterwards, she worked freelance for various startups with social and sustainable business models in business development and marketing. In 2017, she founded READYMADE, Germany's first sharing economy startup for sustainability and a more conscious approach to furniture. Furthermore, she is doing a PhD in philosophy at the University of Fine Arts in Saarbrücken about demarcation and transition.

[illegible]



[illegible]

# The Dilemma of How to Navigate a Rock: Developments in the Catholic Church in Germany and Resources for Navigation in the VUCA World

Michael Kempf and Juliane Schlaud-Wolf

**Abstract**

This chapter focuses on sources to navigate a complex organization in a crisis: which resources come from their historical purpose and aim. The authors introduce the situation of the German Catholic Church with its strategic and organizational challenges. Are there any resources with which the system and its members can face the upcoming radical transformation phase? It is an impulse for dialogue and also shows paths for different organizations on how to navigate in disruptive times. They combine different perspectives—theological and organizational development—bringing up impulses for different kinds of organization in their journey.

## 1 Rationale for This Article

When investigating the question of organizations navigating through uncertain times you come across an article about the Catholic Church in Germany! Yes, you read it correctly.

What can you expect from this article? On the one hand, insight into the change process in a major institution, lest we forget one of the largest employers in Germany (German Bishops Conference, DBK, 2021). This view draws on external and internal perspectives of leadership and consulting. On the other hand, you will read about the resources that this institution can make available to people and organizations to help them navigate in uncertain and complex times. Why? Because

M. Kempf (✉)
Bad Honnef, Germany
e-mail: michael@kempf-cp.com

J. Schlaud-Wolf
Limburg, Germany



M. Kempf, F. Kühn (eds.), *Navigating a Travelling Organization*, Future of Business and Finance, https://doi.org/10.1007/978-3-030-95326-3_12

helping to navigate through the depths of life has always been the core business, the message of the Church. That is its purpose.

"You are Peter and on this rock I will build my Church" (Bible, Matthew 16,16). This passage is 2000 years old and, seen from the eyes of the VUCA[1] world, it is a considerable challenge. A rock cannot be navigated, only tectonics can do that. And it may well be true that the institution "Catholic Church in Germany" presents itself as a large, heavy, even immobile, tanker with a degree of outdated charm. It comes across as behind the times, more ponderous than agile, sometimes agreeable, sometimes something to be ashamed of. It moves rather cautiously rather than agilely navigating the world's oceans. In VUCA times this proves to be increasingly difficult. For contexts change at breakneck speed, good decisions require one to move elegantly and swiftly up to system boundaries. It is well known that large ships need a long time to change course. There are just a few exceptions—for example, the way the Church acted when it came to tackling the refugee crisis in Europe.

So the Church is an institution that might have long since passed the point-of-no-return. This is a question mooted by its members, in academic discourse and also at the management level (Marx 09/2021). For the Church's current organizational form is at risk of making its own purpose impossible. In order to make the Church fit for the VUCA world, it needs different structures in a different culture. This involves functionality for its mission, changes to its business models, organizational structures, and a systemic understanding of leadership. What is needed is a contemporary portfolio of service provision, comprehensible language, especially in religious communication, and viable strategies for handling its property portfolio, for example.

The Church is not alone in having to tackle the challenges that arise in the VUCA world. What is new, though, is that the decision makers and figures of responsibility in the Church are not only inviting this discourse but also actively engaging in it. It is a question of fundamental reconstruction rather than mere cosmetic touching-up. In this sense, the Church is the learner. And it is discovering in its own reservoir potentials that are significant for fundamental social and organizational change situations. These are to be made available. This fits its own purpose. The Church is there to help one navigate through life.

The aim is to find the best way to jointly shape the VUCA world. Christians find interesting navigation principles in their own DNA that might provide food for thought for non-Christians, too. It is a question of mindset, of essential principles of life that motivate a lifestyle that makes a difference.

[1] While VUCA is still a meaningful model that furthers understanding, BANI goes one step further. This model not only explains the challenges of the current situation it also explains its ongoing consequences. The acronym BANI stands for: Brittle, Anxious, Non-linear, Incomprehensible.

Thus, this model provides a lens through which not only unstable structures can be understood but also even chaotic ones. https://www.resilienz-akademie.com/bani-statt-vuca-die-neue-welt/

**Application of the Three-Pillar Model**

The Three Pillars (Wollmann et al., 2020, 2021) are defined as:

(1) Sustainable Purpose—The raison d'être of an organization, bringing new orientation and certainty to the people for their joint endeavor and success.
(2) Travelling Organization—The mindset of an organization in a permanent state of flux, interacting with the market and customer journey, with rapid adaptivity.
(3) Connected Resources—Interconnecting all needed resources inside and outside the silos, creating consistency between goals and concepts, strategies and processes, competencies, and roles.

The German Catholic Church is in a deep historical crisis—but it has on the other hand deep resources from its history. The purpose seems to be clear, but it is not obvious enough to give the organization the strength to navigate in a good direction in these disruptive times. Which narratives can be used for navigation inside and as well outside this kind of organization—this topic is discussed and shown from two perspectives in this chapter.

## 2 Hypotheses and Derivations

Quite apart from the observable developments that have led to this situation, a matter-of-fact look at the facts is sufficient to be able to derive the need for a fundamental transformation of the Catholic Church in Germany. Improvement and cosmetic repair are no longer enough. The Catholic Church in Germany is one of the biggest employers and one of the organizations with the largest membership (DBK, 2021). The 22.2 million Catholics reflect the social development of the aging of society and reinforce, in parts, the demographic trend.

Within the institution of the Church, too, worsening social polarizations are reflected. This is a high risk for this organization too. "In the Church we are experiencing a profound shock" (Bätzing in DBK, 2021). In concrete terms: a loss of faith due to cases of sexual abuse from previous decades, a rising tendency for members to leave the Church coupled with the financial implications because of the form of church tax in Germany, a fall in financial resources, an excess of property that is barely usable or used; all this demonstrates, in a fragmented fashion, the problem areas. The greatest challenge, however, is that, within, faith and credibility have got lost. There is talk of dual standards, there is a growing divide between claim and reality; and this is happening in an organization that claims to be and is expected to be a moral authority. From a consulting perspective, we describe this as strategic drift (Höfler et al., 2018). This refers to a situation in which an organization has failed to adapt in time to the developments and circumstances in its environment, to adapt to the markets and gear itself to those markets. The need for, and the extent of, transformation rises exponentially and this form of organizational crisis can only be overcome by radical change. Otherwise, the importance and the visibility of the organization fall dramatically.

This situation affects a strongly hierarchical and differentiated organization that has many ramified sub "companies" and that has a presence in many different fields and locations. The strategic competences of the subcompanies are usually lacking as is their strategic professionalism. From an organizational theory perspective, the Catholic Church is still in the differentiation phase (Glasl & Lievegoed, 2004). Moreover, it is strongly characterized by content and theology and driven by structure and finances and less by the impact it can deliver. Its performance processes resemble those of a classic authority and are hence less contemporary, that is, less agile and digital (Gilles in DBK, 2021).

Alongside the structural challenges, a look at the Church's perceptible attitudes is necessary. On the one hand, an openness for humankind and for people is evident; on the other, however, a dysfunctional orientation toward power and opacity in its actions can be discerned. Different facets of organizational reality become clear (cf, among others, Dessoy & Lames, 2008; Dessoy et al., 2021).

Yet there are other sides: Serious development processes on the part of the Church, a new direction and a spirit of optimism to make the Church fit for the future (DBK, 2021). 660,000 children and young adults between 7 and 28 years old are members of youth associations; 3.15 million people take part in the 149,000 or so education and training courses that are offered by the Church. In many dioceses, sexual abuse has been consistently addressed and much work, highly respected socially, has been done in the prevention of the abuse of power. Furthermore, there has been a notable increase of women in leadership positions in the Church; likewise, we have seen indications of lateral and team-oriented leadership concepts and practice. The communication of faith, the Church's core purpose, is making greater use of digital media concepts and competences. Diverse experimental fields of Church-led innovation are being developed, e.g., Church co-working spaces and cooperation with other social stakeholders. The Church's Caritas organizations offer a broad spectrum of aid and support to the whole of society.

But is this enough in these VUCA times? Are these developments sufficiently viable to overcome the strategic drift? Are they sufficiently viable to improve the navigation of this travelling organization?

## 3 Two Navigation Points from the Reservoir of Christianity

### 3.1 An Introduction

When organizations are there to reduce complexity they have to face reality and shape society. If the Church has the mission of shaping society, it is facing the VUCA reality and the specific challenges this reality brings. It is doing this at present by critically appraising its own organizational form and by reflecting on itself. The

Church fulfills this purpose by offering people and organizations points of navigation. It sees these as both suggestion and proposition, coupled with its desire for these points to function as meta perspectives for navigation. Even if the Church has stowed away these treasures in its cargo hold so to speak this does not mean that they are being adequately used to navigate its own organization. It is a long journey from the depths of the cargo hold to the bridge.

The aim is to use the Christian message to open up perspectives, suitable for both life and organizations, that make a difference and hence serve as support on the journey into an unknown future. In this respect, it is a question of how people relate to what they do.[2] The behaviors described here are not meant as the exclusive mindsets of individual pious people behind thick walls. They are aimed at the heart of life and at the actions of decision makers and those with responsibility in organizations in the VUCA world. They should be understood as a co-creative contribution drawn from Christian cultural heritage.

"What's missing if there are no Christians?" (Sellmann, 2021), is the title of a work by pastoral theologian Matthias Sellmann. It is a brief summary of the life competence of Christians that may be useful for non-Christians too. "Being a Christian is a specific form, namely a spiritual form, of wisdom (phronesis). This wisdom motivates one to three competences that, when implemented, constantly complement each other: running away less and less (physis), emerging from oneself (kenosis), taking power from outside (dynamis)" (Sellmann, 2021). The founding teachings of the Church, the Gospels, which translate the Good News, tell of experiences of faith and life, of behaviors and competences. They are about happiness, boundaries, growing, and dying. The aim is a good and just life for all people (cf. Bible, John, 10, 10). To do so, Biblical tales spin red threads.

Life means change, and allowing oneself to transform requires the courage to transform (Haas & Shedletzky, 03/2021) and faith (passion for the possible). There is no life without ambiguities and contrasts. A Christian lifestyle can reinforce the competence to manage ambiguity (Bauer, 2018), question traditional success criteria and empower one to inner freedom; this is how patterns are broken which, for example, turn success logics upside down (Kaduk, 2020).

[2] What we are discussing here is, for Christians, the core of their faith and the expression of their understanding of God. By means of this point of navigation, which is outside their self, Christians discover an unavailable assurance. For them this assurance of good life is a person: Jesus Christ. We want to take this Christian faith very seriously, and propose it as a lifestyle that can shape non-Christian life plans too. Theologians among the readers should exchange their theological spectacles for those of non-theologians. We are not discussing high theology here, even if the development of organizational theology and the cybernetics of Christian leadership in the VUCA world both within and beyond the Church organization appears very interesting.

### 3.2 Passion for the Possible

In order to secure the functionality of organizations in the future something has to enter our field of vision before it is there. "I say that something is coming from the future. There's a cause for it, but the cause lies in the future and, logically, the effect is more to be found in the present than the cause to be found in the future" (Beuys, 2021).

We need a mindset that transcends fragmented connections to a fragmented world. A mindset that unites track records with the logic of giant leaps. It is about faith beyond the world of what is currently visible, about a faith that enables the future in the laws of the present. This mindset supports a balance in the tension between work and new work, between leadership and new leadership. It nurtures a mindset aiming at a balance between business models guided by exploitation and models geared toward exploration, as described in the management theory of ambidexterity (Frey & Töpfer, 2021) and discussed with a view to their functioning in the VUCA world.

The responsibility of being able to deliberate, in your day-to-day work, which innovations from the future could lead to a breakthrough without having truly reliable data, requires images as power sources that go beyond what is already known and readily available. For neither the temptation of the oft-invoked gaze into the crystal ball nor the myriad of manuals and recipes for success, which are more reminiscent of magic potions, can do justice to the complexity of the reality and the responsibility of the navigators. It is not about getting off this world. Professional management in unpredictable times profits from competence in what is possible in the present. From a Christian perspective, this means a mindset for which a decision is required and which develops by being constantly tested. Just as posture changed when humans learned to walk, the decision as to what is possible can also develop from condensed knowledge of life. We encounter this in a particular way in religions, in literary genres of life narratives. Let us take a look at the resource of Biblical narratives.

The Bible tells in prominent places of this passion for the possible. This seems to distinguish Christians[3] (Loffeld, 2020) and their particular form of "world adaptation" (Rosa, 2019).

> *This is what the kingdom of God is like. A man scatters seed on the ground. Night and day, whether he sleeps or gets up, the seed sprouts and grows, though he does not know how.* (Mark 4, 26–28)

The narrative form is a parable; parables tell tales using simple images and are intended to awaken the reader. The protagonist, the sower, behaves professionally

[3]Faithful Christians put it thus: They trust in God. That is the heart of the Christian message: the assurance of God that the world is created good, that we are accepted without having to do anything in return. They are in the world to shape it in a goodly fashion. This big story has to be related to the small stories of humankind.

and follows all the rules of the trade: create a framework, formulate goals, make resources available, check the result, an excellent orchestration of the growth process. But there is a trick in this parable: the sower cannot explain why it happens, how it happens. He cannot do the growing. But what he can conclude from his reflection is the mindset behind his action. He has faith that it will work out. Passion for the possible opens up a particular perspective for him when it comes to navigating in uncertain times.

Why are we formulating this as modern food for thought? Whether something is successful or not is increasingly difficult to calculate. The world is more than complicated, it is complex. It describes behavior that is so professional that it means that the entire success stems from one's own actions (give everything). And at the same time, it describes a mindset that expresses that one cannot make one's own success (let everything go). This does not mean that measurement, figures, dates, facts, setting frameworks do not have to be constantly reinvented as state of the art in order to enable adaptable growth processes. But it means developing a particular inner mindset concerning these tools at the same time. Familiar tools are essential because they help us to assess things. And at the same time they are inadequate because, ultimately, they cannot do complete justice to the context. The sower makes himself available to the growth process and finds inner security in this role. He does what he can but knows that he cannot do the decisive thing. He lives from the passion that everything possible can become reality.[4] Here, we see a point of navigation in uncertain times which, in complexity, by having faith in the future, makes one able to act.[5]

### 3.3 Considering a Different Success Logic

Our second serving of food for thought takes faith in what is possible and reinforces it. It makes us think about a particular understanding of success. This helps us to navigate through the challenges of the VUCA world. Once again, a Biblical text is the inspiration. This, too, is rife with confusion and could barely be more contradictory to the common assumptions of its and our time. The hero of the text is described with surprisingly different success criteria. And it is precisely this difference that makes the difference for the author. The text we are referring to guides the actions of Christians. For non-Christians, it could encourage them to adopt a different lifestyles (Theobald, 2018). The hero we are referring to is Jesus, the new universal ruler. The

[4]In the Gospel of Matthew, which was written somewhat later, the parable is expressed more pointedly. It is supplemented by the weeds, which are confusingly similar to the sowed seed. Cf. The Bible, New Testament, Matthew 13, 24f.

[5]In order to describe the success of the proclamation the New Testament uses the image of fishing (cf. John 21, or Luke 5,10). The point: it is always necessary to cast your nets without knowing whether there are any fish to be caught. Professional behavior and passion for the possible form a tandem.

language in this text is unfamiliar. It is a lyrical text, just over 2000 years old. It constitutes a brief summary of Christianity (Sellmann, 2021).

> In your relationships with one another, have the same mindset as Christ Jesus: who, being in very nature God, did not consider equality with God something to be used to his own advantage; rather, he made himself nothing by taking the very nature of a servant, being made in human likeness. He humbled himself by becoming obedient to death—even death on a cross! Therefore God exalted him to the highest place. (Philippians 2, 6–11)

In this description of success, the attributes and images of power change considerably. People knew what a King needed to be like. The Ruler described here, however, is not distinguished by ascension, power, wealth, rejoicing, respect, and all the other usual trappings of success. Quite the contrary: the familiar is turned upside down. The Universal Ruler is described as a slave. There is talk not of ascent but descent. Descent from Heaven. God becomes human. The hero is truly powerful or efficacious because he humbles himself. He humbles himself in the sense of forgoing status, making himself vulnerable and open to attack.

This is a description of someone who surrenders himself fully and entirely to reality. He does not run away and yet he fails. It could not be prevented despite his ever so sophisticated strategy and even with divine assistance.

The hero fails spectacularly because of the guarantees of success of his time. Essentially: it is not despite failure that he wins but he wins by failing. Because he humbles himself he becomes great. This is a paradox intervention and it could not be greater today.

Where could the points of navigation for the VUCA world and for travelling organizations be in this example?

What is described above shows a fundamental difference in the understanding of success and effect. A person wins by taking a risk. We are not suggesting a trite transfer, especially since we are not martyrs. But this inverted movement of ascent and descent deserves consideration. In situations that are characterized by other contradictions, this could suggest changing one's perspective and strengthening one's ability to manage ambiguity in a servant leadership (Hunter, 2019). Navigating in uncertain times will not be possible without this. And when everything around us changes, this is an interesting guiding principle for navigating the self in taking responsibility for oneself, for organizations and for the world. It can help you to keep going even if you feel like running away (Sellmann, 2021). This inverted image of success might offer a criterion that is critical for successful navigation. Christians are helped by the assurance of God. Succumbing entirely to circumstances helps one to experience inner freedom. A dynamic develops that has confused, fascinated, transformed, failed, and won for 2000 years. It is the question of how we relate to what we do, even, and indeed especially, when it is about success show greatness through humility (Frank, 2020).

## 4 Outlook

What conclusion can we draw from these observations of internal and external consulting and leadership perspectives? Our conclusion encompasses a double train of thought. The first is aimed at the resources of the Church. The second makes clear how the organization Church needs to become more professional. Taken together these trains of thought help to increase the effectiveness of navigating in uncertain times.

**Firstly:** In the history of the oldest organization in the world, there is unexpected actuality for the current challenges involved in navigating the VUCA world. A timely look into the narrative opens perspectives for relating to the challenges of unpredictability, complexity, and insecurity. Here we can find clues that help us to maintain our inner and outercourse when navigating. History can serve as a source for the future because it marks key points of existential experiences of insecurity. It focuses our attention on the possible, on what cannot be recognized, calculated, and forecasted. Christianity lives from the dimension of the unavailable. This experience, namely that the unavailable determines time and space and even ourselves, is part of the VUCA world. It is not about arbitrariness but about the realization that the conventional logics of navigation is inadequate for meeting the requirements of current challenges. We are experiencing the fact that, despite all the professionalism in the world when it comes to navigating, there are some fundamentals that we simply cannot determine; something different is needed. This applies, for example, to the question of how success and effect can be measured when linearity and causation are replaced by unpredictability and fragility. The Biblical servant leadership model provides us with an incentive to rethink the familiar movement of ascent and descent. The Biblical logic of success and the Biblical way of dealing with the unpredictable are worth testing in the VUCA world.

**The second thread:** Looking at the development of the Church as an organization, let us summarize: The Church's place as an institution is at the center of the world. Therefore, it goes without saying that its business model, its core brand, its products, its language have to be measured by the standards of this world. Consequently, it needs to professionalize its organizational processes, its leadership models, its presence. Navigating the Church requires organizational development for the sake of its profile and its own core brand. To enable the Church to become more professional as an organization more discourse with other societal stakeholders and professions is needed. The expertise of consulting is needed, exchange of know-how and ideas with representatives of other organizations that have competence in marketing, organizational development, management, and communication. This would enable the Church to make its dysfunctional structures functional and, as a result, increase its visibility and effectiveness. The Church does not need to become effective for its own sake since the Church's reason for existing does not lie in its own survival; its reason for existing lies outside itself: it lies in its purpose to give the world and the people living in it their own Biblical narrative and to give them God.

This sounds like an exchange or true intercultural, interprofessional, and multinational networking competences: it is about mutual support in each other's own profile, about mastering challenges better together, and increasing each other's effectiveness for society. This awareness is confirmed in the exchange that we have conducted from our perspectives, internal and external, consulting, and leadership. On reflection, it is a classic win–win situation. It is not magic or esoterics or even mere philosophy: it lives solely from the premise that both types of organization—Church and Business—meet one another in the VUCA world, listen to one another, are honest with one another and, in shared dialog, back what is possible. This is how one could begin to tackle the challenge of navigating a rock. The organizational form of the Church is not rock solid; it is solid in the sense of fortifying. What is constant is the focus on what is possible, especially in uncertain times such as those we are living in.

## References


Bauer, T. (2018). *Die Vereindeutigung der Welt. Über den Verlust an Mehrdeutigkeit und Vielfalt.* Reclam.

Beuys, J. (2021, 09). . . . aus der Zukunft heraus bewegt sich was. Retrieved January 09, 2021, from https://www.moenchehaus.de/event/alexander-iskin-die-ursache-liegt-in-der-zukunft

Dessoy, V., Hahmann, U., & Lames, G. (2021). *Macht und Kirche*. Echter.

Dessoy, V., & Lames, G. (Eds.). (2008). *Denn sicher gib es eine Zukunft—Strategische Perspektiven kirchlicher Organisationsentwicklung*. Paulinus.

Deutsche Bischofskonferenz (DBK). (2021). *Katholische Kirche in Deutschland Zahlen und Fakten 2020/2021*. Retrieved January 10, 2021, from https://www.dbk.de/fileadmin/redaktion/Zahlen%20und%20Fakten/Kirchliche%20Statistik/Allgemein_-_Zahlen_und_Fakten/AH-325_DBK_BRO_ZuF_2020-2021_Ansicht.pdf

Frank, F. (2020). *Mit Demut zum Erfolg: Leadership im 21. Jahrhundert*. SpringerGabler.

Frey, C., & Töpfer, G. L. (2021). *Ambidextrie in Organisationen. Das Praxishandbuch für eine beidhändige Zukunft*. Schäffer-Poeschel.

Glasl, F., & Lievegoed, B. (2004). *Dynamische Unternehmensentwicklung* (3rd Auflage ed.). Haupt.

Haas, O., & Shedletzky, S. (2021). Die Führungskraft sein, die man selbst gerne hätte. In M. Eppler, O. Haas, et al. (Eds.), *Wandelmut, Couragiertes Handeln in change—Zeitschrift für Organisationsentwicklung*. Handelsblatt.

Höfler, M., Bodingbauer, D., Dolleschall, H., Schwarenthorer, F., et al. (2018). *Adventure change management*. Frankfurter Allgemeine Buch.

Hunter, K. (2019). *Servant leadership in business*. Independently Published.

Kaduk, S. (2020). *Musterbrecher. Die Kunst das Spiel zu drehen*. Murmann.

Katholische Bibelanstalt. (2016). *Die Bibel*. Einheitsübersetzung, kommentierte Studienausgabe. Katholisches Bibelwerk.

Loffeld, J. (2020). *Der nicht notwendige Gott. Die Erlösungsdimension als Krise und Kairos des Christentums inmitten seines säkularen Relevanzverlustes*. Echter.

Marx, R. K. (2021, 06, 2021, 09). *Die Kirche ist am toten Punkt*. Retrieved January 09, 2021, from https://www.katholisch.de/artikel/30135-kirche-am-toten-punkt-ein-bild-mit-risikopotential

Rosa, H. (2019). *Unverfügbarkeit*. Residenz.

Sebastian, M. (2021, 11). BANI statt VUCA—Die neue Welt. *Resilienz-Akademie*. Retrieved January 11, 2021, from https://www.resilienz-akademie.com/bani-statt-vuca-die-neue-welt/

Sellmann, M. (2021). *Was fehlt, wenn Christen fehlen, eine Kurzformel des Glaubens*. Echter.
Theobald, M. (2018). *Christentum als Stil. Für ein zeitgemäßes Glaubensverständnis in Europa*. Herder.
Wollmann, P., Kühn, F., & Kempf, M. (Eds.). (2020). *Three pillars of organization and leadership in disruptive times—Navigating your company successfully through the 21st century business world*. SpringerNature.
Wollmann, P., Kühn, F., Kempf, M., & Püringer, R. (Eds.). (2021). *Organization and leadership in disruptive times—Design and implementation of the 3-P-model*. SpringerNature.

**Michael Kempf** has been an experienced Management Consultant for over 20 years. The driving force of his professional activities is his strong ambition to design processes and organizations in a sustainable manner. He relishes identifying key challenges, diagnosing complex relationships and assisting in shaping the future. Gaining experience and learning something new are indispensable parts of his life, which is why he likes to seize new opportunities. He began his career as a carpenter before studying social work, education, and business administration. His career has spanned various jobs in social work, 10 years as a manager (HR and logistics) in industrial and retail companies and, since 1998, in advising people, leadership teams as well as working teams and organizations that are all very different. Michael has co-authored numerous publications in the field of leadership and organizational development.

**Juliane Schlaud-Wolf** is a theologian and a passionate organizational developer. She believes in the possibility and opportunity of change and accompanies change processes as a consultant and coach. As a leader, she dares to do new things, and since 2019 she has been leading the department of Church Development and Innovation in the Diocese of Limburg as part of a dual leadership team.

Her work is designed from a coaching approach, and her actions are characterized by clarity, future orientation, and dynamism. For her, organizational development is always also the development of the organizational culture. She has studied theology and philosophy, worked for many years as a freelance writer for a radio station, and was active as a teacher as well as in teacher training. In complex situations, she is able to keep her sense of humor and to get to the heart of things.

# "No Contact without Resistance": Why Cultural Policy Has Such a Hard Time with Navigation

Dieter Haselbach and Frank Kühn

**Abstract**

The funded cultural sector, when viewed as a whole, is an extreme form of hybrid and asymmetric operation, with many decentralized decision-making lines, interests, silos and blockades. We want to demonstrate this using the example of the German cultural sector. And we want to show where hardenings and drift may arise in such a business, which cause an overarching purpose to be lost and which make even a departure, let alone travelling, very difficult. Our aim is not to write another technical article on culture. Rather, it is about a concise, stark example of conflicting organizations. What the example of culture can teach us about the problems of managing complex operations, and how the Three-Pillar Model can help us to understand and navigate operations even under demanding conditions so that Travelling becomes possible and effective, should be transferable to other organizations—or so we hope.

**Application of the Three-Pillar Model**

The reflection on the possibilities of navigating the funded cultural sector in this chapter follows the Three-Pillars Model (Wollmann et al., 2020, 2021):

1. Sustainable Purpose—The raison d'être of an organization, bringing new orientation and certainty to the people for their joint endeavor and success.

(continued)

D. Haselbach
Berlin, Germany
e-mail: haselbach@kulturforschung.de

F. Kühn (✉)
Dortmund, Germany
e-mail: fk@kuehn-cp.com

 
M. Kempf, F. Kühn (eds.), *Navigating a Travelling Organization*, Future of Business and Finance, https://doi.org/10.1007/978-3-030-95326-3_13

2. Travelling Organization—The mindset of an organization in a permanent state of flux, interacting with the markets' and customers' journey, with rapid adaptivity.
3. Connected Resources—Interconnecting all needed resources inside and outside the silos, creating consistency between goals and concepts, strategies and processes, competencies, and roles.

The model clearly shows the challenges of navigation. The diversity and conflicts in the cultural sector and its funding relate to all three aspects: Purpose, Journey, and Connectivity are at all times contested between actors. Interfering, as we are attempting to do here, however, is resisted (Haselbach et al., 2012). Only cultural criticism in the broadsheet newspapers as part of the cultural system is permissible, but this avoids the analysis of the organization and its structures.

## 1 Culture and Cultural Policy

Let us start with some terminology: What is culture, what is cultural policy? We would like to distinguish three levels of meaning.

**Culture I**: The term "cultura" comes from Latin and refers to everything that constitutes agriculture in the broader sense, that is, soil preparation, cultivation, and refinement. Culture represents the work that creates food. This term refers to a contrast between culture and nature, to a culture that works with nature. In this perspective, all intentional and planned human action is culture. With such a concept, nothing can be grasped or distinguished; everything human is meant by this distinction. At the same time, and in an implicit conceptualization, "nature" is conceived as an external and constant background for human action. It should be noted, however, that "nature" is not unchanging, that culture remains bound to nature, just as humans exist as natural beings in dependence on nature, but that, at the same time, human action, i.e., "culture," is increasingly becoming a factor that destroys the constancy, the friendliness of "nature" toward us humans. Climate change may suffice as a keyword here (cf. Latour, 2017). This term is not suitable for understanding cultural policy, the funded cultural sector, as a hybrid enterprise.

**Culture II**: More specific, and often used, is another term: Cultures. This is about differences. How do we do it (our culture), how do others do it (their culture). We eat with a knife and fork, Ethiopians with their hands, Chinese with chopsticks. French people give two kisses on the cheeks as a greeting, Swiss women three, at least when there is no threat of infection, Germans do not usually give any, unless they are acting in a worldly fashion. It is all about symbolic forms and habitual practices. At first glance, this seems simple and looks quite harmless. But the matter of "the cultures" is not without pitfalls. Central to this concept of culture is the distinction between what is one's own and what is foreign. This brings the idea of a "cultural identity" into play. Identities, however, are always concerned with demarcation: "us and them." Identity seems most important to us, but it is where we are most distant from ourselves. For how can we actually know our own as our own without being familiar with the other, the foreign? It is only through knowledge of the other that one becomes one's own. Cultural identity, which is closest to me, is at the same time determined by the foreign. It is only the difference that makes identity. The fact that such a dialectical game can play a major role in organizations does not need to be further explained here. Wars have been, and are being, fought over cultures. Cultures want to be silos, but they cannot be. Whoever talks about culture must always reckon with the fact that people are longing for an identity. Here, the concept of culture has its role. This has to be taken into account in navigation, and this might be best achieved today where the intercultural is en vogue, and not the idea that every culture has its distinct identity, and perceives this identity from distancing.

**Culture III**: When it comes to art and culture as a field, to the culture industry, the conceptual situation is simpler. According to this definition, culture is made up of literature, music, visual arts, performing arts, film, etc., i.e., the various cultural sectors. If one takes the cultural sectors as departments of a decentralized enterprise that produces culture, then this hybrid enterprise is well described by Culture III. Cultural policy provides the producing departments with tasks and with money to fulfil these tasks. The public buys the products that are conceived, developed, and produced in the enterprise, sometimes even paying some of the production costs. At least, that is, how it is supposed to be. It is interesting that in Culture III an interesting game about meanings is played that relates to Cultures I and II. The Sustainable Purpose of the departments and the connectivity in the cultural sector are marked by such a game. Where concepts, plans, and products of Culture III are concerned, it is not uncommon to claim that they at least encompass the meaning of Culture II. To make it illustrative: A play or a performance by a dance company is then declared to be the source of identity or of an engagement with identities. Or a night at the theater is even that which sets us apart from natural beings, animals, for example, which even connects to Culture I. A rather arbitrary argument. But this is immediately followed by the assertion that precisely this night at the theater is "indispensable" for being like this or even for being human as a whole. To be indispensable, however, in the culture industry is what we learned to recognize during the COVID-19 pandemic as "system-relevant": A function without which the system itself falters. Where it succeeds, the rhetorical recourse to "Culture II" and "Culture I" thus immunizes products of Culture III against any change. For it is then about identities or even the core of the human. And not just about an evening watching dance theater.

## 2 Cultural Products and Their Funding

In Culture III, cultural products offered in the context of cultural funding are to be distinguished from those that appear on the market without having received such funding. It may not always be clear to buyers which product they are dealing with. Take cinema. There are commercial cinemas, these cinemas offer their products (the screening) at their own risk: They live from selling popcorn, drinks, and tickets. But there are also municipal cinemas, that is, cinemas that receive cultural funding for running high quality, but not profitable, programs. It becomes even more complex when you look at the production of films, just to stay in the genre. Hollywood, one hears, produces commercially. European films often have a production budget that includes public money or that of public broadcasting. A subsidized film can be shown in a commercial cinema or in a subsidized cinema; via lower distribution costs, the commercial operator may have his share of the public subsidy. The customers are happy to see what they want to see. When they go to the cinema, they do not need to know whether money from cultural funding has flowed in or not: They buy their ticket without any ulterior motive of funding, costs, and public shares. It makes a difference for the operation of the cinemas: They all have to schedule their screenings so that the costs are covered in the end. But funded cinemas have some leeway. They can take higher risks; costs of showing films that are only partially covered are complemented by funding. Or they can sell tickets more cheaply.

In this way or in a similar way, offers of all cultural genres can be differentiated. Where they are funded, they are part of the public operation of cultural funding. Where they are not, the cultural funding agency can offer some products at a reduced price or with a more opulent equipment. Some products, however, are almost only available in publicly funded operations: An opera performance, for example, involves such high costs that admission fees can only cover a fraction of them. Depending on the theater, cultural funding covers 75 to 90 percent of the costs. Without such funding, an opera ticket for a medium-quality seat would have to cost between 320 and 800 euros instead of 80 in order to keep the operagoing—but at these prices, sales would probably drop dramatically, the production as a whole would become problematic. Thus, one could say that opera-goers are "treated" by the public purse.

## 3 Who Controls?

This leads to the question of what part of cultural events receives funding and what does not. In other words: What is being funded? And more importantly: Why is funding provided, what are the decision-making criteria and who decides? But also: Who has the professional competence, who has the authority, who takes responsibility for deciding which parts of the production in the sector enjoy funding and which do not? Every decision is part of navigating the web of the cultural sector and its conflictual journey on contentious terrain.

At the same time, this raises questions for the funding recipients: How autonomous are the grantees, the "departments" of the cultural enterprise on their respective journeys? How much room for maneuver do they have, how far can they make, or at least influence, the decision on whether and how they are funded? What can they do if they are not satisfied with funding decisions? And we also have to look beyond that: What actually happens to those who are not funded? Many questions—they correspond to a rather complex network of actors, decision makers, beneficiaries in the hybrid cultural business. There are also customers; but cultural funding is not really geared toward the customer, despite all the rhetoric. It becomes clear that navigation has to ask for connectivity between competences, interests, and decisions, between experts, influencers, and decision makers if it wants to deal responsibly with products and resources. This is a dynamic undertaking because, as previously mentioned, all stakeholders are on their own journeys, and even asymmetrical organizational set-ups, of their own. Such a hybridity risks fractal governance if it is not united by a common, overarching purpose, even if that purpose has its own unique journey: Is it about pleasurable experiences, support of the respective political system, perpetuation of a social identity, reputation of the community, or even bridges between nature and social structure?

When we speak of "organization" in the following, we have to make a distinction: On the one hand, there is the "Travelling Organization" of the whole; by this, we mean the development of the totality of the changeable interactions between cultural policy, structural implications, and cultural creation ("Cultural Doing"). In various places, we also refer to this as the ecosystem of culture. And on the other hand, there is the structural face of the cultural enterprise with its institutions, departments, and projects, which is geared toward the requirements of funding, at least in its structural image on paper. This distinction is fundamental. We are concerned with steering ***of*** and steering ***in*** the ecosystem of culture, we are concerned with the purpose of this system and with the possibilities of the ecosystem to set out on its journey. Such a perspective must keep the institutions of the cultural system in mind, but also bear in mind that these institutions are part of the ecosystem and are not to be perceived with their inherent (and often selfish) will.

In Germany, culture is federally structured. Let us start with the top of the organization. Cultural sovereignty lies with the 16 federal states (*Länder*). Along with school education, cultural policy is one of only two policy-making fields in which the *Länder* are autonomous and do not act largely on behalf of the federal government. However, a considerable part of the funds allocated to cultural policy (expenditure for their own institutions, subsidies to other organizations) are not disbursed directly by the *Länder*, but by municipalities and municipal associations. In this case, the decision-making authority on the use of funds lies with the municipalities, within the framework of the respective municipal law. Municipalities often work with nongovernmental organizations to achieve their goals. *Länder* have their own projects; here, in contrast to the municipalities, their own institutions are more important in the budgets than cooperation with nongovernmental organizations. The federal government plays a legally subordinate, but economically increasingly important, role in cultural funding. This is due to the fact that, on the one hand, the federal government has a very limited legal mandate in cultural policy, but on the other hand, within the framework of its more flexible budget management, it has deeper pockets and can mobilize a lot of money to support funding activities. This greater flexibility was particularly evident during the Coronavirus pandemic: The federal government was able to mobilize billions for cultural policy with several programs, which were intended to partially compensate for the losses caused by the closure of cultural institutions or to initiate new cultural impulses.

The navigation of the cultural ecosystem is based on decentralized management; the system of cultural funding is the result of a multitude of funding decisions in municipalities and districts, *Länder* and the federal government, and this is not without competition between the different levels. But there are also many interconnections. They range from agreements between municipalities, to municipal alliances, to support for municipal activities by the *Länder*, to joint institutions between the *Länder* and the federal government. At all levels, decisions on funding are made in parliaments within the framework of budgetary sovereignty. These decisions are prepared and supported by the respective cultural administrations (or ministries). The implementation of the agreed measures, or more precisely and in most cases: the public supervision of the implementation at funded organizations in the sense of structures, institutions, units, projects lies with the same administrations. There is no overarching common understanding among the many decision makers and administrators about goals, or in the language of "Three Pillars" the "Purpose" of funding, i.e., the meaning of the operation. And yet we have before us a Travelling Organization of extreme exemplariness, if "organization" according to Luhmann (1995) consists of decisions.

How does funding flow? A distinction must be made between institutional and project-based funding. Institutionally funded cultural producers can count on receiving public money over a longer period of time. This includes institutions that are sponsored by the respective local authorities (public theaters, museums, public libraries, etc.). Project funding is paid out for a specific program, with an end that is defined at the start. In each case, cultural producers must apply for this funding with a project. Such projects can also be awarded to institutionally funded persons. Here, too, there are intermediate forms: Project funding that is reliably handed out to the same producers every year, project funding that is publicly financed but handed out by associations of producers, so that reliability is created here as well.

What exactly is funded? Funding can be directed toward different goals. Cultural production or quality can be promoted. Money is then available to produce more elaborate products (a lavish production in the theater, an opulent exhibition, a large production budget for a film) without this having to be reflected in ticket prices. Distribution can be promoted: In the theater sector, guest theaters are publicly funded, there are municipal cinemas, a website is maintained without the costs being passed on in full. Finally, sales can be promoted (reduced ticket prices, additional services such as the admission ticket including the use of local public transport, but also the improvement of customer communication, etc.). Of course, the economic effects of such funding flow into each other for the cultural producers who receive funding. A sideways look at how the cost and revenue structures of nonsubsidized producers differ from those of subsidized producers is revealing, but the topic cannot be pursued further here.

A look at the second level, the recipients of funding and producers of cultural offerings, again shows a rather colorful picture. At one end of the spectrum, there are the institutions that can count quite securely on a permanent flow of funding and can plan their offerings accordingly for the long term. Against the backdrop of such security, audience appeal is less important. At the other end are artistic entrepreneurs who need funding projects to run their businesses. Such entrepreneurs are often under constant pressure to innovate in order to be successful with funding applications. But audience appeal and the resulting turnover can also play a major role in the economic management of these companies. In between, there are endless forms of participation in funding. But it is inherent in all funded cultures that it must also orient its actions toward obtaining and maintaining sources of funding. The greater the dependence on funding, the more important it is to adhere to the rules of the funding body; the audience, on the other hand, becomes secondary.

Something has already been saying about the audience. One can describe funding as a measure that makes it possible or easier for audiences to experience culture. But it can also be understood as a measure that immunizes artistic production against the influence of audience appeal; this is where funding relieves cultural producers of the pressure to sell their products. A not uncommon pattern of argumentation here is: Artistic quality is proven precisely by the fact that the audience is not easily attracted by the product; quality is seen here in the inaccessibility, in the rejection of the artistic taste of the many. In this narrative, pleasing the audience becomes a sign of a lack of artistic distinction. And the narrative has a very practical effect on cultural policy: It is not uncommon for institutionally funded cultural institutions to compensate for declining audience appeal by increasing their funding.

What criteria are used to decide on funding? There is a broad cultural policy discussion, also about money. But there is no consensus on what purpose and what social effects funding should have. The only thing that is clear is that the business should be preserved. For many decades, the guideline was "Culture for All" and the goal was to make cultural products available to the entire population, locally and at a reasonable price. This has been achieved: In Germany, access to cultural offerings is cheap and easy. However, popularity with the public has not increased because of this: Not everyone wanted the "culture" offered to everyone. There is no consensus, usually not even a serious discussion, on what effects should be achieved with cultural offerings or with the desired effect of many people demanding cultural products. Rather, each institution and each funding recipient fights for its own cause. What does it mean for navigation that there is a refusal to find a common basis for funding decisions?

## 4 Navigation of the Cultural Sector

Navigation depends on what is the understanding of the Purpose of a Travelling Organization, and related to that, what is meant by success. The smooth distribution of funds? Self-fulfillment? The enjoyment of the customers? In the cultural sector, the Purpose itself becomes the object of the journey. Navigation begins where the Purpose is discussed. There is a widespread conviction at the level of those being supported that, in the cultural sector, it is they who own the right to determine their own purpose.

This brings to mind a principle of so-called "democratic photography" (Sussman & Weski, 2008): every object has a right to be included. The problem of democratic photography is obvious. From the right to be recorded, it does not yet follow that all such photographs exist. Today, this can apply to culture as a whole: Not every cultural production is supported. Much, most, is not funded. Everywhere in the cultural sector, however, the self-image prevails that funding decisions must not interfere with artistic content, that distance must be kept from those being funded. With this attitude, funding respects a fundamental (constitutional) principle, that of the freedom of art. To remain in the image of democratic photography: There is no picture of all objects, but the photographed objects are not retouched.

As it stands, we are dealing with a very specific organization. An idiosyncratic purpose produces an idiosyncratic organization. Organization is a distinction. Distinction is organization. More specifically, the individual institution must distinguish itself in order to construct a reason for funding. And the multiplicity of distinctions is a characteristic of the ecosystem of promoted culture. Each organization has to find its point of distinction, to secure its funds. The motivation for creating a cultural organization is twofold: It lies on the one hand in the coordination of people's (collaborative) work, and on the other hand in presenting itself as a case for public funding. The latter motivation is often the primary one. Organization creates tangibility, responsibility, accounting mechanisms that relate to the funding structures. The purposefulness of organization is redefined.

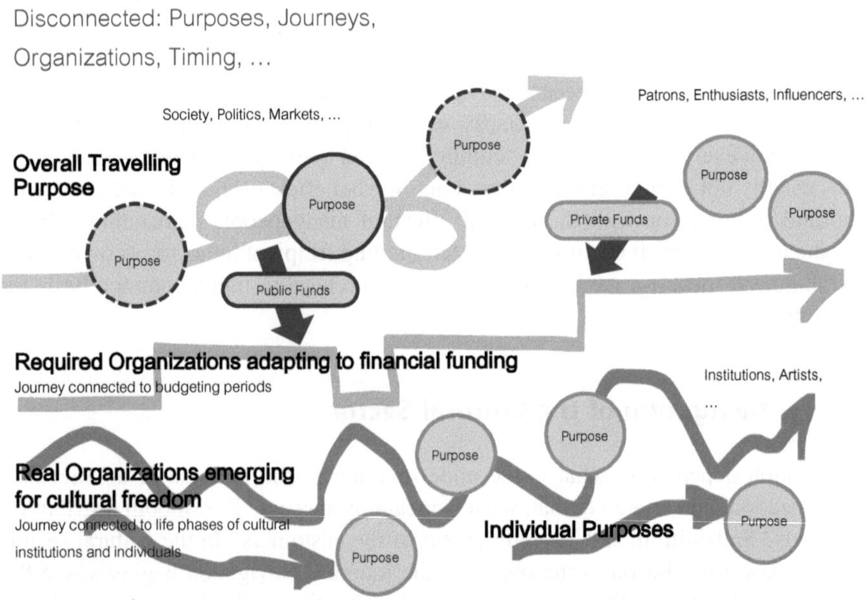


**Fig. 1** Governance of the cultural enterprise: a picture of fractures (Illustrated by the authors, used with permission, all rights reserved)

The ecosystem of culture has many fractures (Fig. 1). The connectivity between the evolving social purpose of culture and the journey of cultural workers is only provided by the budget distribution. In addition, each line is characterized once again by its own diversity of political decision-making processes, funding structures, and cultural operations.

Only those who control the cultural sector from the top, who are supposed to secure the necessary funding from public budgets, are not allowed to be explicit and to control the purpose. That would be a contradiction to "freedom" at all levels. The non-navigation, programmatically demanded by those funded, is called cultural policy. Cultural policy refers to the cultural landscape as a whole and is responsible for each individual grant but must not intervene or steer. Organization and control only arise on the second level, but there, too, with resistance, because every participant in the system also has a personal purpose. Otherwise, they would not be artists.

For the cultural sector, however, the principle of funding without control has far-reaching consequences. Noninterference affects more than artistic content. A change in the level of funding or the conditions of funding can be interpreted by those receiving funding as an attack on their artistic freedom. But when it comes to artistic freedom, it is precisely institutionally funded institutions that easily find support in the political public sphere to defend themselves against any change in their funding conditions. Where everything has to remain as it is, there is a strong tendency toward institutional rigidity. This is also because the financial resources in the cultural sector are limited. If new and different things come into play, they are considered suspicious by existing recipients of funding. Only when these new things are funded on top of the existing funds, such suspicion can be overcome. Conflicts can thus be avoided only when funds are increased and new initiatives are given additional money. New funding recipients will immediately play the same game for self-preservation and shield themselves against the next newcomers. Questions about the future viability of the current form of the cultural sector are suppressed. To ask such questions is not in the interests of those who are most articulate in cultural policy.

However, it is obvious that cultural funding as it is practiced now cannot be taken for granted. Tomorrow, in a more restrictive political system (and the then quickly redefined ecosystem of the cultural sector), things may be very different, and then navigation will also look very different. Without such drastic scenarios already looming, other shocks are also looming: Public money for culture will become scarcer when the consequences of the Coronavirus pandemic have to be dealt with in public budgets. Then the question will have to be answered more urgently as to what should be continued, what should be created, and what can be discontinued. Because taking a little bit away from everyone is a bad policy, it incapacitates many public cultural institutions. An opera house does not operate in the same intimate way as a *Kammerspiel* or chamber play. A museum can reduce its offering, but hardly reduce the costs of maintaining the collection. It is foreseeable that the debates on this will be public, intense, and very aggressive. But is the culture industry capable of change at all? Is there a common journey?

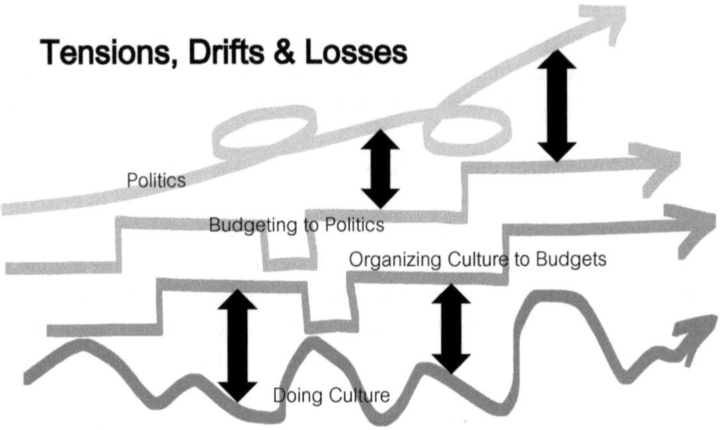


**Fig. 2** Navigating the travelling organization means working on productive tensions, critical drifts, and losses—which needs a readiness of mutual understanding and co-creating better solutions (Illustrated by the authors, used with permission, all rights reserved)

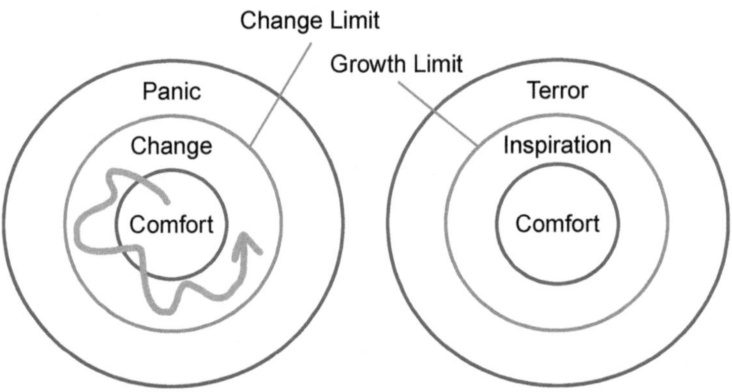


**Fig. 3** Two similar drawings about and around comfort zones, the left one known from Change Management, the right one from a discussion on New Work (Breidenbach & Rollow, 2019) (Illustrated by the authors, used with permission, all rights reserved)

There is agreement that the journey of the ecosystem of culture as a whole consists of many individual decision-making and creative lines and structures (Fig. 2). The Travelling Organization is navigated through a risky landscape with numerous cliffs between political lines, public demands for sensible use of funds, for example, and the demand for artistic freedom. It is a story of tensions, drifts, losses, and compromises.

Only the budgets and the cultural work are real; the organization in between is an agreed chimera. The actual form is an artificial interface between cultural policy and the art business. The latter have won their budget which is the maximum possible.

But have they really "won" or is it just a silent agreement in the comfort zone of conflict avoidance that makes real change so difficult? (Fig. 3).

## 5 VUCA and Culture

The cultural sector is also moving in its own VUCA world. Social developments and digital influences are radical change agents. Only a digitally shared work is a remarkable one, otherwise, it would not have been shared. Only WhatsApp turns the photographed dolphin into an event; without a smartphone, the experience on a stormy sea is only worth half. The opera audience is dying out (but there are about 90 subsidized opera houses in Germany). Classical concert audiences are also shrinking, but hardly the number of orchestras and concert events, at least when there is no Coronavirus pandemic - which is adding new remote art forms. Libraries and museums are not only being digitized, but are partly replaced, partly supplemented by Wikipedia and digitized literature. The concert business is shifting to a multitude of private events of diverse genres.

People deal with the uncertainties of the VUCA world in different ways; some limit their horizons to analogue and digital echo chambers, deepening gaps and their lack of understanding for others.

## 6 Is there a Purpose of the Cultural Enterprise? What Is to Be Controlled?

The way the cultural enterprise is now constituted, the purpose of the enterprise, and its very own structure is primarily defined by those who are supported. It is a multiplicity of purposes, and the funded bodies object to anyone other than themselves when it comes to determining the purpose: for that would violate artistic freedom. If this arrangement is right and sensible, then the question of the purpose of the cultural sector, of cultural funding, is simply indecent, indeed. It would contradict the rights of freedom, and thus a core of our understanding of humanity and society. The question of navigation, of the direction to be taken by the culture industry, would simply be offensive.

But there is a flaw in the argumentation presented by those who receive funding. Artistic freedom is, without doubt, the freedom to do or not do artistically what the artist wants. The funding recipients, however, reinterpret this freedom as the duty of the funding providers to promote their actions.

In this light, is the question really offensive? Against the self-image and practice of cultural funding, it remains to be said that funding is inevitably used to steer. It is not the practice of art that is regulated; that belongs to the realm of artistic freedom. But the funding bodies decide which projects they will fund and which they will not. This decision cannot be avoided, because in a world of limited resources, choices must be made. Not everything that wants to be art can be funded. Artistic freedom does not help with this choice. But where choices are made, particularly choices in how to spend public money, it is legitimate to expect reasons for these choices, namely transparency. If the recipients of funding demand that the purpose of the cultural funding must first come from them, then this must be rejected. The cultural sector is strongly shaped by public monies. The funding agencies have to give reasons for spending this money.

What are possible reasons for or against a funding decision? Every subsidy must have a purpose. The reason for funding is that objectives are pursued. The purpose of funding is fulfilled when goals are achieved. The reason for refusing funding is that there is no objective of the funding agency that the beneficiaries are striving for, or that the activity seeking funding does not appear to be suitable for fulfilling an objective. All objectives sought by public authorities are public objectives. The cultural sector has the obligation to achieve a social good.

Once objectives are set they become a yardstick for measuring operational success. Have the goals been achieved? Have the effects been achieved? Can the hoped-for effect be determined? Funding can only be justified on the basis of its effects.

The impact of cultural activities is the key. The impact must relate to society, to target groups, their condition, their perspectives. Possibilities change over time. Generational change, crises, changing values, political outrage, digitalization, all these factors influence which impact is needed. But is it possible to reach a consensus, and is it possible to have a constructive discourse about the sought-after impact? Or would even such discourse be suspicious?

Meaningful control is possible. Objectives can be defined in cultural policy, impact can be controlled. It is just that the second level, the funded institutions, have succeeded in undermining a public debate about this by making themselves the exclusive owner of all definitions of purpose and objectives. A first step for the funding agencies to reclaim control from the cultural institutions in the cultural sector would be to regain interpretive sovereignty. In order to do this, the funding agencies must put their own reasons for funding, goals and hopes for impact to the fore. They must make explicit choices and decisions. This does not mean intervening in artistic production but clarifying why one artistic production line is funded and another is not.

The control could follow a guiding principle of electrical engineering: There will be no contact without resistance. In other words, cultural institutions get the message: "Don't be safe." The discussion about cultural policy funding, which currently only takes place in the grantees' own echo chambers, must come back into political society. This is where "resistance" can manifest itself.

Such a consideration is neither anti-art nor anti-culture. The impression that art is a public event, an event staged by the state, may have been imposed by the many support and funding programs in the Coronavirus pandemic. But art is not dependent on funding. Artists are autonomous. In some disciplines, this is more true than in others, but cultural work (in the sense of Culture II and Culture III) happens predominantly beyond and independently of the funding establishment.

## 7 Where Should Navigation Be Directed?

It is difficult to impose steering on the ecosystem of culture described above, otherwise, it might already have happened. So far, steering has therefore been limited to the lowest common denominator, the allocation of funding. Public effectiveness was sidelined.

Effectiveness can be defined in two ways: the effectiveness of culture and the effectiveness of the organization of the cultural enterprise. Both must become the subject of navigation. It is not just a matter of adjusting the effectiveness here and now, but of designing the navigation for future development, i.e., for the Travelling Organization.

How can navigation be made better and more acceptable? What helps to understand the challenges of the Travelling Organization and to navigate effectively? Is it understanding how the different journeys of stakeholders between cultural policy and cultural work are organized and how they function, and how they can be better related to each other overall, i.e., more effective through more connectivity even under asymmetrical conditions and motivations? This could result in an abstract discussion about positions and structures.

Or is the better approach to first take a look at the essential differences, tensions, and drifts? Then navigation could first be related to critical "touchpoints" between travellers and their journeys.

For the navigation of the ecosystem culture as a Travelling Organization culture, this would mean, to stay with the image, to first renegotiate the concept of organization and the purpose of organization, to determine the essential differences, drifts, and touchpoints between the individual journeys (Figs. 1 and 2) and, based on this, to invite the stakeholders not only to discourse but also to co-create an overall picture and then to make decisions together. Decisions can also be made over time: We will try something for a year and then review the decision. But decisions must always be made, because it is the decisions that make a difference to the arbitrary (and potentially: eternal) discussion. Active participation in the process must be a prerequisite for receiving funding; refusal to engage in discourse, negotiation, and decision-making is not acceptable.

In many public, and even more so in commercial, enterprises, it has long been common practice that stakeholders not only participate in, but also contribute to, the organization as a matter of course. Change processes are no longer conceivable otherwise.

How can this be organized in the ecosystem of culture? Social change, political developments, and artistic perspectives can undergo rapid changes and upheavals; the navigation process must be geared to this. Therefore, there is no time, there are no resources, there is no patience for administrative overkill. For example, sociocratic approaches (Cumps, 2020) of overlapping expert and decision-making circles can help (Fig. 4). For selected touchpoints (stimulated, for example, by social turning points, cultural policy decision points, cultural events, funding conflicts), there can be respective reflection circles with relevant stakeholders who present their results and ideas in a cultural forum, in which decisions are made. This would be

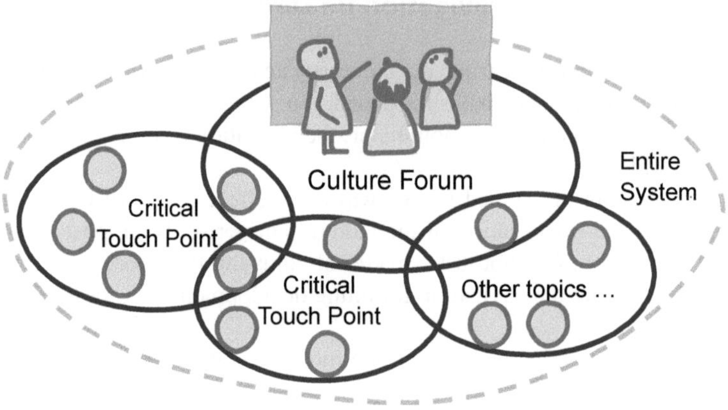


**Fig. 4** Organization based upon the concept of nested circles (Illustrated by the authors, used with permission, all rights reserved)

Connected Resources *par excellence*: responsibility for cultural policy and operations, decision-making authority, and competence in one space.

This process can be started immediately. In Germany, there is currently a wave of planning the cultural landscape, both in municipalities and in the *Länder*. At present, the planning processes are largely based on the premise described above: that cultural policy goals are only set at the second level. However, these planning processes could be used to hold discussions with all those involved about the further development of the whole system. The respective top, the respective cultural policy funder needs to claim the right to shape the planning, which is linked to the allocation of money. It is then not a matter of cultural-political donors intervening in artistic processes or controlling the programming of cultural institutions, but rather of deciding, together with civil society and the departments of the cultural enterprise, what effects the funded cultural enterprise should have and how the—always scarce—public funds can best be distributed for the benefit of such an effect. The sovereignty of interpretation currently claimed by the departments of the cultural sector would be relativized in such a cultural forum.

In addition to the discussion of content, the journey of the cultural ecosystem would then be reflected upon and further developed in the cultural forum. The constructive discussion of the players would, as already described, be a prerequisite for them to receive their funding: It is not only the work in the cultural ecosystem that counts, but also the collaboration on the overall system. This, however, takes those involved out of the comfort zone in which they had previously settled: Funding without a mandate will be a thing of the past. Politicians, fund administrators, cultural institutions, cultural practitioners, will all have to act in a significantly different way. For the cultural forum will certainly not act in the comfort zone; it will be the location where the further journey of a very heterogeneous group of travelers will be renegotiated again and again.

## 8 Takeaways/Essentials

The system of funded culture is here understood as a hybrid, and even asymmetrical, organization. It is obvious that the navigation of this system is different from the journey of other public or private sector enterprises. The intention of our contribution is twofold: first, to make readers from other fields understand that this extremely diverse operation may appear to exaggerate experiences from their own organization a little, but still make them say, "Wow, that's just like ours!" Second, to give hints as to what need for action exists for the cultural enterprise itself; at least that is how our planning for this essay began.

Helpful insights and lessons learned

- It is helpful to have a common image of the different journeys in the ecosystem. This image should be drawn and explained by the participants themselves. This is followed by an evaluation: What does the image mean? How can different journeys be described? What distinguishes our ways of looking at the world? Where do the differences, tensions, drifts come from?
- Purposes and interests are part and parcel of the ecosystem's journey. Travellers will have different views on sustainability and pacing. The discourse, the journey and the stopovers must adapt to this.
- Every organization is as it is because it has meaning or is the result of purposeful action by stakeholders. This is also true for the organization presented here with all its fractures and seemingly absurd features. The question then is: What is the problem for which this organization is a solution? This is the question every organization must ask itself—what is the point of us being set up like this? What are the reasons for it? And what are the costs that come with this solution?
- And most likely, the problem itself has travelled and needs a new organizational response rather than sticking with the old one. What about the journey of the problem? Does the organization simply serve to hand out budgets with as little conflict as possible? Or is it possible to organize cooperation and/or success at touchpoints? Only when an organization knows what its purpose is can it work effectively.
- What does navigation focus on? On the processes and issues of the stakeholders themselves (from policymakers to the public, clients, and institutions to performers) or on their interaction and discourse? If processes and issues are indeed subject to artistic freedom to the extent claimed, the quality of the engagement still remains an object of navigation. Feedback and exchange thus become the central instance of control. But even that can be understood as an imposition. Refusing exchange, however, would be a fundamental decision against the system from which it is financed. Exchange must be a prerequisite for funding, we owe that to a good development of our society. In totalitarian systems, this is exactly what does not work.

## References


Breidenbach, J., & Rollow, B. (2019). *New work needs inner work* (2nd ed.). Vahlen.

Cumps, J. (2020). *Sociocracy 3.0—The novel: Unleash the full potential of people and organizations*. Lannoo.

Haselbach, D., Klein, A., Knüsel, P., & Opitz, S. (2012). *Der Kulturinfarkt—Von Allem zu viel und überall das Gleiche*. Knaus.

Latour, B. (2017). *Facing Gaia—Eight lectures on the new climatic regime*. Polity.

Luhmann, N. (1995). *Social systems*. Stanford UP.

Sussman, E., & Weski, T. (2008). *William Eggleston—Democratic camera*. Whitney Museum of American Art Yale University Press.

Wollmann, P., Kühn, F., & Kempf, M. (Eds.). (2020). *Three pillars of organization and leadership in disruptive times—Navigating your company successfully through the 21st century business world*. SpringerNature.

Wollmann, P., Kühn, F., Kempf, M., & Püringer, R. (Eds.). (2021). *Organization and leadership in disruptive times—Design and implementation of the 3-P.-model*. SpringerNature.

**Dieter Haselbach** is a sociologist by training. Cultural advisor and researcher for more than 20 years. He taught sociology in universities in Canada, England, Austria, and Germany. Managing Partner of ICG Culturplan, then Managing Partner of ICG Integrated Consulting Group Germany, now Business Partner in ICG Public Management GmbH. Director of the Center for Cultural Research in Berlin. Develops business concepts, planning processes, and strategies for institutions and local authorities and supports change management in public administration. Certified Systemic Interactive Coach. Created a furore as co-author of the book "The Cultural Heart Attack (in German)".

**Frank Kühn** has been supporting companies and institutions in the areas of transformation, organization, and leadership for many years. His clients involve him as a development partner for both their urgent change projects and sustainable future concepts. Frank has a degree in engineering and a doctorate in work science. In leading positions in research and industry, he was responsible for labor management, production strategies, and project management. In the early 1990s, he joined HLP Hirzel Leder & Partners in Frankfurt and later co-founded the ICG Integrated Consulting Group Germany in Berlin and was a partner in the European group in Graz. Today, he is an independent consultant, business partner of ICG and is associated with other project partners and think tanks. He brings his experience to the development of methodologies such as the Three-Pillar Model and has published numerous articles in management journals and books.

# Gathering Points Creating Momentum—Navigating the Journey of a Value-Driven Company

Markus Winnen and Frank Kühn

**Abstract**

The chapter is based upon the experiences in a non-listed, value-driven company with an established customer base, product range, and process landscape. The company is a market leader in its industry in Europe and is internationally successful.

At the same time, it has to deal with new market opportunities, digital transformation, and organizational change at a faster pace than ever before. One of its strategic projects, described here, has been a pilot for the transnational introduction of a new matrix structure and level of collaboration across the entire group.

Beyond the usual change or project management routines, the mode of travel and navigation developed in this pilot initiative relied on the momentum that allowed people to experience the journey together and encouraged them in breaking habits and changing organizational patterns. In this way, the journey proved to be a prototype for future international collaboration not only in, but also on, the organization.

Awareness of the diversity of cultures around the table, types of organization, and personal interests involved was crucial. There was always the space to value and listen to people, to encourage them for the uncertain journey, to bring them into dialog on an equal footing, to ensure reliable communication, and to give them social safety in the process.

M. Winnen
Wuppertal, Germany
e-mail: m.winnen@ciret.eu

F. Kühn (✉)
Dortmund, Germany
e-mail: frank@kuehn-cp.com

 
M. Kempf, F. Kühn (eds.), *Navigating a Travelling Organization*, Future of Business and Finance, https://doi.org/10.1007/978-3-030-95326-3_14

Thus, the navigation always provided gathering points where the travellers came together to reassure and reorient themselves, to integrate their findings and results, and to set new milestones. It became clear to all involved that this communicative process was the key anchor for navigating such an uncertain journey—which was a valuable feeling and experience for their future travelling organization.

Each gathering point, each event, has a past, present, and future, for the group and each individual. The corresponding connections between these events supported the preservation of the momentum and the flow of navigation. This navigation happens whether we like it or not. An active, accepted, and effective influence on this navigation can only happen with an honest awareness of our individual possibilities—beyond any illusions of power and control.

This approach has been a great success and the company is already multiplying this success beyond the described pilot project and thus embarking on its further journey.

## 1 Opening Credits

The chapter is based upon the experiences in a non-listed, value-driven company with an established customer base, product range, and process landscape. At the same time, it has to deal with new market opportunities and digital transformation at a faster pace than ever before.

The management team of this company benefits from the advantage that they do not need external communication to regulators, shareholders, the stock exchange, etc. They can decide independently how to navigate their corporate journey, how to organize and steer product innovations or organizational changes in cross-functional, international projects and teams.

One of its strategic projects described here—in its basic considerations and with some key situations—has been a pilot for the transnational introduction of a new matrix structure and level of collaboration across the entire corporate group. The Three-Pillar (3-P) Model (Wollmann et al., 2020, 2021) was used to be continuously aware of the challenges of the journey and to navigate the project toward success.

**Journey to a New Collaboration and Organizational Quality**

For a transnational restructuring project, the transformation process is to be aligned with the current group-wide optimization of the matrix organization and the ongoing review of processes. Each unit involved (from purchasing to finance to sales) has—within the framework of the corporate strategy—its own navigation needs. Now—in the project—it has proven to be an advantage that the key people are involved who are also active in the organizational structure and in the processes, and who will also take on new roles after the

(continued)

restructuring. They form "the bridges," so to speak, in this corporate journey, ensuring connectivity in this hybrid system and ensuring that everything fits smoothly, and that priorities and timing are well aligned. The project management system recently introduced throughout the Group will be used to create a methodical framework and transparency for all those involved.

## 2 Reflecting the Travelling and Navigation Approach with the 3-P Model

We discussed the experiences from the company's management practice along the Three Pillars and then saw that important impulses and parameters for the corporate journey also lie in the interactions between the pillars. So, on the one hand, the key challenge is the navigation of the travelling organization; on the other, we have experienced that this is closely interlinked with the other pillars.

**Application of the Three-Pillar Model**
The Three Pillars are defined as (Wollmann et al., 2020, 2021):

1. Sustainable Purpose—the raison d'être of an organization, bringing new orientation and certainty to the people for their joint endeavor and success
2. Travelling Organization—the mindset of an organization in a permanent state of flux, interacting with the markets and customer journey, with rapid adaptivity
3. Connected Resources—Interconnecting all needed resources inside and outside the silos, creating consistency between goals and concepts, strategies and processes, competencies and roles

Some examples of the company addressed here working in the field of "painting tools":

- The sustainable purpose and the travelling organization following this purpose are determined in this case by the intention to give a more visible meaning to an industry and to offer its customers, as far as the end user, solutions and innovations to optimize their services and issues, which contributes to an increase in the value of the real estate as well as the quality of life of the people in their homes and workplaces. Sensitivity to this has grown in the pandemic. All activities in the various parts of the organization have to suit this purpose.
- The development of good, value-based cooperation between the organizational parts and between the people is a prerequisite for a common journey. This quality of cooperation affects everyone: the people in the company and the external

business partners on the shared journey. Resonance is directly picked up in the daily work, thanks to employee surveys and feedback from the company's business partners.

- A great opportunity for corporate development is seen in the diversity of the different generations, cultures, and development stages in the Group. In order to value these assets and resources in their diversity and, at the same time, unite their capabilities on the shared journey, a strong mission and collaboration culture is needed that is effective across the travelling organization.
- With the described, practiced, and appreciated diversity, a high connectivity to the markets and customers develops. This also extends to the historically evolved leadership styles in different cultures; however, the guidance for the navigation of the travelling organization is always formed by the Group-wide values of respectful and responsible human interaction.
- The development and transformation journey of the organization is characterized by the constructive handling of positive and negative developments. This includes an error culture in the sense of learning together instead of finger-pointing and formulated values focusing on curiosity, team spirit, passion, sustainability, reliability. Each member of the management team has taken on the sponsorship of a value; together, the management team stands for the community of values in the company.

Across the company, there must be a space to discuss which strategic success factors are subject to the navigation of the Travelling Organization. In the case described, the formulated values and principles, which the owner also clearly stands for, play an essential role.

## 3 The Navigation Companions: Complexity, Diversity, Dynamics

The corporate journey develops in the context of dynamic environmental, business, and organizational requirements. It can therefore only be navigated to a limited extent according to a consistent pattern. Standardized process models are suitable for repetitive tasks, other tasks require a creative group of experts, and others must be developed through experimentation—trial and error on unknown terrain (Fig. 1).

It is the deliberate handling of diversity, dynamics, and uncertainty in the travelling organization that makes it possible to select the right approach for balancing a navigation that is neither under- nor over-complex (Dörner, 1997). They will be reliable companions on our journey. In one case, navigation consists more of a comparatively short-term sequence of decisions about whether the direction is still correct: We navigate by sight or by ear. In the other case, navigation refers to the fulfillment of goals and consideration of success factors to enable goal achievement—as planned.

This awareness must be established before thinking about concrete navigation practices, processes, and systems. How much navigation is right at which point?

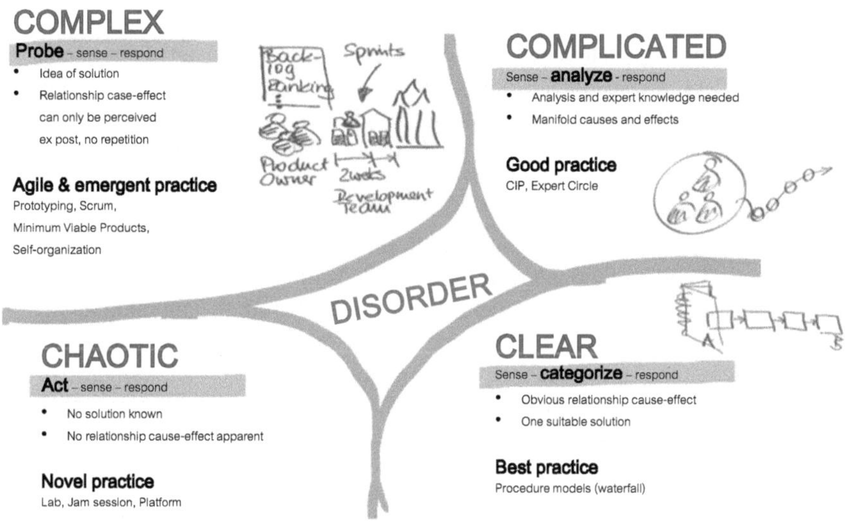


**Fig. 1** Different degrees of complexity of organizational units imply different control concepts (Snowdon & Boone, 2007). (Illustrated by the authors, used with permission. All rights reserved)

What needs to be aligned, connected, integrated, or even disconnected again for the journey? And also again and again: How much navigation and which steps are appropriate to tackle the next stage in the complexity?

> *No more things should be presumed to exist than are absolutely necessary. (John Punch, 1603–1661)*

The requirements are very different and volatile, e.g., when different parts of the business and organization develop with their different, very individual, complexities. What is needed here is an awareness that diversity can be a strength that needs space, where people are encouraged to communicate with each other on an equal footing. Such an encounter creates a unique, shared momentum.

In addition to external dynamics, diversity within the company must also be taken into account. What in the diversity can influence the journey and what can also emerge ***on*** the journey? What different timing may also be implicated?

**Diversity as Advantage**

It is about different

- Cultural, generational, and gender influences on education and training, which determine the "set-up" of the workforce

(continued)

- Professional characteristics in the branches, functions, and departments (controllers, salespeople, product developers, etc.), which determine individual priorities and technical language and often cause misunderstandings
- Interests, opinions, experiences, and knowledge, which organizational form fits best to which task: hierarchy, projects, start-ups, shared services, innovation teams, etc.
- Development stages across and within the organization (Fig. 2) as well as intentions and ambitions toward higher levels of development
- Understanding of roles in organizational charts, based on cultural diversity between nations (centralism and individualism vs. federalism and consensus orientation, open feedback vs. never lose face, etc.)
- Sympathies and linkages between different organizational parts, their protagonists and teams

Productively dealing with these diversities signals that they are valued. This means approaching individuals and encouraging them in diversity, protecting them from being stereotyped and, at the same time, creating common ground: everyone is confronted with a change, everyone is given the same space to express themselves personally on an equal footing, people are offered equal roles and competencies for this—in the organization, in the process, in the workshop.

This mindset leads to completely open questions that affect everyone, whether it is about factual aspects, personal concerns, or momentary feelings: "What's on your mind?" At the same time, it can be useful to prepare teasers and examples (e.g., for substantive solutions, organizational considerations for the common path) to inspire joint work, well-balanced between greenfield, collecting ideas and experiences, and clear specifications. It must be clear where there is openness to change and co-creation, but also where decisions have already been made that need to be implemented.

| 1 - "Tribal" | 2 - "Traditional" | 3 - "Modern" | 4 - "Post-Modern" | 5 - "Evolutionary" |
|---|---|---|---|---|
| Authoritarian leadership | Formal, scalable hierarchy | Innovation, growth, profit, competition | Stakeholder-oriented | Purpose-driven motivation |
| Short term focus | Command & control | Accountability and meritocracy | Culture of empowerment | Realizing the potential of people |
| Works in chaotic environments | Transactional leadership | Situational leadership | Transformational leadership | Self-management, distributed leadership |

**Fig. 2** Only one example of diversity: The stage of organization and leadership can be different between local business units. Some key aspects as described by Laloux (2014) and based on Beck and Cowan (2005). (Illustrated by the authors, used with permission. All rights reserved)

## 4 Importance of Gathering Points

How to provide the space for complexity, diversity, and dynamics—and conduct it toward a joint journey?

Every navigation must begin at a common point and, due to factual diversity, repeatedly needs common gathering points, at which one can reassure oneself together and reorient oneself. These gathering points need space, openness, ritual, and moderation in order to make the momentum tangible again and again.

In an uncertain journey, this communicative process is the only sure thing. That is why kick-off meetings and regular events are so important, providing much more than just information to participants: a shared momentum for the journey together.

*The shift must happen in the room. (Peter Hawkins)*

Each of these gathering points is, at the same time, an important stopping, navigating, and decision-making point that must have reference to the destination but also to the reality of the organization and its travellers:

- Navigation happens all the time, decisions are made everywhere and at all times, more or less consciously and transparently, at every level, in every communication.
- But conversely, navigation also needs interaction between people: without interaction, there can be no navigation.
- Navigation needs a direction: purpose, strategy, next milestone.
- And must also endure other paths: The first way does not always have to be the right one, experimentation is part of it.
- But navigation must also set limits: Deliberate one-way streets are a no-go.

Navigation always happens, whether we like it or not. If we want to participate actively, we have to be aware of the influences that we cannot control. There are many that we do not even know. We can only manage our own influence on this navigation system; we have to make ourselves aware of this again and again, because all too easily we fall into an illusion of power and control.

The following examples show this for different situations.

**Each Journey Has a Starting Point: First Gathering**

The kick-off meeting in a transnational change project that is to play a significant role in the transformation of the travelling organization. We anticipate a wide range of personal uncertainties and concerns on the part of the participants, and we all know that the success of change is significantly influenced by emotions. A good understanding must therefore begin at this gathering point, and the navigation process for the change project must also

(continued)

build on this. Although a process model for project management agreed company-wide should also be used, movement always starts between the people. And the first question is, therefore: "What goes through your mind when you hear about this project?" The question is open-ended, and we are aware that further project planning and navigation may have to adjust to unexpected answers, such as: "What about our jobs?" "Where can I be involved?" "Where are we going to get the capacity?" "I don't know anything, it makes me very uncomfortable, I don't think it's okay either" etc. All of these questions and answers influence the design and agreement of an effective change and navigation process. In addition, these questions, answers, and experiences from the change process also represent important learning points for the higher-level processes of corporate management, especially since the change project described here is also intended to be a pilot for further, similar, steps in the transformation of the travelling organization.

**Readjustment: Critical Gathering Point Creates New Momentum**

In the central corporate function team, a new management concept for the business unit in a neighboring country has been developed and thoroughly tested. Now the colleagues from the country have come to a workshop at headquarters. The presentation by the corporate function team starts, and it quickly becomes clear that this is not the way to go. German thoroughness meets with resistance from the guests, whose culture tends to be a very pragmatic one. In addition, they do not think that the concept sufficiently reflects the special features of their own, decentralized unit—and, even worse, they were not consulted. Before the situation escalates, we take a break. We rearrange the room, and after the break, there are blank pinboards in place of the screen. The message is clear: it is no longer about presentation; it is about co-creation. First, the design criteria ("What is important for the management concept?") and process criteria ("What is important for us to succeed in co-creating the concept?") are clarified. Then the joint work for the new concept starts. The mood quickly turns positive, and the concept is now developed together very quickly: What is needed to manage the foreign unit? How will the concept be interlinked with the Group's management concept? A technical outline is drawn up for the first question, and a communication process to approach the second question.

The navigation of the travelling organization is illustrated in Fig. 3 using three main processes as examples:

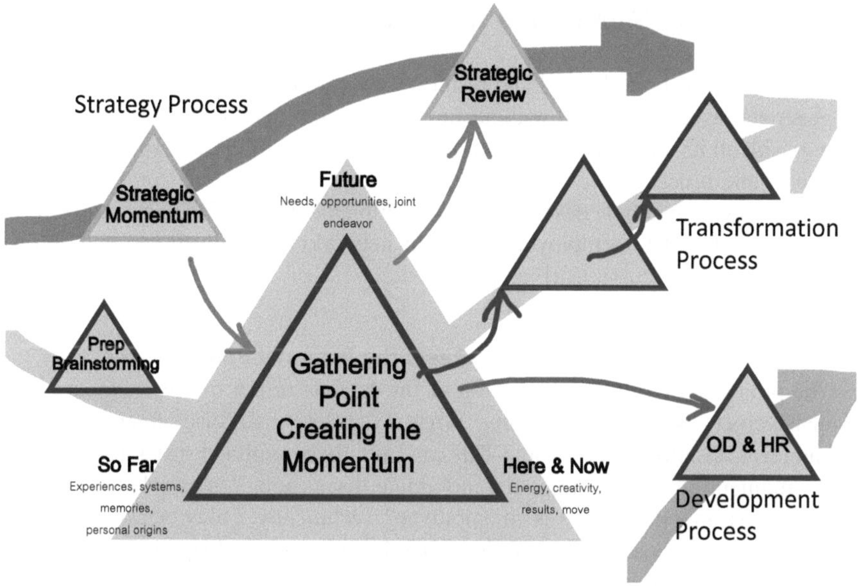


**Fig. 3** The interlinked processes in the travelling organizations. The transformation process in the middle showing the navigation via gathering points—starting with the kick-off event—that create momentum based upon connectivity between past, present, and future; cultures, people, and functions involved; progresses in the processes. (Illustrated by the authors, used with permission. All rights reserved)

- Strategy process
- Transformation process
- Development process

These processes live through their specific events, which repeatedly generate a momentum and impact that creates an energy field in the 3-P model:

- Sense of purpose
- Travelling mindset
- Connectivity of all resources

Each event builds a bridge between past (experiences so-far), future (hopes, fears), and presence (what am I ready for "here and now")—whether we like it or not. It is there. How we deal with it will impact the momentum we want to create together: "The shift must happen in the room." The deliberately open-ended question to participants: "What's on my mind?" can address experiences and ideas, concerns, and questions for all three perspectives.

## 5 Creating Momentum with the People

The momentum is both the fuel and result of navigation. And this momentum must be generated again and again without interruption and networked within the company—with all its different levels of knowledge, interests, skills, and speeds—across structures and processes.

The following example describes how the implementation of the new structure as well as the roles of the employees and their networking are illustrated and agreed upon in personal discussions (Fig. 4).

**Gathering Point: New Structure Meets the Personal Point of View**
The project now raises the question of the various responsibilities for future management within the company. What do professional, disciplinary, local, and legal responsibilities mean? This can initially be outlined structurally, but the momentum only arises in the individual discussion. What "role set" do I have to assume personally as an employee? Technically, I may be assigned to a shared service such as supply chain, but disciplinarily and legally I report to my country head. And in addition to these management relationships, new cooperative relationships also arise with internal colleagues and perhaps external partners. The realization of these new collaborative relationships represents a milestone in the corporate journey.

So how do we create the momentum that is the central inspiration of the navigation understanding described here? Ultimately, the key is face-to-face

(continued)

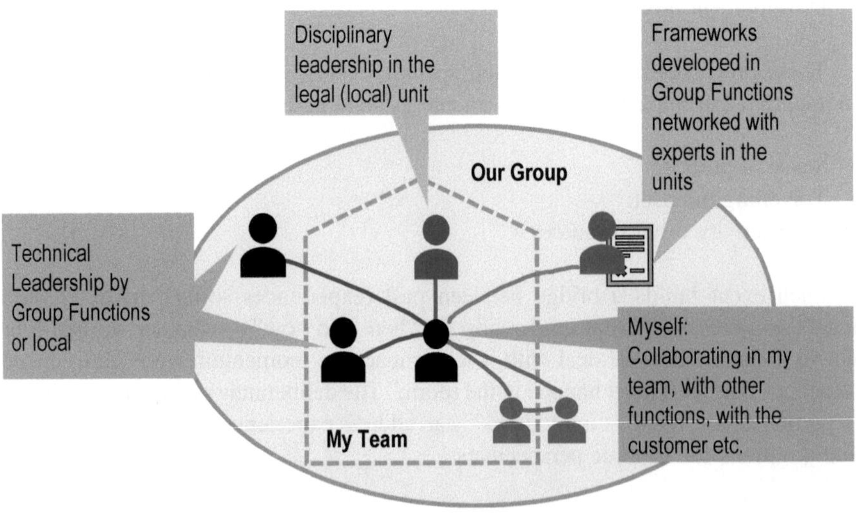


**Fig. 4** People-centered discussion and development of roles and collaborative relationships in the organization system. (Illustrated by the authors, used with permission. All rights reserved)

meetings in which the new work and relationship networks are outlined and discussed with each employee, conversations with colleagues are prepared, and the ways to new collaboration are paved. In the truest sense of the word, this is a fundamental navigation task.

People make relationships and create the movement. We put the people involved in the center of the presentation and the explanation of the new, with total appreciation for them and the joint journey (Bergmann, 2019). What are your questions, worries, and hopes? Where will you be "at home" in the future? What will your social environment be? Who will your colleagues and contacts be?

## 6 Essentials and Lessons Learned

What were helpful mindsets and starting points?

- As a key step in the travelling organization, all participants in the project experience the continuous and transparent networking of the strategy process, transformation process, and support processes through the presence and collaboration of the key players.
- Purpose, strategies, values, and principles, for which the owner also clearly stands, are explicitly referred to for the purposes of orientation and navigation—how do our ideas and approaches, measures, and interventions pay off?
- The conscious handling of diversity, dynamics, and uncertainty in the travelling organization makes it possible to vary the right methods for balancing a navigation that is neither under- nor over-complex.
- The key is always to co-create a shared momentum. The journey stands or falls on this. The foundation is a constructive culture of interaction that enables a highly flexible navigation of the travelling organization. It is always about experiencing good movement.
- The experience and awareness that diversity can be a strength that needs its space, where people are encouraged to communicate with each other on an equal footing, also creates shared momentum.
- The questions that arise from uncertainty and resistance can also be understood as contributing to a momentum that continues.
- Dynamic navigation needs to be agreed upon within the team: How do we embrace relevant changes, internal developments, and external influences (such as COVID)? How do we adjust to the fact that unpredictable things occur? How do we (repeatedly) make decisions about the appropriate course of action?
- Navigation always happens, whether we like it or not. Decisions are made everywhere and at all times, more or less consciously and transparently. If we want to participate actively, we have to be aware of influences we cannot control; many of them we do not even know about. We can only control our own influence

on this navigation system. We must therefore always beware of illusions of power and control.

- Every navigation must start at a common point and, because of the uncertainty of the journey, repeatedly needs common gathering points, where we can reassure and reorient ourselves. These gathering points need space, openness, ritual, and moderation to make the momentum tangible. In an uncertain journey, this communicative process is the only thing that is certain.
- Every gathering point, every event, consists of past, present, and future. Whether we like it or not. Connecting between events helps maintain momentum and flow of navigation.
- Teasers and examples (e.g., for content solutions, organizational considerations for the shared journey) can be prepared to inspire the work, well balanced between greenfield, building on experiences, and decisions already made and now to be implemented. It must be clear where there is openness and freedom to be creative, but also accept which things have already been decided.

People make the relationship and create the movement. They must therefore be at the center of the creation, presentation, and explanation of the new. That is where the momentum is created, not in abstract organizational concepts. What are your questions, worries, and hopes? Where will you be "at home" in the future? What will your social environment be? Who will your colleagues and contacts be?

## References

Beck, D. E., & Cowan, C. (2005). *Spiral dynamics: Mastering values, leadership and change*. Wiley-Blackwell.

Bergmann, F. (2019). *New work, new culture: Work we want and a culture that strengthens us*. John Hunt Publishing.

Dörner, D. (1997). *The logic of failure: Recognizing and avoiding error in complex situations* (4th ed.). Perseus.

Laloux, F. (2014). *Reinventing organizations*. Nelson Parker.

Snowdon, D. J., & Boone, M. E. (2007). *A leader's framework for decision making*. Harvard Business Review 11/2007.

Wollmann, P., Kühn, F., & Kempf, M. (Eds.). (2020). *Three pillars of organization and leadership in disruptive times—Navigating your company successfully through the 21st century business world*. Springer Nature.

Wollmann, P., Kühn, F., Kempf, M., & Püringer, R. (Eds.). (2021). *Organization and leadership in disruptive times—Design and implementation of the 3-P-model*. Springer Nature.

**Markus Winnen** born and raised in Tunisia, has always been committed to recognizing diversity as a strength. Overcoming intercultural obstacles has been a constant companion in his career. Since the beginning of his professional career, he has been responsible for exports in German medium-sized companies. In the early 2000s, Markus built up the international sales of market-leading manufacturing companies in Western Europe, America, Asia, and the Pacific. He marketed the largest global glass brands in the beverage industry in these regions. In the decorative glass industry, he established export as a key area in the company. In 2013, Markus joined the market leader for painting tools as Managing Director responsible for Sales and Marketing. From the beginning, he has accompanied and been responsible for various change and management processes in the group. Starting with the integration of a major competitor after an acquisition, to the establishment and development of a start-up abroad, to the networking of group-wide functions via a matrix organization. The success of this corporate journey has always been based on the conscious handling of diversity and agility in navigation.

**Frank Kühn** has been supporting companies and institutions in the areas of transformation, organization, and leadership for many years. His clients involve him as a development partner for both their urgent change projects and sustainable future concepts. Frank has a degree in engineering and a doctorate in work science. In leading positions in research and industry, he was responsible for labor management, production strategies, and project management. In the early 1990s, he joined HLP Hirzel Leder & Partners in Frankfurt and later co-founded the ICG Integrated Consulting Group Germany in Berlin and was a partner in the European group in Graz. Today, he is an independent consultant, business partner of ICG and is associated with other project partners and think tanks. He brings his experience to the development of methodologies such as the Three-Pillar Model and has published numerous articles in management journals and books.

# Industrial Excellence Meets Travelling Organization: Keeping Promises in the VUCA World

Werner Przybilla and Frank Kühn

**Abstract**

The Industrial Excellence mindset is a main driver in progressive process industries such as the chemical industry. One of their concepts is called T-O-P, displaying the business requirements and change dimensions "Technology, Organization and People," and their systemic interconnectivity around a sustainable purpose. Coming from this interlinkage between the Three-Pillar (3-P) Model and the T-O-P model, the authors present an approach about (1) how to understand the corporate journey's progress and need for navigation by means of a "travelling clock"; (2) how to apply the integral T-O-P concept for shifting and navigating the "connected excellence level"; (3) how to set up a T-O-P roadmap to commit, navigate, and support development and the overall transformation toward T-O-P excellence. A number of use cases explain how the travelling system—based on these findings—can be developed and navigated close to the wind of the wider ecosystem and VUCA world.

## 1 Excellence Mindset

Industrial excellence is a key driver in industries that connects value creation and change performance. Following this, one of their core principles is formulated as "effectiveness over efficiency." In the VUCA (volatile–uncertain–complex–

W. Przybilla (✉)
Schwerte, Germany
e-mail: przybilla@nextspin-consulting.com

F. Kühn
Dortmund, Germany
e-mail: fk@kuehn-cp.com



M. Kempf, F. Kühn (eds.), *Navigating a Travelling Organization*, Future of Business and Finance, https://doi.org/10.1007/978-3-030-95326-3_15

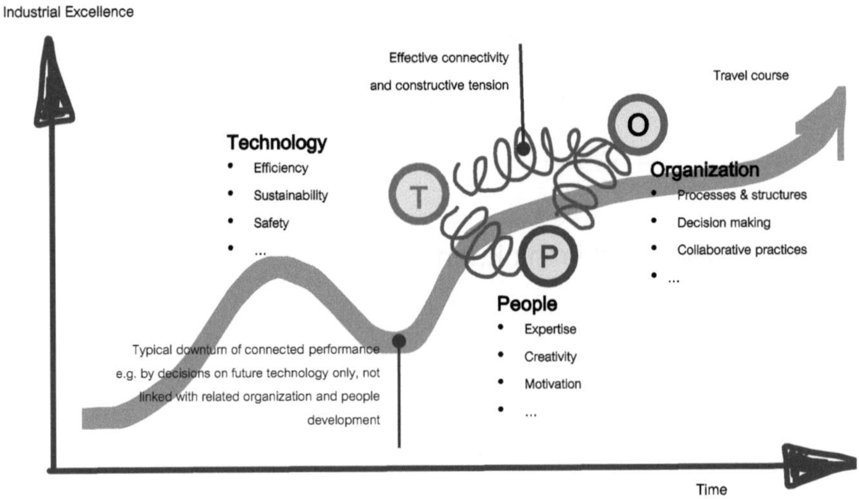


**Fig. 1** Navigation must include the connectivity between the T-O-P dimensions on the journey. (Illustrated by the authors, used with permission. All rights reserved)

ambiguous) world this means to be alert, to respond, and act quickly, which requires agile thinking at its best.

Excellence means both: to be fit for the current business challenges and co-walk and/or co-define the corporate journey toward a sustainably successful future.

One of the excellent approaches is the so-called T-O-P concept. This means keeping the three change dimensions in a joint journey: technology, organization, and people that are building a naturally connected system. Consider Formula 1 motor racing—you can only win the race by having the right car, the right team, and the right pitstop. Navigating this T-O-P system on its journey is challenging as each of these dimensions have their own development logic: Technology is looking for the most innovative and reliable combination of hardware, software, and processes, driven by enthusiastic developers, operators, and maintenance people. Organization then has to develop what seems necessary to face the innovations, changes, and disruptions in terms of communication, practices, processes, and structures. Finally, the people provide their competencies, creativity, motivations, and experiences in order to make the whole constellation work, at the same time as being human beings with values of their own, with personal and societal needs.

How can this T-O-P system support the navigation of the journey?

Figure 1 displays the journey with the connectivity of technology, organization, and people. Ideally, we would see a consistently positive development. In this case, we have a deviation, for example, when a new technology is introduced, and the appropriate organization and people only follow with a delay, which can cause a downturn in the travelling system. Physically speaking, there is a hysteresis between technological development and the other two dimensions.

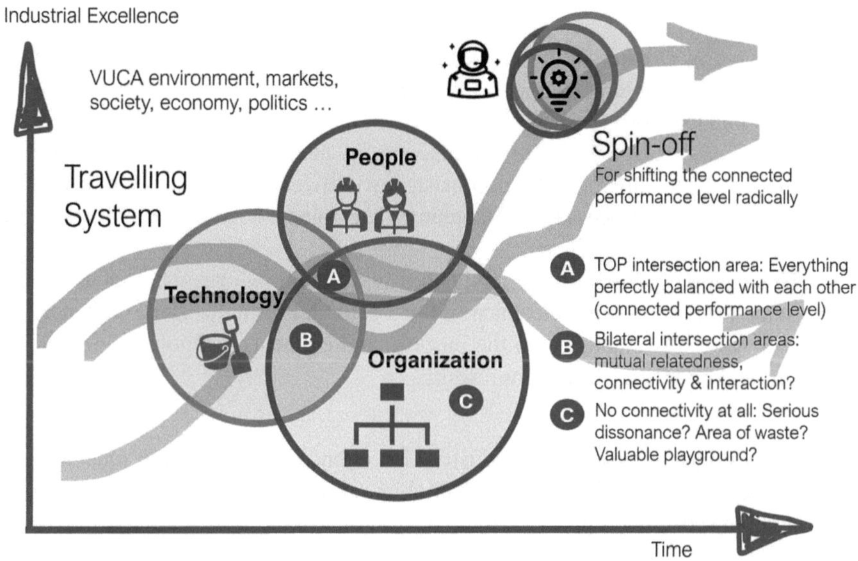


**Fig. 2** What is the optimum degree of connectivity? (Illustrated by the authors, used with permission. All rights reserved)

In Fig. 2, we have extended this consideration. The overlaps replace the springs of balance in Fig. 1, and this gives reasons for new questions: How great is a productive match between T-O-P, where are the precise connections between T-O, P-O, and P-T, where is there a need for free spaces of development perhaps also outside the attempt to balance everything? If the result is not effective enough to cope with future challenges as a company, spin-offs may occur, for example. Navigation must include these considerations.

## 2 Three Pillars Meeting the Promise of Industrial Excellence

Navigating a travelling T-O-P system as described needs a sustainable purpose that gives the direction and is both clear and strong enough to "pull" all three dimensions—technology, organization, and people—and keep them as close together as possible. Regarding these three dimensions as the systems' resources, they have to be well connected and balanced to master the journey.

**Application of the Three-Pillar Model**

The Three Pillars are defined as (Wollmann et al., 2020, 2021):

(1) Sustainable Purpose—the raison d'être of an organization, bringing new orientation and certainty to the people for their joint endeavor and success

(continued)

(2) Travelling Organization—the mindset of an organization in a permanent state of flux, interacting with the markets' and customers' journey, with rapid adaptivity
(3) Connected Resources—Interconnecting all needed resources inside and outside the silos, creating consistency between goals and concepts, strategies and processes, competencies and roles

This chapter focuses on the navigation of a travelling organization and, at the same time, shows the relevance of the 3-P model for industrial excellence. The navigation is aligned with the purpose and connects technology, organization, and people as three core resources.

With regard to the promise of Industrial Excellence, the navigation must always focus on the following strategic target variables, all three contribute to a company's sustainable purpose and challenge the T-O-P dimensions of technology, organization, and people:

1. Reliability of production or value-adding process
2. Sustainability of financial success
3. Avoidance of any waste of resources

These three goals are always valid and must be continuously checked and balanced with regard to the effectiveness of journey goal, next steps, and timing.

In the chemical industry, the reliability of production covers aspects such as quality from the customers' point of view, supply reliability in terms of quantity and time, but even more health, safety, and environment (HSE) aspects. All three target variables are directly related to the three pillars that must be applied as success factors for the journey and achievement of the three target variables.

All three variables can be seen as promises to society, customers, shareholders, and employees. In order to take such promises seriously, we need to make them concrete and describe the underlying assumptions that are the subject of navigation. These include factors such as a working supply chain, the political situation, availability of machinery, skilled staff, crisis management, etc.

**Keeping Promises in the Travelling Organization**
Since conventional structures offer people less and less safety in VUCA times, the importance of reliable leadership and collaboration has come to the fore. This is even more true in change or transformation. This means trust: We want to trust at least promises and agreements: this is the minimum. But what can we promise people in a travelling organization? That we will be guided by a

(continued)

strong vision and a clear strategy, that we will build and have future fitness of skills, that we will realize advantages, that we will implement the action plan consistently (Fig. 3)—or only: that we will keep the journey of the company transparent, that we will communicate news and changes immediately?

We can only promise to achieve the target figures under certain conditions and promise to inform about their development. Agile approaches such as OKR (Doerr, 2018) build on this: We agree on following a number of objectives and key results (OKR), and we agree and promise each other a process in which we regularly discuss the OKR achievements, their further relevance and the way forward together. We cannot do much more than that.

Thus, promises have two challenges: Keeping them is one. The other is to promise only what we can deliver. If necessary, promises need to become smaller and more iterative, just like decisions in the VUCA world. For example: If the (too) cautious professional honestly wants to promise the delivery of a concept only in 6 weeks instead of the expected 10 days (who promised whom the 10 days?), then we have to agree with him on a quicker intermediate step to find other ways to solve the problem; or we have to find another expert who might not keep the promise either. This is where reliable navigation happens in daily team and leadership practice.

Promises kept at short notice build long-term trust.

| | | | | | | | |
|---|---|---|---|---|---|---|---|
| Vision | Strategy | Skills | Advantages | Capacities | Action Plan | ➔ | Journey |
| | Strategy | Skills | Advantages | Capacities | Action Plan | ➔ | Disorientation |
| Vision | | Skills | Advantages | Capacities | Action Plan | ➔ | Confusion |
| Vision | Strategy | | Advantages | Capacities | Action Plan | ➔ | Fear |
| Vision | Strategy | Skills | | Capacities | Action Plan | ➔ | Resistance |
| Vision | Strategy | Skills | Advantages | | Action Plan | ➔ | Frustration |
| Vision | Strategy | Skills | Advantages | Capacities | | ➔ | False Starts |

**Fig. 3** A practical approach to mapping the success factors of the journey that can be used to review the navigation: What can you promise to take the people on the journey? (Adapted from Knoster, 1991) (Illustrated by the authors, used with permission. All rights reserved)

# 3 Use Case A: Getting Back on Track—Co-managed Communication Paved the Way to T-O-P Excellence in Teamwork and Collective Navigation

## 3.1 Perception and Understanding: Need for Action

The economic crisis had hit the chemical company heavily. Fixed costs had to be reduced in order to survive and respond to shrinking market demand. That had a direct impact on the manufacturing setup. Marketing and productivity studies had concluded that the operation shift teams had to be cut down significantly while improving the per head productivity disproportionally. It was evident that the way that operations communicated horizontally and vertically was inefficient and ineffective, reflecting the silo setup. That included the managers, the shift operators, quality control, maintenance as well as supply chain and health, safety, and environment (HSE).

Shift handovers as well as experience exchange meetings between all these stakeholders were mainly relying on the individuals' capabilities, their presence resulting in inefficient and often redundant information flow despite their visible engagement for the site. As information flowed orally or in writing it was prone to Chinese whispers effects and poor retrievability. Additional emails with huge distribution lists added to this sort of organizational dementia. Hence, the idea emerged to implement a digital logbook to support and ensure the communication process as a basis for an agile navigation approach.

## 3.2 Mapping and Prioritization

In the sense of the T-O-P systemic approach, it could be stated that the people slightly drove the system as described above while the organizational and the technological components were weaker (Fig. 4).

The organized flow of information was not embedded in a set of informal meetings and processes as the information was either hand-written or conveyed orally with some basic usage of emails by some selected persons. The technological component was small. That meant that the interactions between these three system dimensions were neither effective nor efficient. This brought the importance of connectors to the fore.

With all the given stress on costs and productivity, it was imperative to give the whole manufacturing T-O-P complex a managed communication system in order to navigate it to the envisioned state of excellence (Fig. 5).

Industrial excellence implies that this change is sustainable and stimulates intrinsically further continuous improvement. This accelerates Plan-Do-Check-Act-feedback loops (Deming, 1982) and it results in a higher industrial fitness with respect to a VUCA setting. Fundamentally, the ability to keep track and navigate through unchartered terrain is the key to future competitiveness and prosperity.

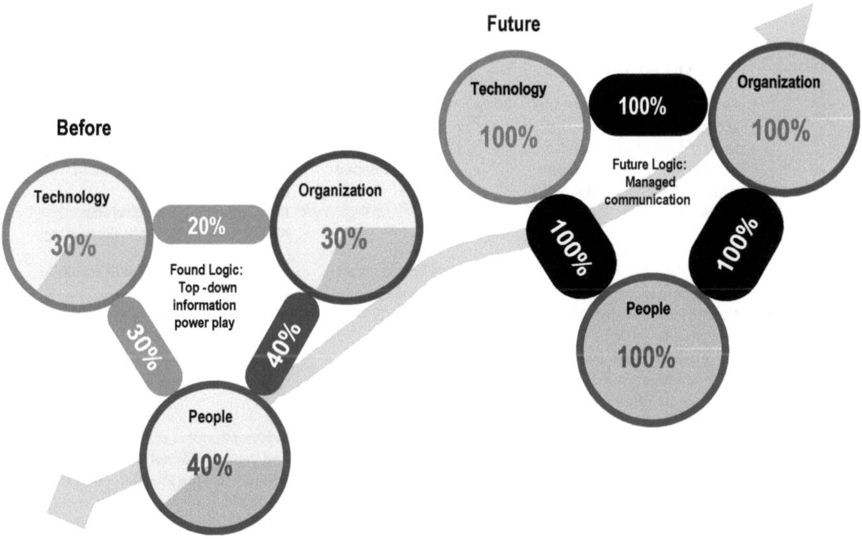


**Fig. 4** T-O-P change journey to implement a logbook for managed communication. In this case, the challenge was to radically improve the connectivity between Technology, Organization, and People and thus make significantly better use of resources in all three dimensions. (Illustrated by the authors, used with permission. All rights reserved)

## 3.3 Co-creation and Development

In a collaborative approach, the future business arena was based on marketing outlooks, while the future state of the overall production lay-out was appropriately designed by applying Lean concepts and an Operational Excellence mindset.

**Lean Design Principles (VDI 2870-1, 2012):**

- Avoidance of waste
- Resource efficiency
- Continuous improvement process
- Standardization
- Zero-defect principle
- Flow principle
- Pull principle
- Employee orientation and goal-oriented management
- Visual management

From that, it was obvious that, with increased per-head-productivity (shrinking headcount), the communication effectiveness of the operations team had to be brought to a higher level where more and more relevant information per time and head is shared and processed. This has led to some key questions of managed communication.

| | TOP | Current state | | Intermediate state | Target – Future state |
|---|---|---|---|---|---|
| | | Characteristics | % | Next objectives | Characteristics 100 % |
| Dimensions | T | • Few computers available and accessible<br>• Mostly paper-based hand-written information transfer with unstructured data<br>• No retrievability | 30 | • Invest and install more PCs in office LAN<br>• Install the needed software | • Multi-user capability<br>• Relational database in LAN run on any Office PC<br>• Easy access to entry PC (1 PC at least per workspace)<br>• Data retrievable and filterable<br>• Ad-hoc reporting and dashboarding |
| | O | • Only certain persons have access rights<br>• No structured information flow process<br>• No retrievable documentation<br>• Shift handovers done<br>• Information often redundant | 30 | • Grant access rights to all stakeholders | • Everybody has Read-Write access to logbook database<br>• All info is read in an organized and structured way (rhythm, dedicated recipients + meetings) |
| | P | • Low IT skills in the workforce<br>• Poor empowerment: Only certain people are capable of using computers<br>• Operators engaged | 40 | • Training of all users and/or stakeholders | • Every operator is capable of usng a PC and the Logbook software – motto: "If you can surf the internet, you can use the tool."<br>• Every operator feels fully informed |
| Connectors | P-T | • Use of email and telephone<br>• Software confusing | 30 | • Use Design workshops in order to guarantee best user experience | • Information is entered asap + anywhere + 1st hand<br>• Easy ergonomics |
| | T-O | • Regular reports missed<br>• Email is used in parallel to oral information<br>• Info is dispersed over different people, paper, folders and files | 20 | • Define and set up the internal cloud<br>• Define minimum data requirements and dataset structure (fields & content) | • Information is structured in a simple way.<br>• Every dataset contains at least time stamp/author/title-content/importance/ shelf-life, if possible, workspace/topic<br>• Automated Reports and Dashboards are used |
| | O-P | • Intra-/Inter-shift information flow is poor.<br>• Long-term organizational memory poor<br>• Poor collaborative learning<br>• All based on personal relationship<br>• Chinese whisper effects | 40 | • Use Design workshops in order to define deployment rules<br>• Set up a minimum policy and standard operating procedure | • Data is entered by anyone, anywhere, anytime<br>• Complete documentation of any relevant event<br>• Every dataset contains at least time stamp/author/title-content/importance/ shelf-life, if possible, workspace / topic<br>• Information is guaranteed to be reliably processed<br>• Any info dataset can be linked to 1:n-measurement and managed |

**Fig. 5** T-O-P analysis future to current state. (Illustrated by the authors, used with permission. All rights reserved)

**Managed Communication**

Managed communication is the basis for performing and learning as a team. The key questions of managed communication are:

1. How does an organization guarantee that the right information is provided and processed at the right time and place, by the right persons in the right way, and triggers the right next actions?
2. How is the level of noise and organizational dementia kept low while reducing remembering and searching/retrieval time?
3. How does everybody in the team participate, feel involved and benefit via understanding communication both as key to immediate know-how development and sharing as well as key to enabling a sustainable personal and organizational learning journey?

Hence, as displayed in Fig. 5, the future state of the communication management system in all three T-O-P dimensions was defined as 100% as well as the desired interaction intensity of the different dimensions. This is especially important as the driving force for intrinsic industrial excellence lies in the connectors' quality, e.g., how the available technology is deployed by qualified and motivated human beings and teams, and vice versa how the human user is best supported by the technology. The latter is often about ergonomics, pilot systems, and automation while the former is about training and a learning mindset. Figure 6 summarizes for each T-O-P connector some of the excellence-enabling characteristics.

All these properties fuel the cyclic intrinsic excellence process described in Fig. 7 by the travelling clock enabling to navigate and move forward. A driver without a roadmap will certainly struggle to arrive at the destination especially when a deviation suddenly pops up. For industrial excellence, the crossover from the 4th to the 1st

| T-O-P Connectors | Characteristics |
|---|---|
| P-T | • T: Ergonomics, availability, assistance systems, automation, modularity, scalability, reliability, digitalization (digitized-data driven, retrievability, real-time)<br>• P: Training, technical affinity, open mindset, trust |
| T-O | • O: Processes, clear RACI roles (responsible-accountable-consulted-informed), agility, management of change, release management<br>• T: Availability, accessibility, modularity, reliability, connectability, scalable, adaptability, digitalized |
| O-P | • O: Clear RACI, vision, change and Excellence story, strategy, Project Management Office (PMO), values, policies, alignment, standards, management of change, culture (trust, empathy, psychological safety), structure, roles<br>• P: Change mindset, leadership, trust, empathy, training, agility, curiosity, hunger for success, will to win |

**Fig. 6** Characteristics of the connectors enabling excellence—not complete. (Illustrated by the authors, used with permission. All rights reserved)

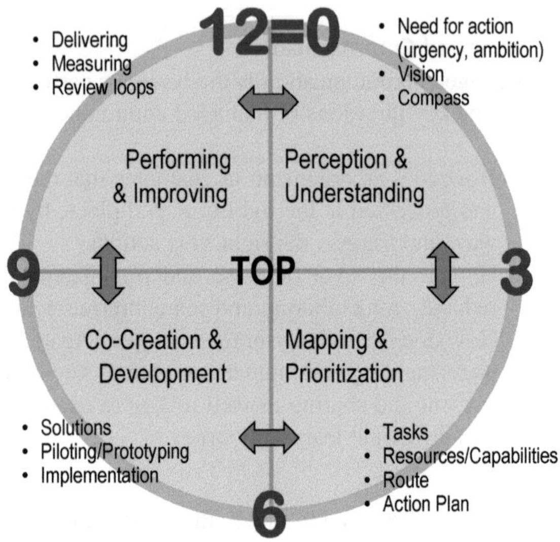


**Fig. 7** Travelling clock for cyclic intrinsic excellence. (Illustrated by the authors, used with permission. All rights reserved)

quadrant needs special attention. The O-P connectors in particular drive that junction. Traditionally, we have pictures in mind of a visionary company founder who, with courage and inspiration, has led the business into a bright present. To what extent is such a development triggered today by the organization or the technology? Can they spark the excellence process or the crossover? Can an organization be set up for intrinsic excellence by installing, e.g., great production systems like that of Toyota in the world? Can there be a technology setup that pushes and pulls the people and the organization? Can Artificial Intelligence (AI) deliver on that promise and bring technology to that active spark level? Only when the first AI becomes CEO or at least CTO of a company we will be able to speak of Industrial Excellence 5.0.

**Working with the Travelling Clock**

Industrial excellence means doing the right things, besides doing the things in the right way. This means working with the clock: Each of the clock phases is always more or less relevant to be continuously checked in its impact and interconnections with societal development, market dynamics, and customer journeys.

The questions to be applied are:

- How good are we in each phase and in the phase transitions?
- How effectively do we balance and distribute our investment of time and energy between the four phases?

(continued)

- What prevents us from being excellent or advancing in terms of technology, organization, people, and their interaction?
- What actions must we take to challenge and balance the T-O-P aspects?

**Potential Next Step?**

In this context, the idea was born to build a digital twin of the travelling organization, such as Google Maps showing the landscape, routes, and current traffic conditions. The travelling clock can contribute to conditions, current location, and road closures. The technology should then be able to automatically recalibrate the route. This idea was agreed upon as the next step after implementing a logbook to support the trip, its communication and navigation, and was included in the strategic roadmap.

## 3.4 Performing and Improving

As this communication improvement project was embedded in the overall manufacturing redesign program it arose from a SWOT analysis during a team workshop. It was one of the main challenges to be tackled, offering an opportunity to develop and improve cooperation in an agile and low-cost way in the short term, thus, creating more momentum in the transformation journey.

The project team members were chosen by the operations leadership team based on their interest, skill set, and their involvement and role in the overall digitalized communication process. With the application of different supporting techniques such as process mapping in combination with Lean Thinking the project team made a significant impact on the new communication process and created more trust and, hence, team spirit.

The chosen IT tool was a relational database that was set up in the network in a front/backend approach, which provided a high degree of modularity and scalability. The start of the first release was within 2 weeks and further improved releases were quickly published based on the feedback from the user community and the project team. Reports and dashboards were developed and embedded in the rhythm of the manufacturing organization.

## 3.5 What Is the Bottom Line?

This case produced some specific key insights and take-aways of its own which also represent a significant shift in navigational capabilities:

- *Logbook navigation instead of memory loss*—From the start, people received a solid benefit from their changed habits which accelerated the use of the digital logbook, improved efficiency of the communication processes like the shift handover, and dramatically reduced the memory losses. People were able to retrieve distinct information from months ago within seconds as opposed to the hours they had needed previously.
- *Rapid solution development*—With the defined dataset structure, people were able to check how often within the last 12 months a certain event had occurred. That tremendously accelerated the sustainable solution development capabilities and empowered them in their team meetings instead of reinventing the wrong wheel again and again.
- *Sustainable solutions for higher reliability*—The reliability of the manufacturing was improved as reflected by higher equipment availability, quality, and process performance.
- *Travelling mindset via communication loops*—The level of alignment on the change journey was always kept at a higher level as the communication loop was faster, democratized, documented, and transparent.
- *The trust level increased with promises kept due to smaller steps and agile co-development.*
- *Joint clocking in the team*—Especially, the agile co-development approach of the process and the tool supported the travelling team in the sense of Tuckman's team-clock (Tuckman, 1965) as well as the travelling clock described in Fig. 7 on their continuous improvement journey to excellence.

## 4 Use Case B: Innovation Leadership—Navigating the Journey Using the Travelling Clock

The analysis of companies in different industries with the travelling clock led to the specific patterns we observed in many cases. It provides us with interesting clues in interpreting the cases from the point of view of how to manage the travelling organization. The following case is based on our experience with a medium-sized financial services company. We found the travelling clock (which provides the structure of the case description) and the T-O-P model (which adds interesting analysis) to be appropriate approaches to represent what happened and what was proving to be a threat to the company's existence and future.

**Some Methodology for Risk Strategists**

Do not think that the story could not happen in the way described here. Try the so-called "disaster story" technique (Kahneman, 2012) together with your peers to analyze the risks in your company. The approach is easy: Put yourself in the future (1, 2, or 3 years) and imagine: the corporate journey was a disaster. Now go through the journey again in your mind: What can you imagine happened? Where and why did navigation fail?

## 4.1 Perception and Understanding

The perception of markets and opportunities was done in the marketing team, digital team, and in the management circle. A multitude of questions and impulses of the staff on site who worked in direct customer contact was taken up rarely or too late. In a recent board meeting, two decisions were made: The employees needed to be further developed in their change motivation; two innovative managers who could imagine implementing digitization within their areas were allowed to do so. But more fundamental organizational preparations for future fitness were not considered.

What does T-O-P tell us about this? People were willing to contribute their insights and move the company forward, the new technology was developed through a few initiatives, but the organization as a whole was not seen as relevant for sustainable change.

The travelling organization's navigation was based on assumptions and perceptions that did not reliably incorporate experience from day-to-day customer interactions.

## 4.2 Mapping and Prioritization

The roadmap, therefore, contained ideas that were essentially contributed by the executives. The opinions of expert teams were included. An effective prioritization failed because no manager wanted to take a back seat with his or her idea.

The T-O-P analysis: it was not a technology problem (nor was the technology challenge really taken seriously); but the organization did not provide a culture and process to prevent the management from dysfunctional behavior and including people's available expertise, skills, and talents.

Navigation was constantly surprised by new initiatives that were difficult to bring into a common direction with a reasonable allocation of resources.

## 4.3 Co-creation and Development

Managers' favorite ideas were also very quickly given preference in the solution-finding process. Proposals from expert teams were accepted if the managers could imagine the proposed concept easily; time-consuming discussion was not popular. Alternatives were rarely tried out; there was no time for experimentation and managers were expected to make decisions quickly. The overload of projects meant that people got bogged down, and therefore everybody was grateful for any shortening of projects.

The T-O-P analysis: There was a disconnect between the need for deeper technological understanding and the resistance of managers to spend their precious time on it. This was due to their self-conviction and role behavior as it has worked in their organizational culture so far: speed takes precedence over sound effectiveness on the journey. "Think fast," never slow (Kahneman, 2012).

Navigation was limited to prioritizing quick projects or shortening them to achieve quick results, which had nothing to do with iterative approaches that require sustained management consistency. Thus, some of their strategic thinkers described their journey as day trips, returning to the familiar organizational home in the evening.

## 4.4 Performing and Improving

When it came to implementation, many solutions developed in this way were difficult to reconcile with the experience, expertise, and working methods of the experts on site. However, the latter were stuck in the performance phase because they knew the difficulties of putting forward their own ideas. Therefore, they increasingly held back their ideas and simply did what they were assigned to do.

What does T-O-P tell us about this? Employees' talents and ideas were being wasted due to the time pressure caused by ineffective organization. There was no time or motivation to test new technological concepts that could have connected the knowledge management processes or mapped the company and its navigation in a digital twin. The organizational culture seemed to be a serious barrier that prevented any transparency and open exchange.

Both the journey and the navigation were dramatically disconnected between senior management engagement and employee experience, between strategists' attempts at navigation, organizational power plays, and day-to-day business realities.

## 4.5 What Is the Bottom Line?

The process minimized effectiveness: From limited perception to power-play-driven project selection, from there to narrow-minded development, from there to half-hearted practical implementation and underperforming organization. The logic behind this was not so much a focus on efficiency, but a reduction to something feasible. The hierarchical culture prevented the superiors from using the potential of the people, new technology was only tried out sporadically, the organization proved to be both barrier and taboo. The people had neither courage nor trust in their own capabilities.

A new CEO came in and found these findings devastating. Together with teams from the staff across all levels, she created, in some loops, a new image of the future and brought in a new understanding of how to navigate a future-fit organization. This included, for example:

- Ideas, questions, and comments from all employees are welcome.
- They are jointly evaluated and routed according to T-O-P criteria.
- The resulting backlogs, roadmaps, and actions are transparent to all staff.

Such points were deliberately designed to develop all three T-O-P factors in interaction and good balance with each other: people (trust, engagement, competencies), organization (knowledge and innovation management, agile practices), and technologies (analogue and digital platforms).

Most important for these points was the principle of only including aspects that could be promised and delivered. This was seen as the essential prerequisite for building new trust and shifting the further journey to a new level of excellence. And it became an outstanding leadership challenge throughout the structure to ask the people for the promise: Are you willing to stick to it and continue the journey together in our team?

## 5 Use Case C: Re-inventing Self-organization—Co-creating the Next Level of Navigation Excellence

The following case focuses on the T-O-P model, its three dimensions, here considered as resources, and the connections between them. The use case shows how this approach supports holistic consistent thinking of the situation, the goal, and the next step, which are explicit components of the journey. This deeper understanding of the challenges enables much more effective navigation.

A retailer company's management team was concerned about the current and future fitness of their organization. Under pressure from crisis and increasing mail order volumes, processes proved to be not flexible and fast enough to deliver quality on cost and on time.

This was taken as a good opportunity to create a greater vision: to transform into an agile and resilient company that should be ready to face and master future market dynamics. Thus, they made the decision to start with their returns department as a pilot area. The goal was to replace conveyor belts with teamwork and test out self-organization.

Thus, the overall vision was described in the management team (compare Fig. 5) and compared to the current situation: What preconditions, motivation, and competencies do we have to go on a journey into uncertain territory? How should we navigate them?

They estimated the levels of readiness for the new via percentages: Technology 70% (minor problem), Organization 30% (due to the need to overcome the established hierarchy), People 30% (motivated, still needed training).

Especially the connectivity between organization and people concerned the management team. The staff on the shopfloor communicated that they had seen the difficulties and barriers in their organization and would have been motivated but were not allowed to contribute their concerns and ideas due to the hierarchical culture. Therefore, they had established informal communication channels among their teams to improve the situation somewhat, at the same time creating serious conflicts with their superiors.

In a series of meetings with managers, employees, and facilitators, the desired vision was radically formulated: a 180° turn from T-O-P down navigation to self-organized and customer-oriented teamwork, with tailored IT support and servant leadership—from power play patterns to a culture that should provide people with the opportunities to organize and take responsibility in line with the promises made to customers.

Following from this, the management team and delegates from the shopfloor teams discussed the T-O-P vision, reflected on the current situation and roadmap.

They committed to the roadmap, knowing that they would have to adapt it to any changes in the market and customer requirements which needed a cyclical or iterative review process. Thus, they developed a shared navigation cockpit for the beginning of their journey and agreed transparency from then on. Currently, they are discussing how to support this process by the OKR concept which provides a process of agreeing on objectives and key results (OKR), working on them, regularly rediscussing their effectiveness, and readjusting their assumptions where appropriate.

For all of them, it was clear that things can change, new ideas and experiences can come in, and that the only promise they could make to each other was transparency. Nothing else—which meant: each disappointment would disrupt the trust needed for this transformation. This was a dramatic outcome: Hierarchical control hindering any journey on the way to be replaced by joint navigation energizing the travelling organization.

In terms of the "clock," they have perceived and understood the problem, mapped the options and prioritized a pilot project, co-created and developed a solution, and tested it for performance and further improvement. Now it is up to the drivers of this initiative to expand this approach to other areas or to the entire organization and start the clock again as a key navigation tool.

## 6 Conclusions and Take-aways

The challenges within each of the three T-O-P dimensions cannot be understood without their mutual interactions or connectors. Do not buy a car when you cannot drive! Do not drive a car when you do not know the highway code (the rules)!

All three use-cases demonstrate the applicability and power of the holistic T-O-P approach combined with the travelling clock. This leads to some important and general conclusions and take-aways for future excellence, transformation initiatives, and navigation approaches:

- If everybody on each level wins something, the reservoirs of motivation and trust increase continuously. This sparks new improvement cycles and fosters the interrelationships between P-O, O-P, P-T, and O-T. Back and forth. T cannot give trust or be motivated. It is just a tool.
- Co-development is key. Welcome everybody's ideas and feedback.
- Small promises for small steps are more easily kept. Payback is frequent and direct, which creates trust and progress. Use agile approaches whenever possible.

- Communicate steadily among the stakeholders. Success and progress are kept promises which are not visible to anybody if not professionally communicated. Not celebrating would be a lost opportunity for trust and excellence build-up.
- Make promises. Keep promises—at least try as hard as you can. Show the will. A relationship or organization without promises is dead.
- Build trust. P in O, O in P, P in T, and O in T. Create opportunities for trust creation.
- Taking smaller steps or being more fragmented on the journey necessitates a very solid kind of progress management office with a clear roadmap and an attractive vision of where you want to be at the end of the journey.
- Good rules, values and feedback processes on how the T-O-P system needs to interact during that journey are needed, even if your vision will change. That is the least duty an excellent leadership should stand for.

With these guiding principles, the road to excellence will be well prepared and the navigation will work effectively. As promises are more likely to be kept and kept more often, the intrinsic and extrinsic trust level will constantly increase, employee satisfaction will rise and customers will foster their relationship with the company. Travelling T-O-P systems will emerge much fitter from this journey to advance to the next level of excellence.

## References


Deming, W. E. (1982). *Out of the crisis*. Massachusetts Institute of Technology.

Doerr, J. (2018). *Measure what matters—OKRs*. Penguin.

Kahneman, D. (2012). *Thinking, fast and slow*. Penguin.

Knoster, T. (1991). Factors in managing complex change. In *Presentation to the TASH Conference*, Washington D.C.

Tuckman, B. W. (1965). Developmental sequence in small groups. *Psychological Bulletin, 63*(6), 384–399.

VDI 2870-1. (2012). *Ganzheitliche Produktionssysteme—Grundlagen, Einführung und Bewertung*. Beuth Verlag.

Wollmann, P., Kühn, F., & Kempf, M. (Eds.). (2020). *Three pillars of organization and leadership in disruptive times—Navigating your company successfully through the 21st century business world*. SpringerNature.

Wollmann, P., Kühn, F., Kempf, M., & Püringer, R. (Eds.). (2021). *Organization and leadership in disruptive times—Design and implementation of the 3-P-model*. SpringerNature.

**Werner Przybilla** has developed his 20+ years of experience in the chemical industry in all manufacturing leadership positions in the life cycle of a production plant. He worked with global champions like the French companies Total and Arkema as well as the American private equity company Hexion. For a decade, he has developed and directed an Operational Excellence culture and real-time performance management systems. He achieves excellence in operations by synthesizing tailor-made approaches based on technological, organizational, and human aspects with key focus on digitalization, managed communication and processes. Today, he is an independent consultant and associated with other project partners, service providers, institutes, and platforms. His experience lies in the field of operational excellence, change management and digitalization. He supports companies in the process industry as well as service organizations to reach the next level of excellence. Werner has a degree in chemical engineering and a doctorate in material engineering. He is a true European citizen.

**Frank Kühn** has been supporting companies and institutions in the areas of transformation, organization, and leadership for many years. His clients involve him as a development partner for both their urgent change projects and sustainable future concepts. Frank has a degree in engineering and a doctorate in work science. In leading positions in research and industry, he was responsible for labor management, production strategies, and project management. In the early 1990s, he joined HLP Hirzel Leder & Partners in Frankfurt and later co-founded the ICG Integrated Consulting Group Germany in Berlin and was a partner in the European group in Graz. Today, he is an independent consultant, business partner of ICG and is associated with other project partners and think tanks. He brings his experience to the development of methodologies such as the Three-Pillar Model and has published numerous articles in management journals and books.

# Beating the Normal Curve—Finding the Path for a Traveling Organization in Disruptive Times

Mohanakrishnan Raman

**Abstract**

Never in the history of humankind had people been asked to stay at home for several months and human movement been completely restricted. However, this actually occurred and it has now been 18 months since the WHO declared the coronavirus outbreak to be a pandemic in March last year.

The pandemic not only affected human beings but also many organizations in different industries. Manufacturing, textiles, automotive, travel, and tourism industries were the worst hit while the pharmaceutical and health sectors have experienced a boom due to the pandemic. However, even they were unable to ramp up their production and create a supply chain to exploit these new opportunities.

In this context, an international community of professionals attempted to understand and offer a model that would help organizations worldwide during such disruptive times. Considering the Three-Pillar Model, this chapter is an attempt to offer a model to help "traveling organizations" during these disruptive times. It is assumed by the author of the paper that traveling organizations need to maintain speed and, at the same time, not to miss the crucial part, i.e., learning to cope well with the challenges and keep moving in the direction of the goals defined.

## 1 Application of the Three-Pillar Model

The Three-Pillar Model is an inspiration to have a fresh look at the current pandemic crisis and at what is going with organizations. Irrespective of the size and scale of the organization, and across national boundaries, many organizations have faced serious

M. Raman (✉)
Mysuru, India

 
M. Kempf, F. Kühn (eds.), *Navigating a Travelling Organization*, Future of Business and Finance, https://doi.org/10.1007/978-3-030-95326-3_16

challenges to their performance and results. The Three-Pillar Model focuses on Sustainable Purpose, Traveling Organization, and Connected Resources (Wollmann et al., 2020, 2021):

1. **Sustainable Purpose**—the raison d'être (purpose) of an organization, bringing new orientation and certainty to the people for their joint endeavor and success.
   Teams working on a project based on the challenges they face, during their performing stages, will experience hurdles, disappointments, failures, and many other challenges, will go through stages from immobilization to understanding and integrating the experience as a learning point. This learning point ensures the Sustainable Purpose of an organization when the teams move to new projects or products or even new challenges. Over a period, the teams will be able to cope well with unforeseen challenges or ones that strike like a thunderbolt such as the COVID-19 pandemic.
2. **Traveling Organization**—the mindset of an organization in a permanent state of flux, interacting with the market and customer journey, with rapid adaptivity.
   The Volatile, Uncertain, Complexity, and Ambiguity (VUCA) world is not getting any easier, rather it is getting much tougher due to technology disruptions and the impact of the pandemic. Traveling organizations will have to have agile methodologies in place and the entire staff must have been trained in using the tools and methodologies that ensure the organization can move or travel without much difficulty.
3. **Connected Resources**—interconnecting all needed resources inside and outside the silos, creating consistency between goals and concepts, strategies and processes, competencies, and roles.
   The resources are the key elements in making the plan successful. The teams that are responsible for the organization's success and meeting the defined targets will have to consider all the above points in order to continue its journey.

The Three Pillars are critical for organizations to face disruptive times. In order to sail through its difficulties and succeed in its efforts to achieve its goals, the traveling organization needs to navigate by means of effective leadership and highly cohesive teams. The coronavirus pandemic and its impact on economies and organizations around the world emphasized the relevance of the three pillars, the strength of the model, its universal applicability, and its value in finding solutions that work well even in extreme situations. This includes learning and developing for future challenges but also increasing awareness of people of the social purpose of organizations, the shared willingness to travel under unknown conditions, and to experiment with how we can connect our resources even under unusual constraints (Wollmann et al., 2021).

The central point of this chapter is to demonstrate to readers how traveling organizations can navigate through the learning process, adapt to fast change/ transformational interventions and implementation. It is about learning and getting ready for future change and faster change through agile methods.

## 2 Stages of Change Adjustment

When calamities such as the coronavirus pandemic strike, they are new, and everyone experiences shocks and fears. However, bold people face the challenge and survive or even thrive. What makes such organizations different and how do they cope with the challenges they face? The interesting model of what happens to people, teams, and organizations is described below.

During such unexpected shocks, there is a need to develop a mindset to cope with the situation. Life changes continuously; be it personal or professional life. The transformation from one stage to another needs a coping mechanism. It is noted that human beings tend to go through seven stages given (Fig. 1), namely:

> 1) Immobilization, 2) Minimizing, 3) The Pit, 4) Letting Go, 5) Testing, 6) Understanding, and 7) Integration toward vision. (Spencer & Adams, 2002)

Traveling toward the vision is not a straight line, especially during events such as the pandemic and, moreover, the world has become more chaotic and Volatile, Uncertain, Complex, and Ambiguous (VUCA).

The seven stages are important for coping as learnings become an automatic process. Learning through various stages is the most important element that is useful for future large-scale change processes. There is a "should line," that is depicted in the following illustration, which comes from leaders or top management. If the leader directs the organization to skip the stages and achieve the results directly, the

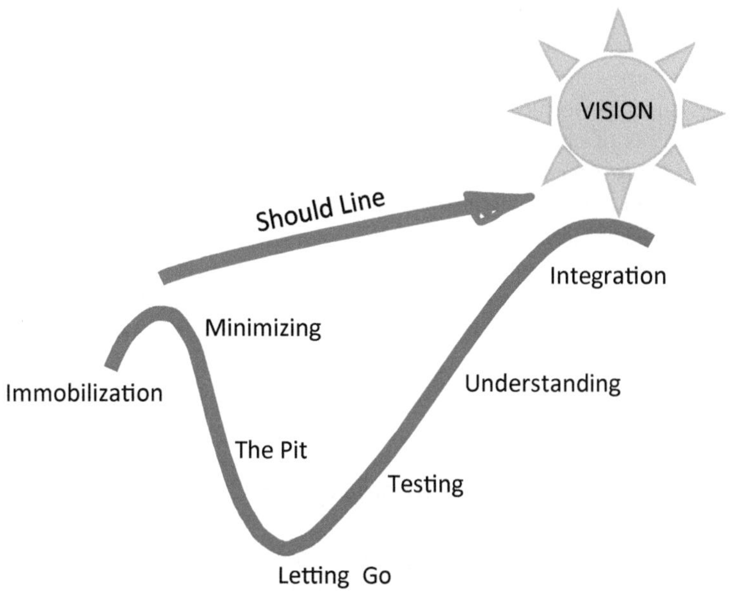


**Fig. 1** Seven stages of change adjustment. (Illustrated by the author; used with permission from Spencer & Adams, 1990. All rights reserved)

most important element will be lost, i.e., "learning." That becomes a strong element in future larger change processes.

The *"Should Line"* indicates *avoidance* of facing the challenges of a major adjustment. If the leader avoids it, he/she will not learn anything and will be equally challenged by the next big change, or perhaps become more cynical about leadership in the future. Therefore, learning "coping mechanisms" is key. It is also important that the team members and the leader go through the process and learn: this can be a useful experience for managing future change projects.

If a leader shares his or her vision of the "new state" while people are still struggling with "The Pit," and merely tells people to "get on with it" or "get over it," the success of the change will be in doubt. The intensity of the change adjustment as described by the curve is a function of *How surprised* people are by the change. That is, how much *novelty and ambiguity* does the change create?

The ways to *speed up* going through the adjustment process for people in an organization are for leadership to reduce *novelty and ambiguity* by:

1. Providing as much accurate *information* as possible about the reasons for the change and how it is progressing (weekly progress reports) to help people have *clear expectations*.
2. As needed, providing ways for affected people to develop *new skills* needed for effectiveness after the changes.
3. Holding events or activities to foster *positive attitudes* about the new state -- new opportunities and capabilities, etc.

The traveling organizations which successfully sail through such difficult times (in recent times, known as called disruptive) adapt to the stages described by the curve at the same time as speeding up to cope with the challenges to survive and emerge as super performers. The purpose of this chapter is to capture the whole learning process of change adapting to seven stages that provide a deep learning possibility, while speeding up the change process to navigate the organization toward the given target or destination. The author attempts to portray the possibility of navigating the organization successfully, continuing to learn, and still accelerating the speed, through the agile process to beat the normal curve of performance or change, compared to other organizations. In one way it is accepting the seven steps described in the curve at the same time as keeping the momentum moving toward the desired destination.

## 3 Advancing Organizational Agility

Agility in general is described as the ability to move quickly and easily. The term is mostly used to describe animals or athletes who move fast in order to survive or win. Can organizations be agile? Can they move faster than expected and navigate to overcome the challenges? What is an agile organization?

The answers to the above questions are explored using case studies and the author's personal consulting experience.

Agile organizations are able to adapt and react quickly to changing circumstances. They embrace a complex and unpredictable environment by being customer-centric rather than profit-centric, adopting fast learning and decision cycles, and building a network of empowered teams and individuals enabled by technology and driven by a shared purpose. Acting with agility will make the difference when striving for sustainable business success.

Therefore, the managers/leaders in navigating organizations must be educated and be aware of the transformation process through the seven stages of change adjustment and remain agile in driving the organization toward the targets. In other words, the leaders go through the cycle of learning and, at the same time, implement change processes simultaneously to survive in disruptive times. These must go hand in hand.

## 4 Linking the Seven Stages of Change Adjustment and Agile Methodologies

The present chapter is conceptualized based on the experiences of the author as a consultant in an Indian and international environment with various clients. The author has noticed consistently how clients undergo adaptation to change by going through seven stages and how the individuals or teams learned while still focusing on the projects/goals that differentiated them from other organizations and that gave them a strategic advantage. Let us go through each of the stages to understand the adaptation and how transformation processes are impacted.

The stages are explained below, based on the article by Spencer and Adams (2002).

### 4.1 Immobilization

Any event, new boss, new job, or a new project within the organization that is new to the employee, any new technology, etc. can create uncertainty. During this stage, focus is affected and makes you unable to think clearly. The important learning in this stage is "stability is only temporary." We all keep experiencing various transitions.

### 4.2 Minimizing the Impact

At this stage, people behave as though everything is normal in order to minimize the impact of change. They pretend that it is "business as usual." It is a time of denial and of expressing surprise that anything has to change at all, making lots of effort to appear normal. This stage helps to protect the individual from the full consequences of change, but it helps to build confidence and courage for the next level journey.

## 4.3 The Pit

Reality hits hard and staying in denial for long does not help. One may develop depression and may also feel powerlessness. This is the stage where emotional outbursts are common from angry reactions to grief and sadness. It is important at this stage to accept that feeling angry, sadness or grief is part of coping. But staying in this stage for too long may push one to stage two and result in one permanently feeling helpless. Accept, understand this stage, fully complete it and move on to the next.

## 4.4 Letting Go of the Past

People tend to spend lots of time on the past and its impact. But once they have overcome such emotions (anger, sadness, or grief) then they can look at the future. Here people enter the confidence stage, where they feel that "I can do it." Once this realization comes, things become a lot easier. This stage, importantly, provides the learning of forgiveness. One will establish a new self, by trying new behaviors and developing new skills.

## 4.5 Testing the Limits

This stage is critical and full of energy and enthusiasm. When they feel they are able to break free from the past with newly gained confidence, people look for ways to test themselves in the new situation and find out how far they can go. The most common experience of this stage is a growing sense of self-confidence and being in charge of one's life and feeling good about the new direction.

## 4.6 Integration

This is the beneficial stage where one consolidates the discoveries and the experiences together into one's everyday life. This integration helps to create the second nature of the person and enables them to look at the world in a new and confident way. An individual is certain to continue to learn new things from the whole experience that he or she has been through, how to be focused on other things, how to be ready for the next major transition.

The above stages are not necessarily linear but can be simultaneously based on the intensity of the experience or impact. It is possible that one may try to skip the painful parts such as the Pit. It may become doubly intense in the event that one tries to avoid certain stages in the process. If one is able to adjust and adapt to the stages of experience then more peace, strength, and confidence will be achieved to face the next challenging experience or assignment.

Having described the seven stages of adjustment changes, it is important to explore the link between how the agile transformation practices fit with the seven stages of adjustment to change.

## 5 Case Study

In a consulting experience with a content solutions company in India, the author describes the best case to link the seven stages of adjustment to change and agile methodologies.

The company was going through serious trouble as one of its senior managers, who had founded the company and made it a self-sustaining and profit-making undertaking, wanted to leave as the relationship between him and the CEO had deteriorated quickly and frequent trust issues had begun to surface. He had to leave the company as a result of these differences and became a threat as he started a rival business in the same industry. There was a risk that many employees would also leave to join the new company founded by the former senior manager. The CEO of the company invited the consultant to intervene and help to overcome the situation and stabilize the organization's performance. There was not much time to respond to the threat. Hence, it was decided that change had to come at a faster pace than normal incremental change. It was decided to use agile methods to transform the organization. Thus, the project began.

The first change that was proposed and successfully implemented was the process of service delivery, which depended on one manager who oversaw Quality Assurance (QA) and Delivery. The process was designed as described: (1) Sourcing the data, (2) cleansing and normalizing the data (production), (3) data quality control, and (4) Quality Assurance. The QA manager was also responsible for delivery, customer interaction and satisfaction. The first three processes were handled by other managers and once they finished processing the data with Quality Control (QC) it was passed on to the QA manager. However, there was a constant complaint that the QC data were not up to the required standard and there was a lot of pressure on the QA manager. It was a one-way process in which the QA never returned the data to the QC; even if they sent it back to the QC function, they were busy with new projects and did not look into the complaints of QA. Therefore, there was constant stress and a power struggle between the process owners and managers. Often the CEO had to intervene to broker "peace" between the managers and functions and ensure delivery to the customers. After analyzing the process and the looming threat of another manager gaining control of the whole organization process and delivery the consultant recommended restructuring the organization and creating Strategic Business Units (SBUs), thus making all the managers responsible for all the processes. This opened the service pipeline and bandwidth of the process management. The SBU structure was helpful to serve more customers and each manager became

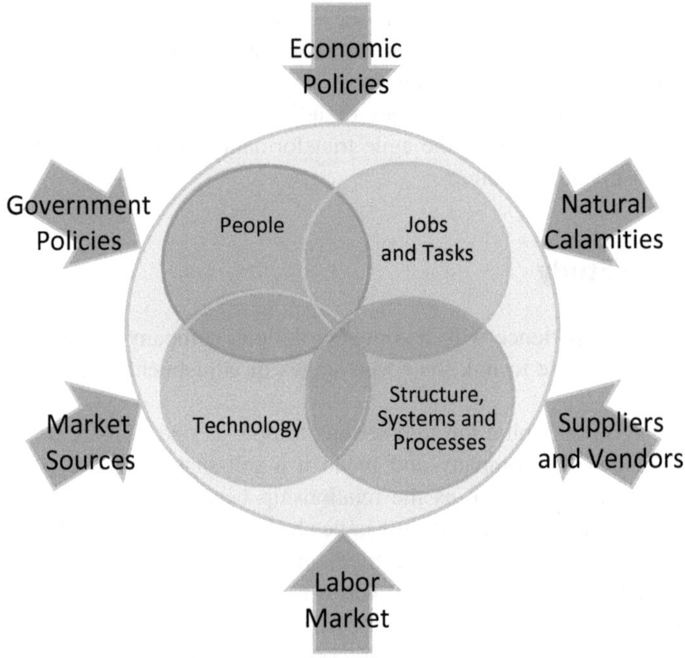


**Fig. 2** The internal and external environments and their elements of an organization (French & Bell Jr, 1999). (Illustrated by the author; used with permission. All rights reserved)

accountable to service delivery. The scenario changed quickly as each one aimed to demonstrate their contribution through high performance.

In this whole transformation process, all the managers went through the seven stages of adjustment to change and demonstrated coping mechanisms. The QA manager was in denial mode (immobilization) for several months, then he was quick enough to adjust by rapidly undergoing each stage. Each of the SBUs started competing with each other and started delivering the services with high vigor, which enabled the company to move from USD 2 million to USD 10 million in 3 years. Currently, it has a turnover of USD 25 million and the company is valued at around USD 50 million.

The entire transformation process and the organizational restructure was achieved using the agile methods using the Agile Transformation model (Fig. 2), conceptualized, and created from various books on Organization Development and Change and the author particularly acknowledges the book by French and Bell Jr (1999).

The organization interventions were designed to bring change to the following areas: (1) Structure—Systems and Processes, (2) People, (3) Tasks—Roles and Responsibilities, and the (4) Technology, generally known as the components of the internal environment of the organization. The agile methodologies were used to bring the changes to all components of the internal environment of the organization.

The case study above explains how the change was achieved by changing the structure and the process.

Simultaneously, interventions were implemented to change the culture of the organization, leadership development programs and processes were introduced to sustain the benefits of change through people. Jobs and roles were redefined along with job redesign. The whole system transformation was done in a record 6 months, while the people and the teams went through uncertain periods and confusion to adjust to the change proposed as defined in the stages.

The change in compensation structure, designations and incentive schemes, career and succession planning, and massive communication efforts enabled the organization to sail through the tough times and challenges and eventually become a very successful company.

## 6 Conclusion

In the Three-Pillar Model, the second Pillar, called the "traveling organization," needs to travel without disruption and to navigate toward the goals defined by the organization. In this context, this chapter attempts to offer a solution that would make the traveling organization speed up its operations and, at the same time, transform itself to deliver better performance without compromising the learning element. It is evident that the seven stages of adjustment to change management (in this context the disruptive events such as the coronavirus pandemic) are crucial and learning through the stages cements the learning points for the people, teams, and organization. However, the seven stages may take time to be coped with and learned, the organization transformation process must be faster by using agile methodologies. The paper concludes that agile methodologies and the seven stages of adjustment go hand in hand. If any leader tends to follow a "should line," it may jeopardize a successful change or transformation.

## References

French, W. L., & Bell, C. H., Jr. (1999). *Organization development—Behavioural science interventions for organization improvement*. Prentice Hall of India.

Spencer, S. A., & Adams, J. D. (1990). *Life changes: Growing through personal transitions*. Impact Publishers.

Spencer, S. A., & Adams, J. D. (2002). *Life changes*. Paraview Special Editions.

Wollmann, P., Kühn, F., & Kempf, M. (Eds.). (2020). *Three pillars of organization and leadership in disruptive times—Navigating your company successfully through the 21st century business world*. Springer Nature.

Wollmann, P., Kühn, F., Kempf, M., & Püringer, R. (Eds.). (2021). *Organization and leadership in disruptive times—Design and implementation of the 3-P-model*. Springer Nature.

**Mohanakrishnan Raman** is a Dr and Ph.D in Industrial and Organizational Psychology. He has 25 years of experience in research, teaching, corporate, and consulting. Having worked in large private telecom, IT and banking sectors, he brings enormous experience in the consulting process for his clients. He practices Organization Development, Leadership Development, Family Business Consulting. He has been a consultant to many family businesses and other entrepreneurial organizations for over 15 years.

# Part IV

# Resume

# Conclusions and Thanks

Michael Kempf and Frank Kühn

**Abstract**

Once again, the Three-Pillar Model has been confirmed, from various perspectives and practical applications. Our thanks go to the authors who, on our common journey, have shown how the model can be applied to urgent challenges, to professional practice, to their consulting and development concepts. They have demonstrated this in impressive ways in different contexts such as in companies, in the university, in the church and in the cultural sector.

It is a great opportunity to write a book, and even more so a book series, together with others in a professional, experienced, and creative multinational community.

We have shared insights and ideas, developed our perspectives and concepts, tested and strengthened them in the written argument. A heartfelt thank you to all who participated!

Once again, our Three-Pillar Model has been confirmed, from very different perspectives and practical applications: as a reflection model for organizations, as a design model in the awakening and transformation of companies, as a thinking model for status determinations and visions of the future. The authors have shown how they could draw a valuable connection to their own challenges, how they applied the model in their specific professional practice, how it helped them to expand and strengthen their consulting and development concepts.

M. Kempf
Bad Honnef, Germany
e-mail: michael@kempf-cp.com

F. Kühn (✉)
Dortmund, Germany
e-mail: frank@kuehn-cp.com



M. Kempf, F. Kühn (eds.), *Navigating a Travelling Organization*, Future of Business and Finance, https://doi.org/10.1007/978-3-030-95326-3_17

This also confirms the approach of offering an open model, but one that requires intensive study. It is not a polished best practice or a simple patent remedy, as is often expected and has dominated management development for decades. But that would not do justice to our uncertain and ambiguous world either, and it would be fixed in the past. And we stand for a better future for Travelling Organizations.

Everyone has to think for themselves in which format they want to apply the Three Pillars, with which objective and in which setting so that it can develop its specific effect. Each company must go on its own journey with it, with its own Sustainable Purpose, its own Travelling Mindset, its own resources that it connects well.

Together with our author community, we have navigated the journey through different stages with diverse outcomes. The first section takes us through these stops. Fittingly, at the beginning was the question of what it means to begin and end, and what prevents us from doing so. Via the role and importance of navigators in the Travelling Organization, the journey led to pragmatic approaches and suggestions for stepping stones and concrete execution. This requires leadership, and this leadership in times of upheaval and transformation also demands personal changes from the people involved. They are confronted with new navigation systems, the transition from MBO to OKR, new agile decision-making practices, and the challenges of a project portfolio that has to be managed in a much more agile way than we are used to. We have arranged the topics and chapters in this order.

Then we moved on to the applications of the Three-Pillar Model in very different areas. Contributors have shown applications in the university setting, in the church, in the cultural sector, and in businesses. This second section of the book shows how the model can be used to reflect on current situations and needs for action, how it can show organizations the way for their new beginnings and upheavals.

What conclusions do we draw from this? Each user of the Three-Pillar Model is asked to design his or her own formula: Relevance of their current issue x exciting objective x Three Pillar application methodology x high-energy agenda x committed participants. We have shown examples of all these factors.

Once again, a deep thank you for this and for the many inspiring impulses and thoughts—especially for our shared development!

Michael Kempf and Frank Kühn

Editors

Bad Honnef/Dortmund, March 2022

**Michael Kempf** has been an experienced Management Consultant for over 20 years. The driving force of his professional activities is his strong ambition to design processes and organizations in a sustainable manner. He relishes identifying key challenges, diagnosing complex relationships and assisting in shaping the future. Gaining experience and learning something new are indispensable parts of his life, which is why he likes to seize new opportunities. He began his career as a carpenter before studying social work, education, and business administration. His career has spanned various jobs in social work, 10 years as a manager (HR and logistics) in industrial and retail companies and, since 1998, in advising people, leadership teams as well as working teams and organizations that are all very different. Michael has co-authored numerous publications in the field of leadership and organizational development.

**Frank Kühn** has been supporting companies and institutions in the areas of transformation, organization, and leadership for many years. His clients involve him as a development partner for both their urgent change projects and sustainable future concepts. Frank has a degree in engineering and a doctorate in work science. In leading positions in research and industry, he was responsible for labor management, production strategies, and project management. In the early 1990s, he joined HLP Hirzel Leder & Partners in Frankfurt and later co-founded the ICG Integrated Consulting Group Germany in Berlin and was a partner in the European group in Graz. Today, he is an independent consultant, business partner of ICG and is associated with other project partners and think tanks. He brings his experience to the development of methodologies such as the Three-Pillar Model and has published numerous articles in management journals and books.

MIX
Papier aus verantwortungsvollen Quellen
Paper from responsible sources
FSC® C105338

If you have any concerns about our products,
you can contact us on
**ProductSafety@springernature.com**

In case Publisher is established outside the EU,
the EU authorized representative is:
**Springer Nature Customer Service Center GmbH**
**Europaplatz 3, 69115 Heidelberg, Germany**

Printed by Libri Plureos GmbH
in Hamburg, Germany